Moments
WITH GOD

Moments
WITH GOD

ONE-MINUTE DEVOTIONS
to encourage, inspire, and spiritually change
YOUR LIFE

BRENDA WALSH

3ABN
books

Pacific Press®
Publishing Association
Nampa, Idaho | Oshawa, Ontario, Canada
www.pacificpress.com

Graphic Designer: Chrystique Neibauer | cqgraphicdesign.com
Copy Editor: Mellisa Hoffman
Cover Image: shutterstock.com/Sunny Forest

ISBN: 978-0-8163-6185-4

August 2016

Additional copies of this book are available through:

Adventist Book Centers®: Call toll-free 1-800-765-6955 or visit online at www.adventistbookcenter.com.

3ABN: Call 618-627-4651 or visit online at www.3abnstore.com

3ABN Books is dedicated to bringing you the best in published materials consistent with the mission of Three Angels Broadcasting Network. Our goal is to uplift Jesus Christ through books, audio, and video materials by our family of 3ABN presenters. Our in-depth Bible study guides, devotionals, biographies, and lifestyle materials promote whole person health and the mending of broken people. For more information, call (618) 627-4651 or visit 3ABN's website: www.3ABN.tv.

Brenda Walsh Ministries: Visit www.brendawalsh.com.

Acknowledgments

Carole Derry-Bretsch

Jason P. Coffin

Michael J. Coffin

Myrtle Coy

Madlyn Hamblin

Tom and Gwen Hanna

Hannah Hoffman

Lance Hoffman

Mellisa Hoffman

Jim and Rebecca Hundertmark

Dale and Pam Knechtel

Pastor James and Bernice Micheff

Chrystique Neibauer

Michael Ortiz

Rodney Reynold

Jerry D. Thomas

Timothy M. Walsh

With Special Thanks

I want to express my deepest thanks and gratitude to my friend, and colleague, Mellisa Hoffman for all her hard work and dedication that made this book possible. She worked tirelessly with me, side by side, carefully checking every detail, organizing files, looking up scripture texts for accuracy, and copy editing the entire manuscript.

I fondly refer to her as my *awesome assistant,* for she surely is that and so much more. It is a privilege to work with someone who loves Jesus so much and shares my passion for spreading the gospel of Jesus Christ. I look forward to being neighbors with her and her family in Heaven soon!

Dedication

I dedicate this book first and foremost to my Lord, Savior, and Best Friend, Jesus Christ. He is the reason I live, the reason I get up in the morning, and the reason I can face each day!

I treasure our special time together, and I pray God will use this book to bring others into a closer relationship with Him.

Secondly, I lovingly dedicate *Moments with God* to my precious parents, Pastor James and Bernice Micheff, who have committed their entire lives to serving our wonderful heavenly Father.

Thank you, Mom and Dad, for your commitment to ever inspire me to be more like Jesus. Because of you, my greatest passion in life is to share God's love with others. It is my deepest desire that the prayer you have prayed my entire life be fulfilled, when "someday soon we will all be gathered together in heaven as a family . . . without one lost!"

I love you, Mom and Dad!

Take Time to Pray

*But whoever is united with the Lord is
one with him in spirit.*

1 Corinthians 6:17 (NIV)

When we understand the sacrifice Jesus made on Calvary, we can't help but fall in love with Him. And once we have given our hearts to God, we cherish the time we spend with Him through prayer and Bible study. It's not drudgery or something that we feel obligated to do. If we want to experience the fullness of His presence, we must make our worship time a high priority.

The more time we spend with Jesus, the closer we will be to Him, and it is then that we'll experience His power to defeat the enemy and walk away from temptation. All too often we avoid prayer until we are in trouble—and *then* we get on our knees. Our problem is that we have become accustomed to meeting our own needs, trying to fix our own problems, and relying on *self* for everything, even when we are doing God's work!

God blesses our feeble efforts. However, when we enter into a prayer relationship with Him, we'll receive blessings beyond our wildest imagination! Talking *one on one* with God gives us wisdom, strength, and power that otherwise we would not have. Only when we surrender *our will* to *His will* can we fully become *one* with Jesus! Determine today to make God your highest priority, and *take time to pray*!

Father, Forgive Me

*No temptation has overtaken you except such as is
common to man; but God is faithful, who will not allow
you to be tempted beyond what you are able, but with the
temptation will also make the way of escape, that you
may be able to bear it.*

1 Corinthians 10:13 (NKJV)

Jesus has promised in Matthew 1:21 (NKJV) that "He will save His people from their sins." Notice that it does not say *in their sins*, it says *from their sins*. There's a big difference between those two words. We are all sinners and have come short of the glory of God. However, there are some who feel they can live a wild life, do anything they want, and as long as they ask for forgiveness each week, then they can keep sinning! But they are wrong! God makes it very clear in that one word—*from*—that He doesn't mean for us to keep sinning those same sins.

God wants us to confess our sins and ask forgiveness with a sincere and repentant heart—but then He expects us to turn away from those sins and stop doing them! And through the grace of God, it is possible! Ask Him to give you a hatred for your sins and to reveal any sins that you are not even aware of! Begin with "Father, forgive me!"

Choosing the Right Friends

*Two are better than one, because they have a good return
for their labor. If they stumble, the first will lift up his
friend—but woe to anyone who is alone when he falls
and there is no one to help him get up.*

Ecclesiastes 4:9-10 (ISV)

G od gave each of us the gift of friendship—but He wants us to choose our friends wisely. That's why it's important to look to Jesus as our example. He was *friendly* with everyone, but He carefully chose His *friends* and His *disciples,* who were His closest companions.

Everyone needs a friend, someone special we can trust, who knows our faults and weakness and loves us anyway—the kind of friend we can depend on, trust with our secrets, and know beyond a shadow of a doubt that they'll never betray our confidence! Real friends give . . . without expecting anything in return, and they'll be there in bad times—not just the good!

Usually it's when you're going through your darkest days that you find out who your true friends are! Friends should draw you closer to God, so evaluate the friends in your life. Are they a positive influence or are they dragging you down? Ask God to help you choose friends who will draw you closer to Him!

Gentleness Requires Strength

And the Lord's servant must not be quarrelsome but must be kind to everyone, able to teach, not resentful. Opponents must be gently instructed, in the hope that God will grant them repentance leading them to a knowledge of the truth.

2 Timothy 2:24-25 (NIV)

Sometimes we confuse *strength* and *gentleness*. Those two words seem to contradict each other, but they really don't. It takes a tremendous amount of strength to control our emotions in a gentle manner when faced with a frustrating, hostile situation for it's human nature to respond in anger.

Gentleness requires strength! The Bible tells us in Philippians 4:5 (NIV), "Let your gentleness be evident to all. The Lord is near." A strong person doesn't have to walk around wearing a sign announcing how strong they are. When Christ lives in us, His presence is reflected in our every action.

God is a strong, all-powerful God, yet He is gentle and full of love. Even when we make mistakes, His correction is consistently gentle. He doesn't scream and holler at us, telling us what idiots we are. He speaks to us in a still, small voice as He gently calls us to repentance.

Jesus instructs us in Matthew 11:29 (NASB) to learn from His example: "Take My yoke upon you and learn from Me, for I am gentle and humble in heart, and you will find rest for your souls."

Fear Destroys Faith

But He said to them, "Why are you so fearful?
How is it that you have no faith?"

Mark 4:40 (NKJV)

Fear and faith cannot possibly coexist in the same life! In fact, fear is the opposite of faith. Some might be surprised to learn that the devil uses fear as a powerful weapon to destroy our faith in God. He knows when we are most vulnerable and strikes when we are at our weakest. But fear has no place in the life of a Christian! A life lived in fear is a miserable existence.

The only cure for a life consumed by fear is allowing Jesus to come into our hearts and putting our faith and trust in Him. We need to get on our knees and immediately ask God to remove all fear and give us more faith! When Jesus lives within us, fear cannot survive. There's only one place to put our trust and that is in our Lord and Savior.

When you feel *fear* lurking around the corner, cry out, "Jesus, help me to trust *You* more! Give me more faith!" Thousands of angels can be released in an instant to give you the strength that you need. Help is only a prayer away!

Be a Blessing

*And let us continue to consider how to motivate
one another to love and good deeds, not neglecting
to meet together, as is the habit of some, but
encouraging one another even more as you see the
day of the Lord coming nearer.*

Hebrews 10:24-25 (ISV)

At the end of a stressful week, spending time with your church family is like fresh, cool water in the midst of a desert. Having other believers to share and worship with is a beautiful picture of God's love. Sadly, not all church families are *loving*. Because of this, many have chosen not to go to church at all. They tell themselves that they can worship at home; they don't need a church family. But rarely is this true. All too soon, God becomes distant and not even in their thoughts.

The devil doesn't care how he does it—his plan is to separate you from God any way he can! If he can cause hard feelings among God's people, then he is ecstatic, because he wins. Oh how important it is to stay close to Jesus! You'll have a different experience at church if you change your expectations. Instead of going to church with the sole expectation of receiving a blessing—go determined to *be* a blessing, and you're sure to walk away filled up and overflowing with God's joy!

No More Excuses

But whoever keeps His word, truly the love of God is perfected in him. By this we know that we are in Him.

1 John 2:5 (NKJV)

Christians talk a lot about *faithfulness*, but many times their actions don't support it. When asked to participate at church, they may say *yes*, but when it comes right down to it, they'll either not show up or find someone else to take their place. Promises are made but not kept. As long as they can justify it with a *good excuse*, there seems to be no remorse. If something better comes along, it's all too easy to find a way to wiggle out of the commitment so they can do what they want.

I'm so glad our God is faithful, and He always keeps His promises! He will never let you down—you can count on His Word. No need for an ironclad contract! God wants you to keep your promises. In fact, not doing so is dishonest, and there'll be no dishonesty in Heaven.

God's children need to keep their hearts pure, clean, and white as snow! When you allow the Holy Spirit to dwell within you, there's no room for lies or selfish desires. Invite Jesus to come into your heart and remember that He is counting on you . . . to stay honest, true, and faithful!

Stronger Faith

Draw near to God and He will draw near to you.

James 4:8 (NKJV)

If you want to have stronger faith and trust in God, then you must have an intimate relationship with Him! And the best way to do that is to set aside special time in your day just to spend in prayer, praise, and worship! Don't just have *good intentions,* because even the best of intentions will fail. Stop making excuses and put God on your calendar *first*, before anything else gets added to your schedule! The more time you spend with Jesus, the more you will love Him, and the more you will want to spend time with Him.

As you see real answers to prayer and witness firsthand God's working in your life, your faith will grow. You'll develop a trust so strong, so genuine, and so real that it will affect every aspect of your life. Best of all, your faith will be a tremendous blessing, not only to you, but to everyone you meet.

The Bible tells us in Deuteronomy 32:20 that if we don't have faith, God will hide His face from us. Wow! That is powerful! God's Word makes it very clear just how important faith is. Pray and ask God to give you more faith and don't be late for your daily faith-building *appointment with God*!

Married or Single

"The LORD your God will be with you wherever you go."

Joshua 1:9 (NIV)

God created man and woman and sanctified the bond of *marriage.* When God *sanctifies* something, He makes it holy. Through the bonds of matrimony, God teaches lessons on faithfulness, trust, love, humility, service, gentleness, and much more, refining our characters for heaven! Having said that, though . . . it is not God's plan that everyone should marry. The Bible says in 1 Corinthians 7:8-9 (NKJV), "But I say to the unmarried and to the widows: It is good for them if they remain even as I am; but if they cannot exercise self-control, let them marry." There are some who are single by their own choice or as part of God's plan for their lives.

Others may be divorced or widowed. If you are single for whatever reason, you may be surprised to learn that you are in a *highly-favored position.* God says that He's the One who will provide for you and defend you.

You can look to our Lord and Savior for love and companionship! He's more faithful and wise than any human spouse. So whether you are married or single, rejoice in the Lord always! Seek His perfect plan for your life . . . and serve God with all your heart!

A Compassionate Heart

This is what the LORD Almighty said: "Administer true justice; show mercy and compassion to one another."

Zechariah 7:9 (NIV)

———◆———

Real compassion is putting your *caring* into *action*! It is much more than sympathy or concern. Feeling sorry for someone when you see them hurting is one thing, but doing something about it is *compassion*.

When Jesus was here on earth, His heart was full of compassion. He reached out to all those who were hurting. He didn't just pass a beggar on the street and say, "Oh, that's sad." No, not at all! He did something about it! Sometimes it's as simple as just *being there* and letting someone know you care—a simple smile or word of encouragement. Other times it may be donating to a worthy cause or giving an offering to a mission project.

Helping others doesn't always mean financially, although that's often the first thing people seem to think of. That's why it's important to pray and ask for Holy Spirit guidance and direction so you know how to respond. Ask God to put compassion in your heart for others, and ask Him to guide and direct how you should show it! Open your eyes and look around you, and you'll see a world filled with hurting people. Ask yourself, "What can I do to help make someone's life a little better?"

We Are All Sinners

"The Father gives me the people who are mine. Every one of them will come to me, and I will always accept them."

John 6:37 (NCV)

Many people push God out of their lives because they feel unworthy—crushed under the weight of their own sin. They can't possibly comprehend or even entertain the thought that God truly loves them. The resulting pain denies them the *peace* that only God can give. But here's one thing that we all need to understand: *no one is worthy*! We are *all* sinners and have come short of the glory of God.

However, when we reach out to Jesus, He covers us with His robe of righteousness! He is the Forgiver of sin and the *only* One who can set us free from the guilt and pain. And here's the best part: Jesus loves each of us so much, He has promised never to turn His back on anyone who comes to Him! It doesn't matter what sin we have committed—Jesus is willing and able to forgive. We need only to confess our sin and ask Him to forgive us. Isn't that amazing? What an awesome God we serve! Wouldn't it be wonderful if we could forgive others in the very same way?

God's endless love reaches out to everyone—the good, the bad, and even the filthiest of sinners. He loves all His children! However unworthy you may feel at this very moment, you are not alone, for God is only a prayer away. Reach out to Jesus, and He will take you into the safety of His loving arms where no one can snatch you away from Him!

In God's Eyes

*"For the Lord will not forsake His people,
for His great name's sake, because it has pleased
the Lord to make you His people."*

1 Samuel 12:22 (NKJV)

Most of us have insecurities that we live with. We look in the mirror and wish God had created us differently. We don't like the shape of our nose or wish we had smaller ears or flawless skin. We fret that we're not smart enough, rich enough, educated enough, lovable enough, and the list goes on and on. In fact, we worry more about what others think of us than what God thinks.

The good news is, we don't have to let our insecurities shape our lives. We can place our faith in God and trust in His opinion! After all, He created us in His image! We can go forward with boldness and confidence, ready to take on whatever assignment God wants to give us . . . and we don't have to wonder if we are *good enough*, because in God's eyes . . . we are perfect!

Relinquishing Power

"For I, the LORD your God, will hold your right hand,
saying to you, 'Fear not, I will help you.'"

Isaiah 41:13 (NKJV)

Trust Jesus with everything—your wants, desires, posses-sions, finances, job, and yes, even your loved ones. To do that though, you need to give up control. Everyone struggles with relinquishing power, and many lose the battle altogether. There's only one way to win this war and that is to consciously make the decision to *let go* and allow God to take over!

As you trust God more and more, the fear will melt away and your confidence in Him will grow. With Jesus by your side, you can feel safe and secure in any situation. Whether you are in the midst of making an important decision, facing a health crisis, waiting for a test result, or struggling through your worst trial . . . Jesus will never leave you or forsake you! He is the same yesterday, today, and forever!

Don't keep worrying about how you will survive, which way to go, or what to do. Instead, release your troubles to God, and you'll sleep like a baby, free from all worry and care, for Jesus is your security blanket—which no one can take from you!

Resisting Temptation

For our high priest is able to understand our weaknesses. He was tempted in every way that we are, but he did not sin. Let us, then, feel very sure that we can come before God's throne where there is grace. There we can receive mercy and grace to help us when we need it.

Hebrews 4:15-16 (NCV)

Jesus walked among sinners and was surrounded by evil pleasures, but He never sinned. He was tempted the same as we are, but He did not fall into Satan's trap, not even one time! Jesus showed us the importance of a close connection to our heavenly Father. He leaned on God to give Him the strength He needed to resist temptation. He talked to God about everything, and, in fact, He was constantly in an *attitude of prayer*.

The devil works hard to make sin look attractive, but whatever worldly pleasures we partake in, they will not satisfy our souls or give us true and lasting joy. Instead, they will leave us in deep despair, with a mountain of guilt and regret. Jesus wants us to know that we too can have the victory over sin! All we need to do is lean on Him.

As busy as Jesus was, He *made time* to pray! He spent long hours talking to God. Yes, Jesus, the Son of God and Savior of the world, took time to pray, and if we want a close relationship with Him, we will do the same. Jesus is willing and able to give us the strength, power, and desire to resist temptation and claim the victory over sin!

Flames of Discouragement

*Though he may stumble, he will not fall, for
the LORD upholds him with his hand.*

Psalm 37:24 (NIV)

Discouragement is a weapon that Satan uses to destroy any happiness you have in your life. It leads to resentment, bitterness, and self-pity—none of which will bring you closer to Jesus. If the devil can separate you from God, then he wins, so he is always looking for anything he can to keep you focused on the negative side of life.

When you feel the heat from the flames of discouragement creeping in, immediately cry out to Jesus and ask Him to stomp them out! Don't give the devil reason to gloat because he caused you even one minute of distress. Instead, give all of your burdens to Jesus!

Remember you are a child of God, King of the universe! Instead of bathing in self-pity, bask in the light of God's presence, asking Him to give you an extra measure of His joy! You don't have to fight the battle alone! Jesus is on your side and is ready to lift you up and set you free!

Knowing God's Voice

*In all your ways acknowledge Him,
and He shall direct your paths.*

Proverbs 3:6 (NKJV)

Many people don't understand how to communicate with God. They pray without even an ounce of faith that God actually hears their prayers. The question has been asked over and over, "How do you know when God is speaking to you?" and the answer is this: the more time you spend in prayer and the study of God's Word, the more you will recognize the prompting of the Holy Spirit.

For instance, when you first meet someone and they call you on the phone, you might not recognize that person's voice. But after you've become friends and called each other countless times, you only need to hear, "Hello," and there is instant recognition. So it is with God. The more time you spend with Him, the closer you'll become and the more you will *know* His voice. And if you're still unsure whether it's God's voice impressing you—then double the time you spend alone with Him! It's in those quiet times that you will hear His voice the loudest!

Stretching the Truth

*Lying lips are an abomination to the LORD, but those
who deal truthfully are His delight.*

Proverbs 12:22 (NKJV)

———◦◇◦———

Lying is a sin! No sugar coating! No prancing around it . . . there's no room in a Christian's life for lying. The Bible says in Proverbs 12:22 (NLT), "The LORD detests lying lips, but he delights in those who tell the truth." But in our society today, lying is looked upon as *no big deal* and even *necessary*. There are all forms of *acceptable lies* in our culture. Some people refer to them as *little white lies*. However, the reality is that there is no such thing. A lie . . . is a lie! Even exaggeration is a form of lying. *Stretching the truth* is done to make something more powerful or meaningful than it really is. Bottom line—there's not a good reason to lie. Not ever!

Lying destroys relationships, especially our relationship with Jesus. Planning to deceive others with untrue statements, denying access to information someone is entitled to, or trying to avoid punishment or repercussions for your actions is just plain wrong in God's eyes. People have become desensitized to all forms of dishonesty and no longer agree on the rules that manage behavior. But God expects us to tell the truth, to stand for truth, and teach the truth!

Holding Hands with Satan

*Commit your way to the LORD; trust
in him, and he will act.*

Psalm 37:5 (ESV)

If we truly want a life of joy and fulfillment, we need to live a life that is pleasing to God. Life is too short to live each day with superficial goals. We can't decide to be a Christian one minute and then dabble in sinful pleasures the next. Many are deceived, thinking they have time to hold hands with Satan and then, right before Jesus comes, quickly give their hearts to God so they can be saved!

Sadly, many will miss that heavenly flight! Seeking fame, fortune, and worldly pleasures is meaningless. To experience true joy and happiness, we must choose every day to commit our hearts to God. We need to set our standards high and keep our eyes on the heavenly goal. Jesus *is* coming soon! Choose today to live eternally with Jesus Christ, our Lord and Savior. Don't wait a minute longer, for tomorrow may be too late!

Lean on Jesus

*Blessed be the God and Father of our Lord Jesus,
the Messiah! He is our merciful Father and the God of all
comfort, who comforts us in all our suffering, so that we
may be able to comfort others in all their suffering, as we
ourselves are being comforted by God.*

2 Corinthians 1:3-4 (ISV)

When life seems unfair, and you're screaming inside at the injustice . . . lean on Jesus. His reassuring words are powerful and life-changing! When your heart is breaking with pain . . . lean on Jesus, and He'll wipe away your tears and comfort you with His arms of love and understanding. He is the only One who can *calm the storm*, give you rest from your burdens, and give you an abundant life with Him (see John 10:10). When you are too weak to go on . . . reach your hands out to Jesus, and He will give you the strength to keep going and open your eyes to let you see there are better days ahead!

In Jeremiah 31:13 (NIV), God says, "I will turn their mourning into gladness; I will give them comfort and joy instead of sorrow." And in Isaiah 40:11 (NIV), we're told, "He tends his flock like a shepherd: He gathers the lambs in his arms and carries them close to his heart." Through every difficult circumstance, every trial, every loss, every heartache . . . lean on Jesus. Our Lord and Savior is full of love and compassion for His children! He will heal your brokenness, relieve your pain, dry your tears, and give you peace, comfort, and more joy than you have never known!

God Has a Better Plan

*For I know the thoughts that I think toward you,
says the LORD, thoughts of peace and not of evil,
to give you a future and a hope.*

Jeremiah 29:11 (NKJV)

When you give your heart to Jesus, one of the most obvious changes in your life is your attitude. That's because, when you fall in love with Jesus, His love flows through you and affects everything that you do. Without God, life is dark and hopeless! But when you give your heart to Jesus and are fully surrendered to Him, your whole attitude changes. You won't be asking, "Is life worthwhile?" or "Why am I even here?" because God will fill your mind with pure thoughts, and the Holy Spirit's strength will cause Satan and his evil angels to flee.

So when your day doesn't go the way you planned—you were passed over for that promotion, the rent is due and your bank account is empty, or you didn't get the diagnosis you were hoping for, instead of pouting or blaming God, remember your life belongs to Jesus. Choose to have a Christian attitude and say, "God has a better plan!"

Most Important Choice

*So whether we are at home or away, we make it our
aim to please him. For we must all appear before the
judgment seat of Christ, so that each one
may receive what is due for what he has done
in the body, whether good or evil.*

2 Corinthians 5:9-10 (ESV)

There are many things in this world that, no matter how much we would like to, we simply can't change. It is what it is, and we can't change it. We have no control over the country we are born in, the parents we are born to, or how we look when we enter this world. We can't choose our genetic make up, such as whether we have a big nose or little feet, blue eyes or brown eyes, blonde hair . . . or no hair! We have zero control over the economy, the weather, or people and how they feel about us. All that being said, one of God's greatest gifts to us is the *gift of choice!*

What an incredible privilege we have been given to be able to decide for ourselves *whom we serve.* This decision is not forced on us. We can choose where we want to spend eternity! God leaves this big choice to us. And it's the most important choice you will ever make.

The Bible tells us in Joshua 24:15 (NCV), "You must choose for yourselves today whom you will serve." Have you made your decision yet? Please, wait no longer—there's no time to waste. Jesus is coming soon!

Reflecting God's Love

Whoever claims to live in him must live as Jesus did.

1 John 2:6 (NIV)

———◇———

There are many descriptions in the Bible that describe God's character, such as loving, merciful, compassionate, and kind. When we make the decision to become a *Christian*, we are choosing to be *Christlike*, and we take on the characteristics of Christ in our actions and behaviors. There's no room for selfishness, meanness, or hardened hearts.

It is through God's grace that He gives us the strength to be like Him. He empowers us! We sometimes forget whom we represent when confronted with an angry spouse, a defiant child, a difficult co-worker, someone who cuts us off in traffic, or someone who takes the parking spot we've been patiently waiting for! But we need to represent Jesus at all times—not just when it's convenient. After all, our character is the very essence of who we are. It is something that defines us.

We need to ask God to seal His character in our hearts so that even when confronted with the most difficult situation, we will react in such a way that others can see Jesus in us! In other words, let us strive in our hearts to *be more like Jesus*!

Nothing Stays the Same

*"You will keep him in perfect peace, whose mind is stayed
on You, because he trusts in You."*

Isaiah 26:3 (NKJV)

There are many things in life that come and go, but one thing in this world that we can count on for sure is . . . change. Nothing stays the same! Some people deal with change better than others and are able to see it as a positive rather than a negative. But many people struggle with change. They stress out about changing jobs or schools, getting a new haircut, moving across town, kids growing up, friends moving away, getting a new pastor, and the list goes on and on! But worry and stress do not belong in a Christian's life.

Each day is a new day to experience all the blessings that God has given us. It's a new opportunity to witness for Him and it's a second chance to have a fresh start! Whether we realize it or not, each day we are growing in the Lord. When we allow the Holy Spirit to dwell in us, we are being transformed from the inside out, thus reflecting God's glory that burns from within.

Sometimes God gives us a gentle nudge through His Holy Spirit, urging us to take care of a certain issue that needs forgiveness. Slowly but surely God is perfecting our characters and changing us so that we can be more like Him!

Controlling Anger

*He who is slow to anger has great understanding, but he
who is quick-tempered exalts folly.*

Proverbs 14:29 (NASB)

God created us in His image, and He gave us the ability to express our feelings when faced with various life situations. We laugh and feel excitement and joy when something wonderful happens, and we are sad when we are disappointed or faced with loss. Being sad doesn't mean that we don't trust God—it just means that we are expressing human emotions that God gave us when He created man.

Many think that *anger* has no place in a Christian's life, yet even Christ expressed anger while here on earth. Remember the corrupt money changers in the temple? It's not a sin to feel anger, as this is a normal response to injustice. It's how we express and deal with it that is most important. If anger is allowed to fester resentment in our hearts and rage out of control, then that's a huge problem, as it destroys not only our own souls, but harms others as well.

The best way to handle anger is to determine the cause, face it responsibly, and ask God to help control it! The Bible gives us wise advice in Psalm 4:4 (NLT): "Don't sin by letting anger control you. Think about it overnight and remain silent." We can all enjoy victory in Jesus by giving God control over our hearts, lives, and yes, even our anger!

You Are Not an Accident

But you are a chosen people, royal priests, a holy nation,
a people for God's own possession. You were chosen to tell
about the wonderful acts of God, who called you out of
darkness into his wonderful light.

1 Peter 2:9 (NCV)

If you're convinced that your life is meaningless, and you have no idea why you are even on this earth, think again! There's no such thing as an accidental or ill-timed birth. God made each one of us unique and special with our own individual physical features, talents, and personalities. He loves us all equally, and it doesn't matter what country you're from, whether rich or poor, famous or unknown, or whether your birth was planned or unplanned—Jesus loves you, and He has not forgotten you! In fact, He has never left you.

Remember, God never leaves people; it is people who leave God. He is right there pleading for you to run into His arms of safety. God has a special plan for your life, and He wants to give you the desires of your heart. So don't give up—don't be discouraged. Surrender your life to Jesus right now. Today! Before it's too late! Jesus is coming soon, and He longs for you to be in the safety of His arms!

Modern-Day Miracles

The LORD said to Moses, "Is the LORD's
power limited? Now you shall see whether My
word will come true for you or not."
Numbers 11:23 (NASB)

Many people believe in miracles that happened way back in Bible times . . . but do not believe in *modern-day miracles.* They simply have no faith that they still happen today! But to deny the possibility of miracles is to discredit the Bible.

When we pray for help, and God intervenes on our behalf, why is it that we have trouble giving Him the credit? We excuse it away as a *coincidence* or rationalize how it could have happened anyway. When we do this, we are the same as a thief and a robber, because we are stealing God's glory. Instead of questioning—we need to praise God for His goodness and mercy. We should fall down on our knees and truly give thanks for the privilege of witnessing God's power!

One of the ways that God reveals Himself to us is through miracles! It is often in our darkest hour when we cry out to Him, acknowledging Him as our Lord and Savior, that we experience His divine intervention. Pray often and pray passionately—expecting an answer, because God is still on His throne and in the *miracle-making* business today!

Ready or Not

"Behold, I am coming quickly! Hold fast what you have, that no one may take your crown."

Revelation 3:11 (NKJV)

Jesus *is* coming again and sooner than we think! When we study God's Word, He tells us what to look for so that we can know when His coming is near. And all those signs are already taking place *right now*! Many will say that they are not worried about it because they are a good person, so they are going to Heaven. Thus, they blindly go about their usual routines, not even thinking about God. But, don't be deceived. It's not enough to *be a good person—we must know our Savior*!

We need to get our hearts ready to meet Jesus. There's no time to enjoy the evil pleasures of this world! We need to recommit our lives to God and also get serious about soul-winning, letting people know that Jesus loves them so much, He can't imagine Heaven without them. And, oh, what a day of rejoicing it will be when Jesus comes in those clouds of glory, and we see our Savior face to face! The Bible tells us in 1 Corinthians 4:5 (NCV), "God will praise each one of them." What a wonderful promise! And God Himself will give us the praise—personally—for our crowns will be given one at a time. God Himself will look into each of our faces and say, "Well done, good and faithful servant. . . . Enter into the joy of your lord" (Matthew 25:23, NKJV).

Answer to World Peace

Cast your burden on the L̲o̲r̲d̲,̲ ̲a̲n̲d̲ He shall sustain you;
He shall never permit the righteous to be moved.

Psalm 55:22 (NKJV)

Unless you have been living in a cave and completely out of touch, it's impossible not to hear of all the horrible things happening in the world—wars, massive earthquakes, famines, tsunamis, terrorism, school shootings, robberies, murders, and on and on. The crime rate is higher than ever before, and it's difficult to feel truly *safe*. And if that wasn't enough, your internal stress-o-meter is higher than ever—trying to meet unrealistic goals and expectations from bosses, coworkers, friends, family, and even our spouses!

It's no mystery why so many people are turning to drugs and alcohol for a way of escape! However, numbing our senses and living a life of sin will not bring the peace and security we seek. *Jesus is the only answer to world peace!* We may not know what the future holds, but we do know *who holds the future*! When we are surrendered to our Lord and Savior, there is no need to worry and fret. God has it all under control! We can live each day with full confidence knowing our future is bright because we can trust in *God's perfect plan!*

Pray for Patience

Rest in the LORD, and wait patiently for Him . . .
Psalm 37:7 (NKJV)

We belong to the *now* generation. We want what we want, and we want it *now*. And if we can't get what we want right away, then we pout, get angry, or blame God. Unfortunately, this attitude has carried over to our prayer life. We pray, and if our prayers are not answered immediately, then we lose complete faith and wallow in self-pity, feeling God has ignored us or simply doesn't care. Even worse, we may feel that God doesn't love us! Oh, how sad this must make our heavenly Father, who loves us so much, He gave His only Son to come to this earth and die on a cross—so that we may live eternally with Him! How soon we forget His incredible sacrifice.

If you need more strength and patience, pray and ask God to provide more faith to trust Him more, and He will. Remember that God created *you*, loves *you* more than anyone else on this earth ever could, and wants only the *best* for *you*! He is worthy of your trust! And here is the kicker that so many struggle with the most—God's timing is not the same as yours. His timetable of making things happen doesn't always match up to what you think it should be—so keep this in mind when waiting for your prayers to be answered: *God's timing is perfect!* Pray for patience, keep praying, and don't ever stop praying, even if it takes years—because God will never let you down—not ever! He *always* answers prayers.

Gold in the Fire

For our light and momentary troubles are achieving for us an eternal glory that far outweighs them all.

2 Corinthians 4:17 (NIV)

Wouldn't it be wonderful if everyone had complete faith and trust in God? We need the kind of faith that Job exhibited when going through trial after trial, each one getting worse, but yet he held firm to his love and faith in God! Instead of blaming God for all his troubles, he declared in Job 1:21 (NIV), "The Lord gave and the Lord has taken away; may the name of the Lord be praised." Wow! *That* is *real trust* and *faith*!

Sometimes our problems are the direct result of our own human mistakes, while other times we suffer at the hand of others. Whatever the reason—we need to take our burdens to the Lord and trust Him to know what to do. We cannot see the end from the beginning, but God can! He knows how much we can handle and promises not to give us more than we can bear.

Many times when we are experiencing pain and heartache, we think God has deserted us—but that's not true. It is during the bad times that God is the closest. Just like refining gold in the fire, He is preparing us for eternity with Him—we need only trust Him more!

No More Loneliness

For I am persuaded that neither death nor life, nor
angels nor principalities nor powers, nor things present
nor things to come, nor height nor depth, nor any other
created thing, shall be able to separate us from the love of
God which is in Christ Jesus our Lord.

Romans 8:38-39 (NKJV)

If you are struggling with loneliness, struggle no more, because you are *not* alone—Jesus is always with you. Satan loves to see God's people feeling weak, depressed, and lonely, and he knows that this is the time when you're most vulnerable to his attacks.

It's easy to let the injustices of this world get you down. But stop for a moment to see things through God's eyes. No matter how bleak or discouraging the world looks around you—there is beauty to behold and blessings to praise God for!

There are endless reasons to rejoice and embrace life. Don't wallow in discouragement and allow Satan even one moment to gloat. Reach out to Jesus who has His hands outstretched, ready to wrap His arms around you so that you might feel His amazing love! There's just no better place to be than that! You are never alone, because Jesus is with you every hour, every minute, and every second of the day! Close your eyes and feel His presence, and all sense of loneliness will melt away!

Showers of Blessing

"It is more blessed to give than to receive."

Acts 20:35 (NIV)

⬥

In today's world, it seems we just can't escape bad news! It doesn't matter which television station you go to, every news channel tells of one horrific story after another—a fatal car accident, devastating fire, murder, drug overdose, school massacre, and the list goes on and on. Unfortunately, we live in a sinful world where there is pain and suffering, and no matter how much we want a perfect world—it's not going to get better until Jesus comes and sin is destroyed forever! That's why we need to passionately pray for one another and support each another, not only through our prayers, but also by our actions.

Jesus set an example here on earth when He said in Matthew 5:3 (NIV), "Blessed are the poor in spirit, for theirs is the kingdom of heaven." Get involved! Give of your time to help someone else. Ask God to show you who He wants you to help today! And even in your prayer time, spend more time praying for others than you do for yourself. When you do, you'll receive *showers of blessings*! The more you give, the more you will receive! The best blessing of all is the incredible joy that will fill your heart when you allow God to shine through you. It's the best feeling in the world!

Don't Clean the Fish

"Do not judge others, and you will not be judged."
Matthew 7:1 (NLT)

I t is not *our job* to point out the faults of others. However, too often, we feel it is *our duty* to do so. When God called us to be *fishers of men*, He did not say, *"Clean the fish!"* Many who make it their job to point out the faults of others will lose their own souls because they are so blinded by their own *self-righteousness*. There are people who have left the church because of *well-meaning Christians* who felt it their duty to point out sin.

Only God knows our hearts. We are all on different levels in our relationships with Christ. The more time we spend with Jesus—the more we *want* to become like Him. The Holy Spirit convicts our hearts to change. A weaker brother or sister can't stand up to the criticism and may fall away! When we see the faults of others—instead of letting them know about it—*pray* for that person! And I do mean *passionately pray*! And keep on praying, trusting in our heavenly Father to lead and guide. It's dangerous to try and do the job of the Holy Spirit, and it's not our job to save. *Jesus is our Savior!* Ask God today . . . for strength to stop judging, a kind heart, a humble spirit, and more love for others!

Live Life Joyfully

*Our mouths were filled with laughter, our
tongues with songs of joy . . .*

Psalm 126:2 (NIV)

God wants us to be happy, and He loves giving us the things that we long for. He tells us in Psalm 37:4 (ESV), "Delight yourself in the LORD, and He will give you the desires of your heart." Of course, when we give our hearts to Jesus, we no longer long for the things of this world. Our desires become one with what God wants for us. And giving our hearts to Jesus is a great stress reliever because we can give all our worries and cares to Him. We can relax, laugh freely, and not take ourselves so seriously.

When we desire God's will above all else, life becomes much less threatening. We can stop worrying about things that are out of our control and find freedom in trusting God and knowing *He has our back!* Proverbs 15:13 (NKJV) tells us, "A merry heart makes a cheerful countenance." In other words, laughter is good for our souls and lifts our hearts heavenward. God delights in our laughter just as parents love to hear their children laugh. He rejoices when we trust Him enough to live our lives joyfully! If we insist on carrying the weight of the world on our shoulders, we will live a miserable life and, worse than that . . . miss out on the joy of God's presence.

Living Under the Radar

Let another man praise you, and not your own mouth;
a stranger, and not your own lips.

Proverbs 27:2 (NKJV)

God made you special! He created you to be uniquely different with your own set of talents and characteristics that make you who you are. There are some people who seem to shine brighter than others and get lots of recognition and attention for their accomplishments. But for every shining star there are many other stars that don't seem to shine as bright—almost as if hidden by the brighter stars. Some people behind the scenes tend to feel useless, as if no one cares, never realizing their worth and are unable to comprehend that to God—everyone is important! Although it's true that some may not get the acknowledgments given to others, all God's children are valuable to Him, and He loves everyone equally!

Ask God to give you compassion in your heart for those living *under the radar* and while on your knees, don't forget to ask Him to give you opportunities to affirm them and to help ease their burden! If your neighbor doesn't know their worth—tell them how much you appreciate them! And most of all, let them know they are loved! It doesn't matter how large your bank account, the prestige of your job, or how talented you are, no one is better than anyone else. Remember, God wants all His children to shine for Him!

February 5, 2020

A Person of Integrity

Whoever walks in integrity walks securely, but whoever takes crooked paths will be found out.

Proverbs 10:9 (NIV)

God values integrity. He wants us to stand up for what we believe, no matter the cost! The dictionary describes integrity as *adherence to moral and ethical principles; soundness of moral character.* But what does *integrity* mean to you? Someone with integrity is usually described as *decent, good, honest, moral, righteous, virtuous,* and *incorruptible.* Is it any wonder God places so high a value on integrity?

Many people exhibit qualities of these high characteristics—until something happens to rock their world. All of a sudden, when the chips are down, they make compromises they wouldn't normally make. It becomes easier to justify a dishonest business deal, telling a *little white lie,* cheating on taxes, or not standing up for what they believe. Justifying bad behavior is a dangerous slippery slope. We can easily rationalize ourselves right into hell! That's why it's so important to stay close to Jesus.

No matter the circumstance or how dark the hour you may be facing, be courageous and allow your heart to influence your actions. Pray for strength to be firm in your convictions, no matter the cost! God will give you the strength to be a person of integrity!

What God Thinks

"God blesses those who are persecuted for doing right, for the Kingdom of Heaven is theirs."

Matthew 5:10 (NLT)

It's much easier to accept an undeserved award graciously than being accused of making a mistake you didn't make! Human nature wants to jump and down, wave a flag, or whatever it takes to make sure everyone is aware of the unfair accusation! Only someone walking with Jesus is equipped to humbly respond in a *Christlike* way. When we're surrendered to God and walking with Him, we are stripped of *self*! We don't have to prove ourselves, argue our point, or defend ourselves because we know God knows our hearts. He knows if we are right or not!

And more than anything, it matters what God thinks of us! If we are *made fun of, ridiculed,* or *put down* for standing up for Jesus and doing the *right thing,* remember this: *it's a privilege and honor to suffer for Christ's sake!* The Bible says in Romans 12:12 (NIV), "Be joyful in hope, patient in affliction, faithful in prayer." Instead of getting discouraged and moping about how unfairly we're treated—get excited, praise the Lord, shout with joy, and say, "Thank You, Jesus!"

Praise God for Hope

*The hope of the righteous will be gladness, but the
expectation of the wicked will perish.*

Proverbs 10:28 (NKJV)

Hope is as important to our lives as breathing, for without it, we die. People without hope lose their dreams of a better future and just give up! We must have hope to survive in this world, and trusting in Jesus gives us new life and hope for eternity! Sometimes, if our prayers don't get answered *the way* we want them to or *when* we want them to, we give up on God But the good news is . . . God *never* gives up on us! He is waiting right there beside us, calling us to come back to Him because He loves us with an unconditional, everlasting love!

When we are waiting for *that big promotion, a miracle of healing, the perfect mate,* or some other great need in our lives, don't give up hope. Trust in Jesus! He knows better than we do exactly what we need. He loves answering our prayers and giving good gifts to His children. He also loves it when His children have faith in Him, knowing that *He knows* what is best! So put your hope in Jesus, because without Him, there is no hope!

He Holds My Hand

"Fear not, for I am with you; be not dismayed, for I am your God. I will strengthen you, yes, I will help you, I will uphold you with My righteous right hand."

Isaiah 41:10 (NKJV)

There's a battle going on between good and evil, and make no mistake, it's a fierce one that Satan intends to win. But as Christians, we have nothing to fear! We know with absolute certainty that God wins the war! When life seems frustrating, wrong, and unfair, remember that it's not the end of the story, just the end of a chapter.

The book God is writing has many, many chapters. So when the days seem dark and dreary, and our hearts are heavy with sadness, remember that this world is temporary! We don't have much longer on this earth—Jesus *is* coming soon!

There's a song that gives encouragement to those who have grown weary, and the words go like this: "I don't know about tomorrow, I just live from day to day. I don't borrow from its sunshine, for its skies may turn to gray. I don't worry about my future, for I know what Jesus said. And today He walks beside me, for He knows what lies ahead. Many things about tomorrow, I don't seem to understand, but I know who holds tomorrow, and I know who holds my hand."

Listening to Gossip

*Keep your tongue from evil, and your
lips from speaking deceit.*
Psalm 34:13 (NKJV)

We hear a lot about the sin of *spreading gossip*. But did you know that it is equally sinful to *listen to gossip*, even if you are not commenting or adding to it? When we take in what others are saying about another person, it influences how we feel about them—many times without us even being aware.

We should never condemn someone based on something someone *told us*, even if the person telling the story is someone we trust or hold in high esteem! Remember, there's always *more to the story*! Form your opinions based on your own personal experience, not what others are telling you!

The Bible could not be any plainer about the consequences of gossip. In Matthew 12:36-37 (ISV) we're told, "On Judgment Day people will give an account for every thoughtless word they have uttered, because by your words you will be acquitted, and by your words you will be condemned." Wow! Killing someone's reputation is not only wrong . . . it is a sin that will receive the ultimate death sentence!

Standard of Perfection

"Repent therefore and be converted, that your sins may be blotted out, so that times of refreshing may come from the presence of the, Lord."

Acts 3:19 (NKJV)

No one is perfect! The Bible says in Romans 3:23 (NKJV), "For all have sinned and fall short of the glory of God." We would be eternally lost except for Christ's incredible sacrifice on Calvary where He paid the price for our sins! In return, He wants us to commit our lives to Him.

God has given us a standard of perfection to live by in John 14:15 (NKJV): "If you love Me, keep My commandments." There's no mistaking how God wants us to live! He knows we are human, and there are times when we will make mistakes, so He has made provision for us.

We can claim His promise in 1 John 1:9 (NKJV): "If we confess our sins, He is faithful and just to forgive us our sins and to cleanse us from all unrighteousness." That doesn't mean go and sin all we want, and as long as we ask God to forgive us, we can sin the same sins over and over again with no consequences! No, not at all! God knows our hearts, and He wants us to come to Him, truly sorry for what we've done—with a deep desire *not* to commit that sin again!

All Who Are Weary

Because of the L<small>ORD</small>'s great love we are not consumed,
for his compassions never fail.

Lamentations 3:22 (NIV)

Many people have an image of God that depicts Him as a stern judge, just waiting for them to make a mistake so He can condemn them. But God is not like that at all! He is a loving God, full of grace and mercy. He wants everyone to have eternal life, desiring that no one should perish!

When you pray, take your troubles to Jesus. Visualize God with His loving arms around you, whispering, "I love you. It's going to be okay. Relax and trust that I can take care of you." Picture a tender, loving Father who hears the cries of His child and then allow God's holy presence to fill you with His peace. With God's strength, you will be able to handle your problems according to His will.

Jesus invites those who are weary to come to Him, and He will give them rest! He will never turn away anyone who comes to Him! You can trust your problems to Jesus, knowing He will never throw them in your face, call you a failure, or betray your confidence. He is a loving, tender, and merciful God who loves you with an everlasting love and will always be in your corner!

God's Holy Word

Your word is a lamp to my feet and a light to my path.
Psalm 119:105 (NKJV)

Most of us own at least one Bible. In fact, we probably have more than one, but few treat it as if it were precious or important. Far too often, it sits dusty on a shelf or coffee table, never even opened. But when we make God first in our lives, prayer, worship, and Bible study become our priorities—not an afterthought or something we put off because we are *too tired* or *too busy*. Instead, we are anxious to hear what God has to say!

Before making any decision, large or small, we should go to God's Word for guidance and allow the Holy Spirit to lead and direct. We can hold on to God's promises and claim them for our own. When we pray and study God's Word, we can expect answers and experience the peace that will wash over us even before we've received His answer!

The Bible is holy and should be treated with the utmost respect, for God is speaking to us on every page! The Bible says in John 6:63 (NKJV), "The words that I speak to you are spirit, and they are life."

Busy, Busy, Busy

*Commit your works to the LORD, and your
thoughts will be established.*

Proverbs 16:3 (NKJV)

Being busy . . . is not a sin! Jesus was busy and so were His disciples. Nothing is accomplished without effort, hard work, and persistence. But what we are *busy* doing is what's important. If we are busy in endless pursuit of things in this world, it will leave us empty, hollow, and broken inside. Worldly pleasures are fleeting and will not bring lasting happiness. All too often, we fill every second of our day trying to earn enough money to *buy things* that we forget about laying up treasure in Heaven, and lose sight of our highest priority.

Nothing here on earth compares to eternal life with Jesus! All the money in our bank accounts will be worthless when Jesus comes. Money that could have been spent on evangelism and winning souls for the kingdom is sadly wasted. A Christian's life should be busy . . . filled with the Holy Spirit leading, guiding, and keeping us focused on our heavenly goal! Pray for God to keep you *busy* working for Him!

Out of the Driver's Seat

"Do not worry about tomorrow, for tomorrow will worry about itself. Each day has enough trouble of its own."

Matthew 6:34 (NIV)

Since the beginning of time, people have been intrigued with the *future*. It's human nature to want to know what's going to happen before it actually does. Some even hire *fortune tellers* who claim to know the future. But *only* God knows the end from the beginning and what is to come! Because of His great love for His children, He puts blinders on our eyes so that we can't see. He really wants our *complete* trust.

There's a beautiful song titled, "If We Could See Beyond Today," and the words of the last verse go like this: "If we could see, if we could know, we often say. But God in love a veil doth throw across our way. We cannot see what lies before, and so we cling to Him the more. He leads us till this life is o'er. Trust and obey, yes trust and obey."

Trusting Jesus is what it all boils down to! If you knew what would happen next week, next month, or several years ahead— you probably wouldn't be leaning on Jesus! There's no need to fear the future if you allow God to control your life. Consult with Him on all your decisions and plans! Jeremiah 29:11 (NIV) says that He has "plans to prosper you and not to harm you." God is the only One who absolutely knows your future, and He's excited about guiding you through it. All you need to do is get out of the driver's seat, move on over to the passenger side, and allow God to do the driving!

True Dependence

The godly may trip seven times, but they will get up again.
But one disaster is enough to overthrow the wicked.

Proverbs 24:16 (NLT)

As Christians, we tend to measure how holy we are by our track record of not stumbling or making mistakes. But it's through problems and failures that we learn to rely on God. True dependence is not simply asking God to bless what *we've* decided to do; it is coming to Him in the spirit of full surrender and inviting Him to plant *His desires* within our hearts.

God may have a plan in mind that seems far beyond our reach, and it would be unobtainable if we were depending solely upon ourselves. But when we rely completely on our heavenly Father, there is nothing we can't do! True dependence is a *faith walk*, taking one step at a time, leaning on Jesus completely.

This doesn't mean that our journey will be without mistakes or that we will never fall. However, each failure is followed by a growth spurt, where our faith becomes stronger, and we learn to rely even more on God! It is only when we live in complete and total dependence upon our heavenly Father that we will enjoy the sweet peace of a victorious life in Jesus!

Share God's Blessings

A man has joy by the answer of his mouth, and a word
spoken in due season, how good it is!
Proverbs 15:23 (NKJV)

When God works a miracle in our lives, He wants us to share our blessings with others. Our personal testimonies of God's miraculous interventions are some of the most powerful soul-winning tools for Jesus. They are faith-building to others who may be struggling along life's journey. God doesn't just bless us and want us to keep it all to ourselves; He wants us to share so that we can help strengthen their faith too! We can bring encouragement by sharing how God helped us through the tough times, and in doing so, our own faith will be strengthened!

When we surrender our lives to Jesus and ask Him to open the door for opportunities to witness, He will do just that. Many times, a hurting soul that has heard a heart-warming, faith-building story will say, "Wow! If God can do that for him . . . He can do that for me!" What a powerful testimony! So, be bold. Speak up, share the blessings, and let Jesus shine through you!

Rejoice Always

Though the flock may be cut off from the fold, and there be no herd in the stalls—yet I will rejoice in the LORD, I will joy in the God of my salvation.

Habakkuk 3:17-18 (NKJV)

Everyone seems to be consumed with *worry*. We *worry* about our friends, families, jobs, finances, and especially our futures. However, the Bible says in Philippians 4:6 (NIV), "Do not be anxious about anything." This is a *divine command*, so that we might be able to live without stress and anxiety.

No matter what crisis we're facing—God wants us to *rejoice always*! Now that's easy to do when everything is going smoothly in our lives, but how is it possible to *rejoice always* when our loved one just died, our bank accounts are empty, or our spouses want a divorce?

Here's the secret to *rejoicing always*: we must live a life *surrendered* to our heavenly Father. It really is *that* simple! We can't *be good* on our own. No matter how hard we try, we will fail! It's only by living by faith, walking hand in hand with Jesus, that we will experience a joyous, carefree life of peace! When we fully trust God with our whole hearts, we won't be tempted to push the panic button. Instead, no matter how bad it gets, or whatever the devil throws our way—there's no need for fear—because we can trust God in all things and *rejoice always*.

Jesus Is the Only Answer

Not that I speak in regard to need, for I have learned in whatever state I am, to be content.

Philippians 4:11 (NKJV)

The only way to experience the abundant life that God wants you to have is to surrender your will to God's will. He has a special plan for your life, but sadly, you will never know what that is if you don't allow God to have complete control. Only a heart given to Jesus can fully know the joy and fullness of living a life in Christ.

If you're searching for deeper meaning in your life, you only need to look in one direction, and that is up! Feast your eyes on Jesus—the only real source of true happiness, peace, and contentment! When you are walking with your Lord and Savior, you are prepared to handle any problem that comes your way!

Having a close relationship with God opens the door to His strength, which enables you to overcome any obstacle the enemy may throw in your path. When life seems too heavy to bear, remember—Jesus *is* the answer, and He is the *only* answer!

God's Hands in Action

*Don't be interested only in your own life, but
care about the lives of others too.*

Philippians 2:4 (ERV)

When we pray over the sick, minister to the weak, give clothes to the needy, or care for the needs of others, we are *God's hands in action*! We share God's love in so many ways by reaching out to our fellow man to make their lives better. Sometimes it's a phone call, a handwritten card, a loaf of bread, or giving fresh produce from your garden! God has blessed each of us with talents, all unique and special. We can use those talents to God's honor and glory or for selfish gain—the choice is ours.

On Judgment Day, we will have to give an account to God as to how we used the gifts He gave us. For some, it might be helping a neighbor fix the computer that he needs in order to keep his job or maybe it's cleaning the home of an elderly woman who just broke her leg. There are many ways we can use our talents to shine for Jesus! If we pray and ask God to use us *in a special way*, He surely will! It's called *living God's Word*.

In Matthew 25:40 (NKJV), the Bible tells us, "Assuredly, I say to you, inasmuch as you did it to one of the least of these My brethren, you did it to Me." Reach out and *touch* someone today, and be *God's hands in action*!

Trust God's Word

All Scripture is given by inspiration of God, and is profitable for doctrine, for reproof, for correction, for instruction in righteousness.

2 Timothy 3:16 (NKJV)

When you're struggling with a decision, there's no need to get all stressed out, not knowing which way to turn. Instead of sleepless nights, go to God in prayer. With Holy Spirit guidance, He will give you the answers you seek.

Many people take prayer for granted, not fully realizing what a privilege it is to have direct access to our Creator God! Not only can you commune with Him through prayer, but He gave His Holy Word for divine guidance. Your Bible becomes more precious once you realize that God speaks to you through the Holy Spirit as you prayerfully read His words. When spending time with God, both in prayer and in His Word, you'll develop a close, personal relationship with Him. The more time you spend in prayer, praise, and worship, the closer you'll become.

God gave His Holy Scriptures to help guide and direct, for the Bible is not merely a book like any other book—it's *God's Holy Word*! And there is *power* in His Word! Before opening the Bible, pray and ask God for divine wisdom, understanding, and guidance. You'll be amazed at the peace that will come even before you've experienced His answer! You can always trust God's Word!

Thank God for Our Trials

*Not only so, but we also glory in our sufferings,
because we know that suffering produces perseverance;
perseverance, character; and character, hope.*

Romans 5:3-4 (NIV)

We often complain about our hardships in life, but it's through our trials that God perfects our characters, and we develop more patience, faith, and trust in our Creator. The Bible says in James 1:2-3 (NLT), "When troubles of any kind come your way, consider it an opportunity for great joy. For you know that when your faith is tested, your endurance has a chance to grow."

It is when we're in our darkest hour and everything seems hopeless that we cling to God all the more! If everything were always *perfect* in our lives, we would not be *leaning on Jesus*! In fact, over and over throughout time, history has shown that when times were good, people turned *away* from God. Many times, God allowed trouble to strike in order to save His children! And it's still like that today. When things are too good, instead of praising Jesus, we forget where the blessings are coming from and soon forget about God altogether.

Through the difficult times, our characters are strengthened and our faith grows stronger. When we trust God to help us through our problems, we become *who* God wants us to be! So, *thank God for our trials*!

Pray Anytime Anywhere

Rejoice always, pray without ceasing, in everything give thanks; for this is the will of God in Christ Jesus for you.

1 Thessalonians 5:16-18 (NKJV)

God loves you so much that He doesn't want you to face your problems alone! He stands ready to send ten thousand angels to your rescue if need be. And the good news is, God doesn't put limits on how many prayers He will answer or how long you can talk. He not only listens—He is interested in everything you have to say.

You can talk to God anytime, anywhere—while driving, working, taking a shower, or even walking down a grocery store aisle! And although you can talk to God throughout your day, it's still good to take time to pray alone in a quiet place, and if possible—on your knees! Kneeling before the throne room of God shows respect and reverence. It reminds us that our Lord and Savior is to be worshiped!

Too many times people try to bring God down to our *level* and then forget that He is our holy, almighty, and powerful God who is the *King of the universe*! He is worthy of our praise and worship—so pray anytime . . . anywhere!

Living Without Regret

*Godly sorrow brings repentance that leads to salvation
and leaves no regret, but worldly sorrow brings death.*

2 Corinthians 7:10 (NIV)

Too many of us look back over our lives with sadness and regret—wishing that we had done things differently. If only we had done this, or if only we hadn't done that—then our lives would have turned out better. It's human nature when faced with difficult circumstances to react out of emotion, without weighing everything out. Anytime we have a knee-jerk response, there's a high probability we will regret it—especially if we haven't had time to get all the facts.

Many times when we hear the *whole story*, our eyes are opened, and we feel bad that we did or said the things we did. But there *is* a way to live without regrets . . . and that is to *walk with Jesus*! Allow God to lead, guide, and direct, and we won't have to worry about if we are doing the right thing or not.

Before responding in anger or forming opinions based on limited information, stop and pray about it. Ask God for discernment and wisdom. And don't forget to ask Him for an extra portion of His love, so that in all situations you can respond in a *Christlike manner*. With God in command of our lives, we can live *without regret*!

Jesus Loves Our Children

*If any of you lacks wisdom, let him ask of God,
who gives to all liberally and without reproach,
and it will be given to him.*

James 1:5 (NKJV)

— ‹◆› —

Raising children and helping to develop their characters for heaven is one of the most important jobs on earth. That's quite a heavy responsibility! How can we be assured that we are doing it *right* and making the *best* decisions? We can read books, go to parenting seminars, and even get counseling, but our *first* place to go *is to Jesus*!

Just as our children come to us with their problems and concerns, we need to go to our *heavenly Father* with our burdens, asking Him for guidance, wisdom, and discernment. The Bible says in Proverbs 22:6 (NKJV), "Train up a child in the way he should go, and when he is old he will not depart from it." What a beautiful promise! God is the *best resource,* and He will lovingly guide us during life's most challenging moments!

Our children are precious to us, and we wouldn't hesitate for a moment to protect them with our lives. We are *God's children*! He not only created us, He *did* protect us with His life when He died for us on Calvary! Just as we love our children—Jesus loves us. And here's the hardest part to comprehend: *Jesus loves our children . . . even more than we do!*

What Real Love Is

"For God so loved the world that He gave His only begotten Son, that whoever believes in Him should not perish but have everlasting life."

John 3:16 (NKJV)

Jesus came to this earth with one goal in mind —*to save His children from sin*! He loved us so much that He left Heaven, took on the form of humanity, and willingly gave His life so that we might have eternal life with Him. What an incredible sacrifice! It's almost impossible to comprehend why He would be willing to do that. The truth is—Jesus didn't *have* to do it! When Adam and Eve sinned, He could have easily just said, "Oh well, that's the price they'll have to pay for disobedience." But that thought never even crossed His mind! His unfathomable love for us made all the difference in His reason to provide us with a means for salvation. Every day of our lives should be spent in praise and adoration for our loving Lord and Savior who loves us that much!

While here on earth, Jesus worked from sunup to sundown helping the sick, the poor, the hungry, and the weak. Even though He was flocked by people pushing, shoving, and arguing with each other, He was never rude or unkind. He was gentle, loving, and so fun to be with that even children ran to Him. He showed love to everyone He met, even His enemies! His life on earth is an amazing lesson of what *real love* is and a wonderful example for all to follow!

A World Without Sin

*There shall be no more pain, for the former things
have passed away.*

Revelation 21:4 (NKJV)

Can you imagine what it would be like to live in a world without sin? Think for a moment just how awesome that would be! No one would be doing anything wrong, so there would be no dangers to avoid, no evil to fear. You would never have to say, "I'm sorry," because you yelled in anger or lost your temper at those you loved the most. Nor would you experience the horrible feelings of shame and guilt.

There would be no more pain or suffering. No more disappointments. No more tears. It would be safe for children to go anywhere, anytime without fear of being kidnapped or murdered. That's right, there would be no death when living without sin. Can you imagine living in a world like that? Well, it's not just a dream, because that's exactly what heaven will be like. Oh, how glorious that will be! And you won't have to wait long, *because Jesus is coming soon*!

Make sure you are ready and your heart is fully surrendered to Jesus! Ask God to forgive each sin you've been hanging on to, and then fully surrender to Him. There's no sin, no matter how pleasurable, that's worth missing out on heaven. Our Lord and Savior loves you so much that He can't imagine heaven without you!

Is Life Worthwhile?

*"Let your light so shine before men, that they may see
your good works and glorify your Father in heaven."*

Matthew 5:16 (NKJV)

———⊰⟨◈⟩⊱———

Christians never have to ask, "Is life worthwhile?" because one of the great benefits of walking with Jesus is, you have a goal and a purpose! Without God, life is dreary and dismal and things seem hopeless, but when you give your heart to Jesus, you look at life in a whole new light. Allowing the Holy Spirit to lead and guide takes away the stress trying to figure out what you should do and where you should go. Whenever you take God out of the equation, you'll be in trouble every time! Satan is all too quick to jump in there and lead you down the wrong path. There's no better plan for your life—then God's plan.

Working for Jesus is the most rewarding and fulfilling work you can do, and you won't have to ask if your life is *worthwhile*—because you will experience the joy that comes with making Jesus the center of your life and the evidence will surround you! When powered by the Holy Spirit, you'll receive strength to face your own problems *head on*, knowing with full confidence that Christ is by your side fighting the battle for you! There's no need for worry and fear, for when you are weak, God is strong. What a tremendous blessing to be a child of God where you can confidently face each day knowing that God is leading in your life and you are safe in the arms of Jesus!

Best Financial Advisor

Wealth gained dishonestly dwindles away, but whoever
works diligently increases his prosperity.

Proverbs 13:11 (ISV)

God cares about our finances and how we spend our money! No matter how little we can afford to put aside, it's important to save for future emergencies. God wants us to live as if each day were our last—but at the same time, plan for the future!

The Bible offers good advice about staying out of debt, making good investments, being generous with others, and giving our tithes and offerings to support God's work. Many times, it's because of our own foolish spending and poor financial planning that we find ourselves in a crisis. But should that happen, run to Jesus *first*! Cry out to God for help! Ask Him to forgive you for not being a good steward. God is so full of grace and mercy. He's not sitting up in Heaven saying, "Nope—it's your own fault there's no food on your table! Get your own self out of this mess!"

That is not who God is at all. He is a God of forgiveness. Ask Him to be your *Financial Advisor,* and determine to honor Him by making good financial decisions. God promises that if we are faithful in our tithes and offerings, our cup will be running over with blessings.

Only One Life

Do not be anxious about anything, but in every situation, by prayer and petition, with thanksgiving, present your requests to God.

Philippians 4:6 (NIV)

L iving in this fast-paced world, more and more people are struggling with anxiety and depression. The stress level is off the charts and rest and relaxation is something that few people experience anymore. The financial strain just trying to pay the bills leaves people exhausted and discouraged. In fact, many describe their lives as similar to a hamster that is in a cage running around and around inside a wheel, turning endlessly, yet going nowhere.

Joy and contentment seem out of reach, if not impossible. But here's the good news: Jesus *is* the answer! He wants to give you peace and joy, and without a doubt, He's better than any anti-anxiety drug out there!

Allow God to be in charge of your calendar, your time, and every aspect of your life! You only have one life to live—so live it to the fullest with God in charge. Then and only then will you find real happiness, peace, and contentment!

Our First Priority

*If then you have been raised with Christ, seek the things
that are above, where Christ is, seated at the right hand
of God. Set your minds on things that are above,
not on things that are on earth.*

Colossians 3:1-2 (ESV)

Sometimes our daily lives can be so jam-packed with things to do that we don't even want to get out of bed in the morning to face the day! The stress-o-meter is off the charts, and our to-do list is downright overwhelming. At times, it seems we are just spinning our wheels, and it's difficult to know just what to do first! That's why allowing God to guide our steps and set our priorities is so vitally important! He knows how busy our lives are! He also knows the expectations of this fast-paced world we live in, so hold on tight to His hand, and He will lead us each step of the way.

God has a special plan for each one of us, and it's far better than anything we could ever imagine. If we go it alone, we will end up spinning out of control because, without the guidance of our heavenly Father, we would have no way of knowing what pitfalls to avoid, what dangers lie ahead, or the earthly goals He wants us to achieve. God should be our *first priority* in all things, because it is through Him that we accomplish everything we need to do!

Out of Your Comfort Zone

*If I ascend into heaven, You are there; if I make my bed
in hell, behold, You are there. If I take the wings
of the morning, and dwell in the uttermost parts of the
sea, even there Your hand shall lead me,
and Your right hand shall hold me.*

Psalm 139:8-10 (NKJV)

———◆———

Christianity is trusting Christ, not self! Most people are trying to reach God, find God, and please God through their own efforts. But perfect trust is relying totally on God, not on self. Some people say, "I really want to serve Jesus, but I just can't figure out what God wants me to do!" And that's the problem. We are not supposed to figure it out. All we need to do is stay surrendered to Jesus and allow Him to lead and guide us in all that we do.

Most people will never know God's plan for their lives because they simply will not surrender. They are so busy doing all the things they want to do that they don't stop and say, "Lord, what do *You* want me to do?" When we allow God to push us way out of our *comfort zones*, it is then we are really leaning on Jesus! There is no better place to be on this journey of life than holding God's hand!

Witnessing to Our Family

And let us not grow weary while doing good, for in due season we shall reap if we do not lose heart.

Galatians 6:9 (NKJV)

Sometimes our most powerful witness is to our own family. If we live a godly life, our daily influence in our own homes is a soul-winning opportunity. And it's never too late to start! Our example can last for generations and will be remembered long after we are gone. We need to be aware that our daily actions will influence those around us—either for good or bad. That's an important choice and a huge responsibility! Sadly, some families are destroyed and broken by selfishness, ambition, greed, and yes, jealousy.

A person with a godly love for their family allows Jesus' love to shine through everything they do. Some may say it's impossible to *be like Jesus all the time*, but the Bible says in Matthew 19:26 (NIV), "With God all things are possible." He will give us the strength, guidance, wisdom, and courage to be *Christlike* in all our actions.

When tempted to speak a harsh word, react in an unkind way, or explode in a fit of rage, send an SOS to heaven and pray, "Jesus, help me be like You!" Tens of thousands of angels can be sent in an instant to turn that anger into a soft word. Even in the most difficult family situation, Jesus *can* and *will* prevail . . . if you let Him!

Leap of Full Surrender

A man's heart plans his way, but the LORD directs his steps.

Proverbs 16:9 (NKJV)

When passionate prayer becomes part of our daily lifestyle, don't be surprised if God occasionally brings circumstances into our lives to perfect our characters and prepare us to be an even greater witness for Him. When our love for Jesus is our highest priority, we are willing to follow Him no matter what the cost. No one wants to go through tough times. We don't pray for God to test us with trials, heartaches, poverty, or pain. And let's be honest, being pushed *out of our comfort zones* can be downright scary!

God knows each one of us personally, and He knows our weaknesses and the secret sins we struggle with. He alone knows what it's going to take for each of us to become the person of priceless character that's ready for heaven. So go ahead! Take the leap of *full surrender*! You have nothing to fear . . . because God is with you each step of the way!

No Secret Sins

Be sure your sin will find you out.
Numbers 32:23 (NKJV)

Do you have a secret sin? Something you've kept hidden deep within that causes you to live in shame? Don't think for even a second that you're keeping anything from God, because it's impossible! He knows all about you, even your most intimate thoughts—because He knows everything! God sees your sin and wants to set you free from the burden you are carrying. He longs for you to run to Him so He can give you forgiveness and His sweet peace that you are longing for.

There's nothing worth being separated from our Lord and Savior. Whatever sin you are hanging on to, give it to Jesus. When you confess your sins, He will wash them away and cleanse you from all unrighteousness. You'll experience a freedom such as you have never known. Guilt will melt away and the heaviness in your heart will be gone! It is then, and only then, you will experience God's gift of joy as you walk closely and intimately with your Lord and Savior!

Real Joy of Serving Jesus

And we know that all things work together for good to those who love God, to those who are the called according to His purpose.

Romans 8:28 (NKJV)

———◆———

Sometimes when God calls, we hesitate or even refuse to obey. Perhaps we justify our lack of response based on our own feelings of inadequacy. We don't feel smart enough, talented enough, rich enough . . . and the list goes on and on! But the truth is this: God doesn't choose us because we are *perfect* and qualified for the job. He chooses us because His plan is perfect and He sees what we cannot. God will give us all the tools we need to perform the task He's given! And if we think we're just *too busy*, think again. God is better at keeping our schedules than anyone else!

We will never be sorry when we *make time* for Jesus. We can't out-give the Lord—in finances or in time! God's people who are working tirelessly for Him have learned to take bold steps of faith and fully trust in the power of Jesus' name.

So, answer God's call today with full confidence, knowing that His plan is perfect! Ask God to forgive you for ignoring His call and tell Him you want to work in whatever capacity *He* has in mind. Then get ready to experience . . . the real joy in serving Jesus!

God Wins the Battle

"You are to go to all the world and preach the
Good News to every person."

Mark 16:15 (NLV)

———◇◆◇———

Just imagine where you will be the day Jesus comes in the clouds—all ablaze with His glory. You can be assured that you'll not be lost in the crowd! Jesus knows exactly who and where you are, and He will send angels to escort you in the air.

Picture in your mind the look of tenderness and love on His face as you see your Savior for the first time! And then to hear those words, those very precious words, "Well, done, thou good and faithful servant! I'm so proud of you! Because you allowed me to use you, others are here today! Would you like to meet them?" Then imagine that moment as, one by one, people step forward until a crowd is gathered all around and Christ shows you the fruits of your labor! Wow! What a glorious moment that will be. No amount of material goods, wealth, or fame could possibly compare. When you're tired, discouraged, or tempted to think you don't matter, think on this moment. Sear it in your mind!

Satan wants to discourage you from working for Jesus. Make no mistake—this is war! Satan and his evil angels are working overtime to turn people away from God. But, here's the good news: we know the end of the story! We know God wins this battle! So keep working and shining for Jesus!

Living in Fear

The LORD is my light and my salvation;
whom shall I fear? The LORD is the strength of my life;
of whom shall I be afraid?

Psalm 27:1 (NKJV)

When we always see the glass half empty, always assume the worse, walk around with a nagging feeling that something is wrong . . . then we are living our lives in fear instead of faith! Walking around with a negative, heavy heart is a dishonor to God. The Bible teaches us in 2 Corinthians 10:5 to cast down every negative thought and every wrong imagination.

Unless we are walking with Jesus, it's far too easy to give into fear and let our imaginations run away with us. But we *can* overcome fear! And that is by following the advice in Philippians 4:8 (NLT), "Fix your thoughts on what is true, and honorable, and right, and pure, and lovely, and admirable. Think about things that are excellent and worthy of praise."

Determine today to cast out fear! Claim Philippians 4:13, (NKJV), "I can do all things through Christ who strengthens me," and with God's strength, you can stop living in fear and walk by faith!

God Answers Prayer

And this is the confidence that we have toward him,
that if we ask anything according to his will he hears us.
And if we know that he hears us in whatever we ask, we
know that we have the requests that we
have asked of him.

1 John 5:14-15 (ESV)

The Bible says in Matthew 21:22 that whenever we approach the throne room of God, we need to have faith that God *can* and *will* answer our prayer. It's also important to pray *in Jesus' name* because there is power in the name of Jesus! We're told in Philippians 2:9-11 (NIV), "Therefore God exalted him to the highest place and gave him the name that is above every name, that at the name of Jesus every knee should bow, in heaven and on earth and under the earth, and every tongue acknowledge that Jesus Christ is Lord." Just the mere mention of the name of *Jesus* causes the devil to flee and tremble!

When we pray, let us remember to pray *believing*, not *begging*. We need not beg God to listen to our prayers. He is our Father who lovingly listens intently and earnestly to His children. He not only listens, He answers! It may not be the answer we were hoping for or the timing we wanted, but He *always* answers with our best interest at heart. God always hears and answers prayer!

Free in Jesus

*Blessed be the Lord, who daily bears our burden,
the God who is our salvation.*

Psalm 68:19 (NASB)

The life of a committed and surrendered Christian is the most joyous, satisfying and peaceful journey we can take. Of course, that doesn't mean that our lives will be without pain and heartache. But when we're walking with Jesus, we give our burdens to Him, for they are much too heavy for us to bear alone. Jesus stands ready to remove our guilt, forgive our sins, and bury them at the cross. We must not allow Satan to shed even one cloud of doubt on our relationship with God.

Anytime the devil tempts us or tries to make us doubt God, we should say out loud, "Jesus, help me!" The mere mention of God's holy name will cause the devil to flee! God loves us with an unconditional, everlasting love that frees us from fear and sin. *Free in Jesus* means we are free of all the junk that is weighing us down and separating us from our Savior, because we have given it all to Him! It's no longer *our* problem—it's God's problem!

When we increase our devotional and worship time, we will grow ever closer to our heavenly Father, and it is then that we will start to understand His deep love for us. If we fully surrender our hearts and lives to God, we will experience the joy of being *free in Jesus*!

No One Is Perfect

*Create in me a clean heart, O God, and renew a
steadfast spirit within me.*

Psalm 51:10 (NKJV)

Some people believe they have to be perfect to receive God's forgiveness, but nothing could be further from the truth. For one thing, if that were the case, forgiveness would be an unobtainable goal because no one is perfect! God's forgiveness is not for sale. It cannot be earned, bargained for, or purchased for any price. God's grace and mercy are extended to all His children that love Him and believe in Him. The reason why we obey God isn't to gain entry into Heaven, but rather to show Him how much we love Him.

Many people don't understand how loving and caring our heavenly Father truly is. They think He's looking down on us just waiting for us to mess up so He can pronounce us *lost*. But this is just another one of Satan's lies. Jesus loves us so much that He died to save us! He doesn't want anyone to perish, but longs for each of us to have eternal life with Him forever.

What an awesome God we serve! Forgiveness is there just for the asking. 1 John 1:9 (NKJV) says all we need to do is confess our sins, and "He is faithful and just to forgive us our sins and to cleanse us from all unrighteousness." Confess your sins to Jesus right now, this very moment, and experience the sweet peace of God's *forgiveness*!

When God Decides

Every good and perfect gift is from above, coming down from the Father of the heavenly lights, who does not change like shifting shadows.

James 1:17 (NIV)

God has promised to meet all of our *needs*, although sometimes people confuse this statement with *all of our wants*. But that's not what God promises at all. Yes, God does say that He loves to give His children *good gifts*, and He also says that He loves to give us the *desires of our hearts*, but only when those desires and gifts are good for us! He knows exactly what we need and many times the things that we *think we want*, we wouldn't feel the same—if we knew the future. That's why it's important to always pray, "Thy will be done."

We can never go wrong when we are asking God to make the decisions! When we trust in Him completely, we can be certain that no matter what our need, God will provide!

Sometimes we forget what an all-powerful and loving God we serve. The Bible tells us in 2 Corinthians 9:8 (NIV), "And God is able to bless you abundantly, so that in all things at all times, having all that you need, you will abound in every good work." Thanks to Jesus, we will always have sufficient strength and grace to face each day!

Removing the Plank

He raised Himself up and said to them, "He who is without sin among you, let him throw a stone at her first."

John 8:7 (NKJV)

———◆———

There's a big difference between pointing out the faults of others and confronting someone who has wronged you. The Bible clearly states in Matthew 18:15 (ESV), "If your brother sins against you, go and tell him his fault, between you and him alone." God doesn't want us to spread gossip and complain to everyone around us about how we were mistreated. Instead, He tells us to go directly to that person *privately* and work it out! And if you continue reading the rest of that text it says, "If he listens to you, you have gained your brother."

God has given us that instruction so that fences can be mended and relationships saved. He wants us to have peace and unity. Fighting and bickering among us is displeasing to God. However, many people misuse this text to *justify* pointing out the faults of others. The Bible makes it very clear how God feels about judging! Just read Matthew 7:1 (KJV): "Judge not, that ye be not judged." And Matthew 7:5 (NIV) states, "You hypocrite, first take the plank out of your own eye, and then you will see clearly to remove the speck from your brother's eye." Wow! It doesn't get much clearer than that!

Which one of us is without sin that we can set ourselves up as judge and jury? Only God knows hearts and is qualified to be a fair and just judge. Let's try harder to keep our own lives pure and leave the judging to God!

Unconditional Love

Love suffers long and is kind; love does not envy;
love does not parade itself, is not puffed up;
does not behave rudely, does not seek its own, is not
provoked, thinks no evil; does not rejoice in iniquity, but
rejoices in the truth; bears all things, believes all things,
hopes all things, endures all things.

1 Corinthians 13:4-7 (NKJV)

Few people in this world love with real unconditional love. Many profess love for each other, until something happens where they disagree, and all of a sudden, the friendship ends. Sadly, family is no exception.

Sibling rivalry is real, and when God's love is taken out of the equation, it's downright destructive! Something as simple as a misunderstood comment can lead to years of separation. Even a *best friend* that you counted on to always *have your back* turns out to be not that loyal after all! It all boils down to this: if you truly want to love others, you need Jesus in your heart!

God wants His children to love each other as He loves—with real, genuine, unconditional love that's not dependent upon whether the other person shares your point of view or does everything *you* want them to! Human love is *selfish*—and the only way to love as Jesus loves is to ask Him to fill you to overflowing with His rich, beautiful, and unconditional love!

Fear Is Not of God

"I have given you authority to . . . overcome all the power of the enemy; nothing will harm you."

Luke 10:19 (NIV)

The Bible says in 2 Timothy 1:7 (NLT), "For God has not given us a spirit of fear and timidity, but of power, love, and self-discipline." So if *fear* doesn't come from God—then it is quite obvious that it comes from the devil! Fear is one of Satan's favorite manipulative mind games. He wants desperately to separate us from God, and the best way for him to do that is to plant seeds of doubt so that we'll stop trusting our lives to our Creator and start worrying!

The best way to overcome fear is to confront it straight on with prayer and Scripture! We need to use God's *shield of faith* and memorize power-packed Bible promises, so that when fear starts to rear its ugly head, we'll be well equipped to fight the enemy. We are God's children and as long as we stay closely connected with Him, He will take care of our every need!

We have no reason to fear—but every reason to trust the One who loves us more than anyone else possibly could! Let us live each day trusting fully in our almighty God, using the confidence, power, and strength that He gives! Our God is trustworthy!

Follow the Shepherd

Righteousness will go before Him, and shall make
His footsteps our pathway.

Psalm 85:13 (NKJV)

Life's journey is full of twists and turns, and without a guide, we are sure to be lost. However, we don't have to go through this difficult and challenging maze alone, because we have a Savior who will guide us each step of the way. Jesus calls upon us to follow Him and place our feet in His footsteps so that we will never make a wrong turn!

We can claim this beautiful promise in Psalm 23 (NLT), "The LORD is my shepherd; I have all that I need. He lets me rest in green meadows; he leads me beside peaceful streams. He renews my strength. He guides me along right paths, bringing honor to his name. Even when I walk through the darkest valley, I will not be afraid, for you are close beside me. Your rod and your staff protect and comfort me. You prepare a feast for me in the presence of my enemies. You honor me by anointing my head with oil. My cup overflows with blessings. Surely your goodness and unfailing love will pursue me all the days of my life, and I will live in the house of the LORD forever." The only directions in life we need are . . . *follow the Good Shepherd*!

Love the Unlovable

"But I say to you who hear: Love your enemies, do good to those who hate you, bless those who curse you, and pray for those who spitefully use you."

Luke 6:27-28 (NKJV)

All throughout God's Holy Word, He pleads with us to *love one another!* He urges us to especially care for the children, the sick, the elderly, and the less fortunate. The Bible says in Matthew 25:40 (KJV), "Verily I say unto you, Inasmuch as ye have done it unto one of the least of these my brethren, ye have done it unto me."

It's very clear that God wants us to show love to others, and He's not just talking about our family, friends, or people who are nice to us. There's nothing in the Bible that tells us it's *okay* to be mean to others, not even those who hate us. Indeed, it's just the opposite. Jesus wants us to *love* our enemies! In Proverbs 24:17 (KJV), He counsels us, "Rejoice not when thine enemy faileth, and let not thine heart be glad when he stumbleth."

God doesn't want us to enjoy even one tiny moment of pleasure when bad things happen to our enemies! Not even when it is an ex-spouse that has treated us horrifically or a boss that has fired us unfairly or a family member that has cast us out. We are to love, love, love each other—as God loves us—and yes, that means *love the unlovable* as well!

God Our Father

*Let us then approach God's throne of grace with
confidence, so that we may receive mercy and find
grace to help us in our time of need.*

Hebrews 4:16 (NIV)

In Matthew 6:9-13 (KJV), Jesus taught us how to pray: "Our Father which art in heaven, hallowed be thy name . . ." Throughout the years, people have memorized this prayer—although to many it is just repeating something learned instead of praying from the heart. If there is no personal relationship with God, the prayer lacks faith and has no real meaning.

To have an effective prayer life, we must know God as our *Father*, a Holy Being who is to be worshiped with respect and reverence! Some see God as some *spirit in the sky* that they are afraid of—or a stern ruler that is up in Heaven looking down just searching for someone to sin so that He can bring the gavel down and loudly declare, "Condemned! Passport to heaven denied!" How very sad this is.

Sadly, there are some who don't fully understand what a loving and awesome God we serve—a God who loves us so much that He tries everything possible to save us . . . extending grace and mercy time and time again! His love is without measure and without end . . . an everlasting love that satisfies even the deepest corner of our hearts. If we long for a more rewarding prayer life, then we must seek to know God intimately as our Father and our Friend!

Intercessory Prayer

First, I tell you to pray for all people, asking God for what they need and being thankful to him.

1 Timothy 2:1 (NCV)

One of the greatest privileges of prayer is intercessory prayer, however, many don't even know what that is! When a friend or loved one is too spiritually weak to pray for themselves and someone else steps up to the plate to pray passionately for that person—that is intercessory prayer. There are those who have turned their backs on God and don't even know that they even need a Savior, but God makes a way for us to intervene on their behalf.

When we pray for others, we're asking God to work in their lives, to perform miracles, and to bring them closer to Him. Many parents have children who have wandered away from the Lord and are constantly pointing out their sins, but preaching and nagging will not bring them back and, in fact, just drives them further away! *Convicting hearts is the job of the Holy Spirit.* However, God responds to heartfelt prayers of intercession!

Never give up praying for someone just because your prayer is not being answered the *way you want* or *on your timetable.* Remember, God's timing is perfect! Trust that your prayers are being answered according to God's perfect will. We cannot pray too much for our friends and loved ones! And God will honor our prayers even long after we are gone. So don't give up! Keep praying, for it is when we pray for others that God's power is released in their lives!

Not About Feelings

Now faith is the substance of things hoped for,
the evidence of things not seen.

Hebrews 11:1 (NKJV)

A relationship with God is not based on *feelings*. Rather it's based on faith and a real honest commitment to surrender your heart and life to your Lord and Savior. If you gauged your spiritual growth on how you *felt* each day, it would be pretty discouraging because feelings change like the wind. They come and go and run hot and cold! God created you with the ability to experience the whole range of emotions, but it doesn't define how much you love Him.

There are times during prayer that you can *feel* God's presence and then other times when you may not. However, it doesn't mean that you are doing something wrong or not praying in the *right way* or that God isn't listening to your prayers. It's not *feelings* that will draw you closer to Jesus, but rather faith and a knowledge of His unending love!

God loves you, even when you're *having a bad day* and just don't *feel* close to Him! He understands and knows your heart. So the next time you're struggling with *feelings*, ask God to draw even closer to you so that you may feel His presence. That prayer alone will change the whole tone of your day! Thankfully, *it's not about feelings—it's about His love*!

Letting Go

*Stand fast therefore in the liberty by which
Christ has made us free, and do not be entangled
again with a yoke of bondage.*

Galatians 5:1 (NKJV)

When we turn our lives over to Christ, we no longer have to worry about the future because God will gently lead us in the direction we should go. When we are free from the burden of trying to make the right decisions on our own, it's a tremendous load that is lifted from our shoulders.

Many people love the Lord with all their hearts but just can't seem to grasp the importance of relying totally on God! However, if we are worrying about what the next day will bring—we can't be truly happy, nor can we experience the freedom that surrender brings. When we give all our burdens, worries, and cares to Jesus, we can relax and enjoy life; we cease to have any problems—because they are *God's problems,* not ours! And there's no one better to trust our burdens to than *Jesus.* He *is* the answer!

And here's the good news: freedom is available to everyone. Even prisoners in a high security prison serving a life sentence can be *free*—when they give their hearts to Christ! *Real freedom* is not about being able to act, speak, or do anything we want—it's about the condition of our hearts! When we are trapped in sin, we're living dead-end lives of bondage and slavery. It is when we surrender our hearts to Jesus that we'll begin to experience the joy and freedom of *letting go*!

Go to God's Word

*For the word of God is living and active
and sharper than any two-edged sword, and piercing as
far as the division of soul and spirit, of both joints and
marrow, and able to judge the thoughts
and intentions of the heart.*

Hebrews 4:12 (NASB)

The Bible is not merely a book like any other book and should be treated with reverence and respect, because it's *God's Word*. He speaks to us through the Holy Spirit, impressing us as we prayerfully read His words, and it is through studying the Scriptures that we truly get to know Him.

When you're struggling with a decision, *go to God's Word*. When you need comfort, *go to God's Word*. When you need answers, *go to God's Word*. When you need more faith, *go to God's Word*! There is direction for every aspect of your life in *God's Holy Word*! Pray for understanding and discernment before even opening the Bible, and when you do, God will open your mind and heart to receive His messages.

When you pray in accordance with God's Word—you'll experience the peace that comes even before you have received His answer. John 1:1 (KJV) tells us, "In the beginning was the Word, and the Word was with God, and the Word was God." Clearly, the Bible is God's precious gift to us. So for every answer, every heartache, every need—go to God's Word!

Trust in God's Faithfulness

*He guards the paths of justice, and preserves the
way of His saints.*

Proverbs 2:8 (NKJV)

———————◁≪◆≫▷———————

God is reliable, faithful, and trustworthy! If you want to
have a great day—put your life completely and fully in
God's hands. Give Him your schedule, your bills, your wayward
children, your spouse that you've been fighting with, and
everything else that is weighing you down and causing you to
have sleepless nights. You will sleep like a baby once the weight
of the world is off your shoulders.

And once you've given your burdens to Jesus . . . don't take
them back. Leave them at Jesus' feet! He is much more capable
of handling them than you ever could be. God knows the end
from the beginning, and He knows all the answers. To put it
simply—God *knows* and *wants* what is best for you! *He's got you
covered!* God is your Creator and Father and loves you more
than anyone else ever could! He has promised in 1 Peter 4:19
(TLB), "So if you are suffering according to God's will, keep on
doing what is right and trust yourself to the God who made
you, for he will never fail you." There's no better time than right
now to take your burdens to the Lord—*and leave them there!*

He Cares! He Listens!

We know that God does not listen to sinners.
He listens to the godly person who does his will.

John 9:31 (NIV)

Most of the time people are encouraged not to dwell on the past but look to the future. However, there are times that *looking back* helps us to grow. For instance, examine where you were spiritually two years ago, then ask yourself: how does my prayer life compare today? What about my tithes and offerings? Has there been an increase in both the amount I give and blessings received? How active am I in church? How much time do I spend in Bible study—both my personal worship time and the time spent studying with others? How do I measure up? Am I growing spiritually or slowly slip-sliding away? Do my prayers lack sincerity and honesty?

Some people struggle with *faith* and go through the motions of prayer, not really believing that God cares and answers! But don't be discouraged. Instead of backing away from God, increase your prayer and worship time! It doesn't matter how awkward your prayers or how feeble your attempts at communicating with God—He cares, and He really listens with His heart!

Never forget that the privilege of prayer is always ours— but the power of prayer is always God's! We don't need fancy words or a college education to commune with our heavenly Father; we only need to pray with sincere, humble hearts.

Listen for God's Voice

Your ears shall hear a word behind you, saying, "This is the way, walk in it," whenever you turn to the right hand or whenever you turn to the left.

Isaiah 30:21 (NKJV)

To live the abundant life that God wants us to live, we must keep our minds firmly fixed on Him! There are many distractions in the world today—all traps set by the enemy to separate us from Jesus! Satan will try and tempt us down all kinds of wrong paths, but only God's voice will tell us the right way to go. The Bible says in Psalm 16:11 (NKJV), "You will show me the path of life; in Your presence is fullness of joy; at Your right hand are pleasures forevermore."

God wants to give us a happy life, and it is only by maintaining a close relationship with Him that real joy is possible. If we get all caught up in the sinful pleasures of the world, we will drift further and further into the darkness of sin and pain. Listen for God's voice. Even *well-meaning* Christian voices can lead us astray: *Do this! Don't do that! Pray this way! Don't pray that way!* If we listen to all those voices, we will become increasingly confused. Instead, let us be quiet and listen only to the gentle voice of our Lord and Savior, Jesus Christ!

Little White Lies

*Do not lie to one another, since you have put off
the old man with his deeds.*

Colossians 3:9 (NKJV)

Sadly, dishonesty is an accepted form of behavior in our world today. *Little white lies* are thought of as *no big deal*, and intentionally giving someone the wrong impression is considered *okay* as long as we have a *good reason*. An agreement with a handshake or a person's word means nothing anymore. However, there's no such thing as a *little white lie* in God's book. Dishonesty in any form . . . is a sin! When we don't tell the truth, we are liars!

The Bible has quite a bit to say about how God feels about lying. In Proverbs 12:22 (NLT) we're told, "The LORD detests lying lips, but he delights in those who tell the truth." God places such a high importance on truthfulness that He even included it in the ninth commandment: "Thou shalt not bear false witness" (see Exodus 20:16). God makes it very clear that there will be no liars in heaven. Revelation 14:1, 5 (NIV) says, "Then I looked, and there before me was the Lamb, standing on Mount Zion, and with him 144,000 who had his name and his Father's name written on their foreheads. . . . No lie was found in their mouths; they are blameless."

Wow! It doesn't get much clearer than that. As Christians, we should strive to be *Christlike,* and that includes being truthful in all things—our salvation depends on it!

God's Instruction Manual

Good and upright is the LORD; therefore He teaches
sinners in the way. The humble He guides in justice, and
the humble He teaches His way. All the paths of
the LORD are mercy and truth, to such as keep His
covenant and His testimonies.

Psalm 25:8-10 (NKJV)

There's no need to struggle with indecision, wondering what to do, which way to turn, or where to go, because life comes with a book of instructions! The Bible is God's Instruction Manual for living a happy life, and it's filled with all kinds of advice and direction on which way to go. There are many examples of people who struggled with trials and challenges yet when they followed God's advice—made it through the toughest of times, emerging victorious. We can learn a lot from the characters in God's Word because, through it all, God's love for us is evident on every page!

Pray about everything! Before you start your day, ask God for direction, and keep asking Him for step-by-step instructions throughout your day—and yes, even about the little, seemingly insignificant things. Don't forget the big things too. God doesn't leave you hanging with nowhere to turn. He has the answers you seek! Before making a life-changing decision, such as a career path, which college to attend, accepting a new job, choosing a spouse, or even buying a new car, don't forget to read *God's Instruction Manual* first!

Deserving God's Love

*"For the mountains shall depart and the hills be
removed, but My kindness shall not depart from you,
nor shall My covenant of peace be removed," says
the LORD, who has mercy on you.*

Isaiah 54:10 (NKJV)

Y ou can't buy or earn God's love! It's a gift given freely by
our heavenly Father. Just as a mother loves her newborn
baby even while it is growing inside of her, God loves us even
more. So much so that He gave His only Son to die on a cross
that we might live! There's no greater sacrifice! It's difficult to
comprehend that kind of amazing, unending love!

Even when we sin and fail miserably, God still loves us. He
hates the sin, but loves the sinner. His love for us is clearly defined
in Zephaniah 3:17 (NIV), "The LORD your God is with you, the
Mighty Warrior who saves. He will take great delight in you; in
his love he will no longer rebuke you, but will rejoice over you
with singing." Many can't accept God's gift of love because they
feel so unworthy. But the truth is, we are all unworthy!

There's nothing we can do to *deserve* God's amazing,
unending, unfathomable love He has for us! We can only
humbly and gratefully accept His incredible gift and show our
thankfulness by living a life fully surrendered to Him!

No More Tears

Many are the afflictions of the righteous, but the LORD delivers him out of them all.

Psalm 34:19 (NKJV)

It doesn't matter the reason for our pain, there is something about suffering that immediately shakes us up from our normal routine and brings us to our knees. It's when we are going through our worst trials that we cling to God, the only one who we know can help us. People who don't even believe in God will seek Him when they are at the end of their rope and all looks hopeless.

When we really want to feel God's presence, we need to be still and listen, waiting for His comfort and guidance. Being impatient and forging ahead, trying to answer our own prayers is not the answer! The Bible says in Psalm 46:10 (NKJV), "Be still, and know that I am God."

Remember, God has a special plan and purpose for our lives, and we can trust Him to lead in good times and bad. Just because we are suffering and crying more tears than we ever thought possible—*life is not hopeless*! God has *not* forgotten us! He loves each of us more than anyone else ever could. So much so that He died to save us and is coming again soon to take us home to live with Him forever! There's only one place to put our trust and that's in Jesus, the only One who can truly fix our problems and give lasting peace and joy!

Jesus Is the Real Deal

*Behold, God is my helper; the Lord is
the upholder of my life.*

Psalm 54:4 (ESV)

Christians often talk about Jesus, the Savior of the world, but when the first sign of trouble appears, they blame God—just like His disciples who panicked in the midst of the storm! Can you imagine? How could they be terrified when Jesus was on the very same boat with them?

Many are just as fearful today. There is no real faith and trust because they don't understand what Christ did on Calvary. If we could fully comprehend the depth of God's love for us, this world would be a different place. Jesus died for us! There is no deeper love that could possibly be demonstrated. No greater sacrifice. Jesus is our reason to live! *He is our everything*! He loves us more than anyone else possibly could, and He gave His life so that we can have eternal life with Him.

Jesus not only saved us from our sins, but He wants to *transform* us so that we can become more like Him. He wants us to love Him with our whole hearts! We can trust Him to be our Healer, Conqueror, Deliverer, Comforter, Encourager, Counselor, Savior, and Friend. Oh, that we could all reach the place where we can say, "Jesus, You are my everything." He truly is the *real deal*!

Justified Anger

*"Yes, if you forgive others for the wrongs they
do to you, then your Father in heaven will also forgive
your wrongs."*

Matthew 6:14 (ERV)

———◆———

When you have been hurt, it is a human response to want to hurt back and get even by making your enemy suffer. But you need to remember that Jesus loves your enemies every bit as much as He loves you. God hates the sin but loves the sinner, and He wants you to love everyone—including your enemies. God's requirement of forgiveness is not based on whether or not the person who wronged you is *asking* for forgiveness! He doesn't say to forgive *only* if that person who mistreated you is *sorry*. Jesus said in Matthew 18:22 (NKJV), "I do not say to you, up to seven times, but seventy times seven." Regardless if forgiveness is asked for or not—you must forgive.

Sometimes the hurt is so deep you may not feel able to forgive, but forgiveness *is* possible because, with God . . . *all* things are possible! God not only commands you to forgive, He says that if you don't—He won't forgive you!

In other words, if you hang on to the hurt and anger, it will destroy any happiness that you could ever have on this earth *and* in the earth to come . . . because *you won't be there!* You have a choice to make: accepting God's gift of joy or hanging on to all that *justified anger.* You can't have both—you must choose. Choose joy!

God Has No Limits

I will instruct you and teach you in the way you should go; I will guide you with My eye.

Psalm 32:8 (NKJV)

⟨◈⟩

There are no limits on what God can do in our lives! He has an incredible plan for each one of us, but sadly, most refuse to give up control and will never know or realize what that plan is. Unless we are willing to step out of our comfort zones and fully surrender to His will . . . we will be limited by our own human efforts!

God doesn't want us to set limits on what He can do, for there is nothing that we could dream of that could possibly compare to God's plan for our future! He has called each one of us to be ministers . . . to point others to Him. It is God's glory that people need to see, His fullness that others need to receive, and His love that others need to embrace. We alone have nothing to offer, but Jesus does!

Ask God for an anointing of His Holy Spirit on your life such as you have never known. Take His hand and blindly follow wherever He leads—with complete trust, confidence, eagerness, and Holy Spirit boldness! Then you will experience the richness, joy, exuberance, and fulfillment of living a *totally surrendered, Christ-centered life!*

Pray Believing

*"And whatever things you ask in prayer, believing,
you will receive."*

Matthew 21:22 (NKJV)

———◆———

One of the most important ingredients for answered prayer is *faith*! The Bible tells us in Mark 11:23 (NIV), "Truly I tell you, if anyone says to this mountain, 'Go, throw yourself into the sea,' and does not doubt in their heart but believes that what they say will happen, it will be done for them." Wow! That is a powerful statement, letting us know just how important faith is to God.

Everyone needs more faith! Instead of praying just *hoping, hoping, hoping* your prayer will be answered, pray believing! Ask God to remove all doubt from your heart and mind. Pray with absolute certainty, *knowing* that God *will* answer in a way that is best for you.

Learn to trust when you pray! Don't believe or even listen to the devil's lies, because doubt and unbelief will flood your soul and destroy the closeness you have with Jesus. Instead, push back the enemy! Refuse to allow doubt to wage war on your mind. Instead, pray with faith! *Pray believing*!

Divine Appointments

But in your hearts honor Christ the Lord as holy,
always being prepared to make a defense to anyone who
asks you for a reason for the hope that is in you; yet do
it with gentleness and respect.

1 Peter 3:15 (ESV)

As Christians, we are standing on dangerous ground if we're merely content to just *be a good person* and do nothing to grow spiritually! When we cease to grow—we die! Willingly going through the motions of living a godly life will not only leave us empty and unsatisfied—but it will rob us of eternal life with our Lord and Savior.

We need to examine our lives and eliminate anything that is hindering our spiritual growth. Whatever weakens our reasoning, dulls our conscience, or smothers our desire to be closer to God—should be removed! Any tool the devil could possibly use to separate us from our heavenly Father—should be erased from our lives! Pray and ask God for a wall of protection around our hearts that we may stay pure and true to Him.

Seek His divine guidance and listen to the Holy Spirit as doors of opportunity are opened for witnessing—perhaps at work, standing in line at the grocery store, or a talking to a random stranger we meet at a bus stop. There are no shortages of *divine appointments,* and every time we witness for God, we grow spiritually!

Poisonous Tongues

A dishonest man spreads strife, and a
whisperer separates close friends.

Proverbs 16:28 (ESV)

—◈—

Many people today are suffering from the sting of poisonous tongues! Just as lethal as a venomous snake, gossip can kill and destroy people's lives and reputations. Some have never recovered because of the devastating results of vicious lies! As appalling as this is, Christians are some of the biggest offenders! As long as they preface their gossip with, "I'm just telling you this so you can pray about it . . ." then it becomes sanctified in their eyes. But that's *not* how God feels about it. He makes it very clear that there will be no gossipers in heaven!

If you are a victim of gossip, remember that you and God know the truth. Just because people are talking about you, doesn't make it true. There's only one way to survive and that is to care more about what Jesus thinks of you than what others are saying. Ignore the lies! Don't spend time rebutting and defending! Let God defend you! Put your faith and trust in Him, and pray for those who are hurting you. Ask God to replace the pain in your heart with love for your enemies. You'll be amazed at the peace that will flood your soul!

All Things Are Possible

But Jesus looked at them and said to them, "With men this is impossible, but with God all things are possible."

Matthew 19:26 (NKJV)

———◇———

Christians have unlimited resources through Jesus Christ, our Lord, and there is nothing that we can't do as long as God is in it! We need not fear, but only to keep doing what God wants us to do. He will guide each step of the way and has promised in Isaiah 45:2 (NKJV), "I will go before you . . ." We are never alone!

When faced with troubled times, cling to Christ even more! We do not have to understand the reasons why, but only blindly trust our hearts, wills, and actions to God's divine wisdom and leading. God will give us all the tools we need in order to accomplish the work He has for us.

Many have trouble letting go and releasing control to God— but there is no one safer to be with than Jesus, and He has a specific purpose in mind for each of us—even before we were born, He had a plan! We are His children, and He longs for us to run to Him and stay close to Him, where He can protect us. Never doubt God's power or what He can do! *With God . . . all things are possible*!

No Deep-Sea Diving

*He will again have compassion on us, and
will subdue our iniquities. You will cast all our sins
into the depths of the sea.*

Micah 7:19 (NKJV)

When you have done something wrong that you regret, guilt often will raise its ugly head and can torment you relentlessly. Thankfully, God has the remedy for removing guilt and that's through repentance and receiving His forgiveness. You will always feel so much better once you have confessed your sin.

There are also feelings of *false guilt* that you impose on yourself—perhaps due to painful childhood memories or legalism imposed by fellow church members or even criticism from others who have set up false standards that you don't measure up to. Whatever the reason, don't let Satan or anyone else use feelings of guilt to separate you from our loving Savior. Confess your sins and allow Jesus to bury them in the deepest part of the ocean! And then . . . don't go deep-sea diving! Leave them buried! If you still have feelings of guilt, ask God to show you the source and then, deal with it in a healthy way!

There's an old but beautiful song that says, "Take your burdens to the Lord and leave them there! If you trust and never doubt, He will surely bring you out. Take your burden to the Lord and leave it there!"

Change a Life for Eternity

Jesus answered, "If you want to be perfect, go,
sell your possessions and give to the poor, and you will
have treasure in heaven. Then come, follow me."

Matthew 19:21 (NIV)

It's easy to reach out and help a friend or someone you know, but much more difficult to reach out to strangers. It pleases God when you are kind to others. The Bible tells us in Hebrews 13:2 (NASB), "Do not neglect to show hospitality to strangers, for by this some have entertained angels without knowing it." You just never know the impact you might have on someone with even a small gesture of kindness.

If the Holy Spirit impresses you to reach out to a stranger, pray for *holy boldness* and go forward, knowing God will be with you and will even give you the words to say! For some, speaking to strangers is natural and not difficult at all. But to those who are shy, it takes courage. Jesus stands by, ready to give you all the courage you need to reach out to others! And instead of focusing on how it makes you feel, focus on the other person and how they feel. Your act of kindness and hospitality has the power to change a life for eternity!

A Rich Inheritance

For thus says the Lord*: "Even the captives of the mighty shall be taken, and the prey of the tyrant be rescued, for I will contend with those who contend with you, and I will save your children."*

Isaiah 49:25 (ESV)

Men and women who die broke and penniless can still leave their family a rich legacy! However, that's only possible when they walk with the Lord in *integrity*. Living a pure and holy life is the richest inheritance you can leave your loved ones. A person who has lived a godly life has lived *by example*, and this in itself is a measure of true wealth!

Parents need to pray for their children continually, even if they don't see the results they are hoping for, because God will still honor their prayers long after they are dead. So never give up and never stop praying!

You need to live godly lives as an example to your children, for they are watching you—even if you don't think they are. They see if you are *walking the walk* or just *talking the talk*! If your children can see Jesus in you, it may be the very means of their salvation. So don't give up hope! Keep praying, and you will leave your children a rich inheritance!

Uniquely Different

Bless those who persecute you.
Romans 12:14 (NKJV)

God made each of us unique and special. This world would be so boring if we were all made the same. But some are *extra-special*! They tend to see life differently than most people, imagining themselves as eagles soaring high . . . looking at the world with endless possibilities. They don't care for the usual *rules*, are more inclined to *do it their own way*, and are often referred to as *risk-takers*. However, they usually don't receive *a pat on the back, applause,* or *recognition*. Chances are they might even lose a few jobs, fail a few courses, and ruffle plenty of feathers.

People who are known for not following a traditional path can make others very uncomfortable. But, if you are one of these *extra-special* people . . . don't get discouraged, because you are in great company! In fact, there are many characters in the Bible that stood out for their strong personalities, such as Peter, Paul, Daniel, and so many others. Just look at how God used them in mighty ways to bring glory to Him! God made you uniquely different, and He loves you just the way you are, so just keep shining for Jesus!

Notify Your Face

*A joyful heart makes a cheerful face, but when
the heart is sad, the spirit is broken.*

Proverbs 15:13 (NASB)

When our world begins to get too serious, we need to . . . stop and smell the roses! In other words, have some good *old-fashioned fun*! Try taking a walk, enjoying a swim, a game of golf, or a family picnic. Spending quality, fun-filled family time can make all the difference in our ability to cope with the stress in our lives. We need to give ourselves permission to enjoy happy moments in life, even though we live in a sinful world with heartache and sadness all around us. This takes practice, but it's worth it!

There are some who are of the opinion that Christians should not have any *fun*, that we should be serious at all times. But God made smiles, and He wants us to enjoy all the good gifts He has given us! He wants to give us the *desires of our hearts*! Jesus is a loving God who, when He walked on this earth, had all the emotions that we have . . . including *laughter*. He played with children, held them, and told them stories, and kids longed to be close to Him. Think about it. Would children run to be with someone who was always serious, grumpy, or never smiled? Enjoy today! Be happy! *And if you love Jesus— notify your face!*

Live by Faith

But without faith it is impossible to please Him, for he who comes to God must believe that He is, and that He is a rewarder of those who diligently seek Him.

Hebrews 11:6 (NKJV)

There's only one way to prepare for the stressful times in your life and that is to live by faith! When you have an intimate relationship with Jesus, you'll find unending amounts of strength to overcome any hardship, trial, or temptation the enemy may throw at you. Those who have strong faith in God will not waver or break under the devil's attacks or be paralyzed by fear.

We could save ourselves a lot of headaches if we would just learn to trust God more! Too often we make decisions without praying about them first, and then things don't turn out the way we want, we get angry with God. Of course, it's not God's fault! We have only ourselves to blame for not allowing God to show us the way. When the navigator sitting next to us has a map and we refuse to ask which way to go—it's our own fault we can't find our way!

We serve such an awesome God, who is the same yesterday, today, and tomorrow! The same Jesus, who walked on water, raised the dead, and calmed the storm is still reassuring us today, "Be strong and courageous. Do not be afraid" (see Joshua 1:9). Put God to the test! Place your complete faith and trust in Him and experience for yourself God's amazing love. It's life-changing!

Make a Difference

Be devoted to one another in love.
Honor one another above yourselves.

Romans 12:10 (NIV)

Whenever there's a hurricane, flood, or some other disaster, people seem to come out of nowhere to offer help, many times working long, hard hours to rescue, rebuild, or restore. Hardship forces us to join hands, pull closer together, and work side by side to accomplish the task, and doing so generates *brotherly love*. *Suffering* never ruined a nation, and *hardship* doesn't break up families—*blind indifference does*! When we choose to reach out and help someone in need, it not only builds character, but it leaves us with the best feeling in the world, which comes with *sharing God's love*.

God loves to see *His love* demonstrated by His children. That's why the Bible says in Matthew 25:40 (NKJV), "Assuredly, I say to you, inasmuch as you did it to one of the least of these My brethren, you did it to Me." We need to do what we can to make a difference in the lives of others. Stand up and choose today to *make a difference*! Don't wait for your friends to stand up too! When the Holy Spirit speaks to your heart, respond with, "Yes Lord, send me." Every time you step out to *be a blessing*, it is *you* who will receive *the greatest blessing*!

Stomp Out Prejudice

For there is no partiality with God.

Romans 2:11 (NKJV)

There's simply no room for prejudice in the life of a Christian! All throughout the Bible, God makes it very clear that we are to love each other, and you can be sure there is not one word condoning hatred or prejudice. Anytime we start to think we are better than someone else, we have allowed the sin of pride and prejudice to creep into our hearts. And as long as our hearts are polluted with pride, we lose our closeness with Jesus.

If we have love in our hearts, God will give us open minds to see the beauty in our differences. Just because there are others who are not *like us*—doesn't make them inferior! It just makes us *different!* How boring this world would be if we were all just the same! We can actually thank God for our differences as His special gift to us!

Unfortunately, prejudice is alive and well in virtually every country around the world. God doesn't love one more than another because of age, gender, social class, or what country we are from. The Bible makes it very clear that all are created equal, and we are to love each other as Christ loves us! There's only one way to end prejudice, and that is to ask God to give us more love in our hearts for everyone—replacing contempt with compassion and hatred with love. Stomp out prejudice one act of kindness at a time!

Wait Patiently

*Be still, and know that I am God; I will be exalted among
the nations, I will be exalted in the earth!*

Psalm 46:10 (NKJV)

It's human nature to want *what we want—when we want it.*
However what *we want* may not always be the best for us.
As humans, we can't see the future, but God can. That's why it's
critically important to stay close to Jesus and allow Him to lead,
guide, and direct all aspects of our lives.

Remember God's plan is always the *best* plan! Instead of
getting all frustrated and angry that things are not working out
the way we want—*trust Jesus!* Trust Him enough to take all our
troubles to Him, knowing with absolute certainty that He will
do what is best for us. He will answer our prayers according to
His *perfect plan,* and if we knew the end from the beginning—
we wouldn't want it any other way!

Nothing escapes the eyes of God, and there is nothing that
surprises Him. He knows all the intimate details of our lives—
even those hidden secrets in our hearts. God covers us with
His grace, and when we trust Him with our lives, He works out
everything for our good. We need only to *be patient* and *wait
upon the Lord*!

Called to Serve

*My brothers and sisters, God chose you
to be free. But don't use your freedom as an
excuse to do what pleases your sinful selves.
Instead, serve each other with love.*

Galatians 5:13 (ERV)

Perhaps God didn't call you to be a missionary in a faraway land or preach behind a pulpit, yet you have indeed been called to *minister*. You don't have to waste a minute of your time though, trying to figure out what God has planned for you. If not knowing what to do is stopping you from serving Jesus—then that's your problem! It's not your job to *figure it out*! Your job is to stay surrendered to God and allow Him to lead each and every day.

When you allow God to push you *out of your comfort zone*, that's when He can begin to use you! It's also when you begin *leaning on Jesus*—and not *on yourself*. So many of us are willing to serve God as long as it is something we are *comfortable* with—but that's not really serving God. That's doing what *you* want to do. The Bible has a very clear message of how God feels about that. Just read Matthew 7:21-23, and it will change your life dramatically!

It all boils down to this: *all God's children are called to serve!* Are you ready to give up control? If so, recommit your life to Jesus, fully surrender, and become a daily witness—yes, *a minister* for our Lord and Savior!

Cure for Loneliness

*A man of many companions may come to ruin, but there
is a friend who sticks closer than a brother.*

Proverbs 18:24 (ESV)

Jesus has a tender heart for all His children, and He truly
understands loneliness. When He was in the Garden of
Gethsemane, preparing to face the most difficult and painful
time of His life, He needed and wanted the support of His closest
friends. But where were His disciples when He needed them
most? Sleeping! His support and comfort was His heavenly
Father. Praise God that He is your Father too, who loves you
with an everlasting love!

When you seen a friend, loved one, or even a stranger who
seems lonely—*be a friend*! Many times, a stranger will walk into
church and sit on a church pew all alone, and instead of just a
warm *Happy Sabbath!* as you walk by—turn around and *go sit
with them*! Sometimes the loneliest place to be is in a room full
of people, so reach out and share God's love.

When your days seem darkest and *you* feel all alone, reach
out to Jesus. He will place His comforting arms around you and
hold you close. There simply is no better place to be! Jesus is the
only cure for loneliness!

Everyone Needs Love

When you talk, do not say harmful things, but say what people
need—words that will help others become stronger. Then what
you say will do good to those who listen to you.

Ephesians 4:29 (NCV)

———◈———

This world is filled with heartache and pain so heavy that sometimes life can seem overwhelming, so when you're given the opportunity to make someone's day a little brighter— do it! It may be as simple as a small compliment, pat on the back, or just a warm smile.

Smiling is a ministry all by itself! When you love Jesus, you just can't help but smile—yes, even through the dark days you can experience God's gift of joy! Start with your family in your own home and keep spreading God's joy throughout your day to all those you meet. And don't just select the people you *think* need a lift. Many who outwardly seem to have it *all together* can inwardly be suffering with the same insecurities that most people face.

The seemingly most confident person still needs affirmation and encouragement. They may be bravely and boldly going through their day not letting anyone know they are hurting, so they are often overlooked when it comes to *appreciation* and *reassurance*. Bottom line—*don't overlook anyone!* Give honest affirmation when an opportunity exists because everyone needs to feel loved—*it's as necessary as breathing!*

Only a Prayer Away

*"It shall come to pass that before they call, I will answer;
And while they are still speaking, I will hear."*

Isaiah 65:24 (NKJV)

When our day turns sour and nothing seems to be going right—instead of sinking into discouragement, we need to turn to our Bibles and read Philippians 4:6-7 (NKJV), "Be anxious for nothing, but in everything by prayer and supplication, with thanksgiving, let your requests be known to God; and the peace of God, which surpasses all understanding, will guard your hearts and minds through Christ Jesus."

Sometimes we forget that God is only a prayer away, and He wants us to trust Him completely, instead of worrying about what to do! Why spend even a moment of time pacing the floor, frantically trying to figure out what to do when God already has the answer to our problems? He knows the end from the beginning and what is best for us. We can relax with complete confidence that He has everything under control!

It's rather foolish to keep searching for solutions when the greatest Problem Solver ever—is only a prayer away! With Jesus—we have *nothing to fear*!

Second Chances

*"I, even I, am He who blots out your transgressions
for My own sake; and I will not remember your sins."*

Isaiah 43:25 (NKJV)

If you want to start your life over with a clean slate, you need only give your heart to Jesus, confess your sins, and ask for forgiveness. Then, with God's help, determine to be done with your past.

Whenever Satan tries to remind you of your former sins, pray for God to give you the victory over self-loathing and guilt. Don't let the devil have a moment to gloat. You can have absolute trust and faith that you have been forgiven. You don't have to keep rehashing it and tormenting yourself or keep asking for forgiveness over and over again for the same sin. It is gone! Buried! Washed away by the precious blood of Jesus!

It doesn't matter what skeletons are in your closet or what private shame you bear, Jesus can wash you white as snow and give you a new life with Him. He places His robe of righteousness around you and gives you a fresh new start! Each day is a new beginning! I'm so thankful we serve a God of *second chances*, aren't you?

Safe in the Arms of Jesus

*"The eternal God is your refuge, and underneath are
the everlasting arms . . ."*

Deuteronomy 33:27 (NIV)

You need not wait until you are exhausted, discouraged, and ready to give up before you seek help. Jesus says in Matthew 11:28 (NKJV), "Come to Me, all you who labor and are heavy laden, and I will give you rest."

Don't wait until you can't take another step—run to Jesus *now*! If you fully understood the depth of His love, you would not hesitate for a moment to put your life in the hands of the One who gave His life for you! Jesus loves you more than anyone else ever could and wants you to experience the abundant life only He can give!

God wants to set you free from your troubles and longs for you to give Him all your heartaches that are weighing you down like an anchor in the ocean! There's no need for you to carry the heavy load when God is standing right there with His arms outstretched ready to carry it for you! Once you are in His arms of safety, you will experience the real peace, comfort, and rest that you are seeking. There's no better place to be than safe in the arms of Jesus!

Never Argue Religion

*A servant of the Lord must not quarrel but
must be kind to everyone . . .*

2 Timothy 2:24 (NLT)

———◄◆►———

Your words and actions can be used in a powerful way to witness for Jesus! But how you treat others determines the response that will be generated. If you speak with an authoritative, *know-it-all* voice, you probably won't get the response you were hoping for. In fact, that person will probably never want to hear from you again! And they most definitely won't be attracted to the religious belief you were trying to share with them!

Too often, zealous, well-meaning Christians turn people away from God because they use the Bible as a hammer! Preaching doctrine rarely wins souls for Christ—but showing God's loving-kindness reaches hearts faster than anything else!

There is never a right time to argue religion. There's a wise old saying: *a man convinced against his will is of the same opinion still.* Simply put—*we need to love people to Jesus!* People are receptive to a heart that is kind, gentle, and generous. Instead of having a condemning attitude, love unconditionally as Jesus does! Allow God's love to shine through you, and you'll be amazed at the results. God allows you the privilege of planting His seeds of kindness, but it is His job to water them! Remember, you are God's messenger—but it's the Holy Spirit that convicts hearts!

The Right Reason

*"And whoever compels you to go one mile, go with him
two. Give to him who asks you, and from him who wants
to borrow from you do not turn away."*

Matthew 5:41-42 (NKJV)

Are you motivated to do good things for the *right reason*?
Perhaps you found a wallet with a large amount of money
in it, as well as the owner's identification. You're not tempted
to keep the wallet, but when you turn it in to the police, are
you *inwardly hoping* for a reward? Or do you simply have a
good feeling inside knowing you will make someone else very
happy? Although it feels good to receive praise, the joy of
making others happy is a much greater reward. It's also good to
praise others for their acts of kindness.

All too often, the goodness of God goes unnoticed. He gives
His children wonderful gifts without expecting anything in
return because His motivation is love. Wouldn't it be a beautiful
world if we all were more thoughtful, more kind, and loved
each other with God's love?

Love God with a pure heart and for the right reasons. You
can start today by rewarding God with your praise and worship,
expressing your love and thanking Him for His amazing gifts of
grace and mercy! Yes, what an awesome God we serve!

Persecuted for Our Faith

But you have carefully followed my doctrine, manner of life, purpose, faith, longsuffering, love, perseverance, persecutions, afflictions. . . . And out of them all the Lord delivered me. Yes, and all who desire to live godly in Christ Jesus will suffer persecution.

2 Timothy 3:10-12 (NKJV)

Many who become Christians expect *all their troubles will be over* once they've given their hearts to God, but that couldn't be further from the truth! Christians will suffer abuse and persecution until Jesus comes. You can be sure the devil will do everything in his power to separate us from our Lord and Savior! Make no mistake—the devil is quite cunning, and he knows our weakness and where we are most vulnerable.

It shouldn't surprise us when we are mistreated, ridiculed, or persecuted for our faith. Jesus said in Matthew 5:11-12 that we should rejoice when we are persecuted for His name's sake because we will be rewarded in heaven. My father often said, "If things are going too smoothly in your life—then you're not doing enough for Jesus!" So keep working and shining for Christ and thank Him for the privilege of being able to suffer for His sake!

Joy Comes in the Morning

For the trumpet will sound, and the dead will be
raised incorruptible, and we shall be changed. . . .
"Death is swallowed up in victory."

1 Corinthians 15:52, 54 (NKJV)

Our prayers are not always answered in the way we want them to be or as quickly as we expect. In fact, we may be tempted to think that God has completely forgotten us or question why He let something happen. Please understand this: God *always* answers prayer! For instance, a prayer for healing may happen instantly or it may not happen until the resurrection morning.

It's important to remember that God sees the big picture, and if we could see the end from the beginning, we would not want it any other way than God's way, for His plan is always the *best* plan! When we believe in God, we gain a complete trust in Him. We see everything in a different light. Jesus wants us to have *life and have it more abundantly*! He does not wish for any to suffer or perish. But when sin entered this world, so did tears, pain, and suffering, and we will live with the results of sin until Jesus comes!

Praise God for His gift of eternal life! When the trumpets shall sound and Christ comes in a blaze of glory, the sorrows of this earth will pass away, and there'll be everlasting peace and happiness! The Bible tells us in Psalm 30:5 (NKJV), "Weeping may endure for a night, but joy comes in the morning." Oh how thrilling to be united with our Lord and Savior for all eternity— for there will be no more sorrow, sickness, or death, but each day will be more glorious than the day before.

Gift of Friendship

*And let us consider how to stir up one another to love
and good works, not neglecting to meet together, as is the
habit of some, but encouraging one another, and all the
more as you see the Day drawing near.*

Hebrews 10:24-25 (ESV)

God gave us the gift of friendship to help each other along
this difficult journey of *life*! Friends and family provide
fun, laughter, and happiness. They give support during bad
times and share our joy in the good times. Sometimes we need
a friend to remind us just how much Jesus loves us, because He
is our Best Friend and our real source of love and strength!

God wants us to share His love with our *church family* too.
There's a reason that God asks us to *gather ourselves together* to
worship Him. He wants us to love and encourage each other
along our spiritual journey, so instead of being critical—have a
spirit of love. Ask God to remove the sins of *criticism* and *gossip*
from our hearts. Let's embrace our family, friends and yes, even
our *church family* with God's unconditional love! After all, if we
can't love each other and learn to get along here on this earth,
we will miss out on our heavenly home.

Let's love each other more, judge each other less—and plan
to be neighbors together in Heaven soon! What a glorious day
that will be—face to face with our Best Friend, Jesus!

Secret of Spiritual Power

"But you will receive power when the Holy Spirit comes on you; and you will be my witnesses in Jerusalem, and in all Judea and Samaria, and to the ends of the earth."

Acts 1:8 (NIV)

Many Christians have a desire for *spiritual power*, but are clueless as how to obtain it. Yet, it is available to everyone. It's really not a big mystery that requires a special treasure map! The secret to receiving *spiritual power* comes down to just two things: surrendering your will to God's will and time spent alone with God!

The Bible is filled with stories of people who were given incredible amounts of spiritual power to glorify God—stories of deliverance from a fiery furnace, surviving a night in the lions' den, courage to save a nation, escape from certain death, and on and on! It's important to read your Bible and refresh your memory so you'll be reminded once again of just how powerful God is.

When you fully surrender your heart to your Lord and Savior, He fills you up with unlimited power to work for Him, and your heart will long for *alone time* with Him! You won't be watching your clock to see if you have fulfilled your self-imposed, obligatory prayer time, but instead, will lose track of time because you don't want to leave His presence—that special quiet time when it's just you and God! It's good to seek spiritual power—not for personal gain—but for the sole purpose of glorifying your heavenly Father!

Sweep Away the Ugliness

*Since you have heard about Jesus and have learned the
truth that comes from him, throw off your old
sinful nature and your former way of life, which is
corrupted by lust and deception.*

Ephesians 4:21-22 (NLT)

God wants you to have complete faith and trust in Him, otherwise you will tend to question and doubt where He is leading. You'll miss special *divine appointments* because you will second-guess what the Holy Spirit is saying. If there's even a smidge of doubt in your mind, then you need to do some major housecleaning in your heart.

You need a pure, clean heart in order to truly listen to the Holy Spirit. If you have a heart full of pride, worry, selfishness, or jealousy—then it's not an environment God can live in. Jesus is the Master *Heart-Cleaner,* and He is willing to sweep all the ugliness away—all you need to do is ask!

When Jesus lives within your heart, you will experience peace and contentment such as you have never known. And when trials come, you won't have to worry because you'll be in tune with the Holy Spirit and depend solely on Him. The good news is, God can use you to the fullest when you allow Him to dwell within. Trust God fully and completely for He has great plans for you—and He's waiting for you to answer His call right now!

A Secret Life

*O Lord, you have examined my heart and know
everything about me. You know when I sit down or stand
up. . . . You know everything I do. You know what
I am going to say even before I say it, Lord.*

Psalm 139:1-4 (NLT)

God is our Creator and knows everything about us. He knows our innermost thoughts, feelings, and dreams, as well as our heartaches, worries, and fears. We can pretend that we are the world's greatest Christians and everything is perfect in our lives, but we can't fool God! He sees behind the pretense and knows who we really are. And if we think all that hypocrisy will bring us happiness . . . think again! Before long, all our pretending won't be able to stop the mountains of guilt and shame! Before we realize it, our *secret lives* will control our every thought and action, trapping us in a prison of despair and hopelessness.

Instead of trying to hide from God, we need to run into His outstretched arms, confess our sins, and start rebuilding our relationship with Him through prayer and the study of His Holy Word. When we commit our lives fully and completely to Jesus, He will give us the abundant life we are seeking! God's grace, mercy, and perfect love will wash over us, and we will experience a joy such as we have never known!

Plan for the Future

*Many are the plans in a person's heart, but it is the
LORD's purpose that prevails.*

Proverbs 19:21 (NIV)

Planning is good! In fact, we are counseled to *plan for the
future, but live each day as if it were our last.* While making
our plans, we need to recognize that even the best plans . . . are
subject to change! We should make out our agendas and set our
priorities, remembering to surrender all plans to God. Then,
with a willing heart, we can take hold of God's hand and go
where He leads!

When we belong to Christ, He lives within us and gives us a
renewed way of thinking, so we need to remember to allow the
Holy Spirit to lead, instead of stubbornly storming ahead with
our own personal agendas! Proverbs 16:9 (NRSV) says, "The
human mind plans the way, but the LORD directs the steps." Set
aside *quiet time* with God each day and take time to listen to
His voice. Be assured that He will direct our every step when we
allow Him to be our *Travel Guide*!

When the Time Is Right

Jesus said to her, "Did I not say to you that if you would believe you would see the glory of God?"

John 11:40 (NKJV)

—◇—

When you are following Jesus, and you are depending fully on His strength to sustain you, expect to see great miracles . . . because you will! Miracles are not always obvious, but when you *live by faith*, you can see them clearly! Trust God's perfect plan for your life even if everything seems hopeless and you don't understand.

Sometimes your path may seem blocked or the answers you are seeking are being revealed so painfully slow that you have to fight every impulse to jump ahead of the Lord. But be patient! Remember, God's plan is always the *best* plan! When the time is right, the doors will open and the path becomes clear! God delights in giving good gifts to His children and that includes giving you the desires of your heart—providing, of course, that your desires are good for you!

It's when you obey and trust God to know what's best that you more fully realize His incredible power and love! Living by *faith* rather than by *sight* enables you to see God's glory, and in your weakness, He will make you strong!

Not for Sale

For judgment is without mercy to one who has shown no mercy. Mercy triumphs over judgment.

James 2:13 (ESV)

All of us want *mercy*, not only from God, but from our fellowmen as well. There have been times when some of us have even begged and pleaded for it. Although we all want grace and mercy, few of us are willing to extend that same mercy to others. God wants us to show tenderness and love for others, even those who are mean and hateful. In doing so, we are painting a beautiful picture of God's love, which represents His character in us.

When we criticize others and do not have compassion, we lose the powerful witness we were meant to have. Don't be uncaring or hard-hearted! Instead, let the light of God's love shine out to all you come in contact with, freely extending God's grace and mercy, not only to those who you feel really deserve it, but to those who don't deserve it as well.

The beautiful thing about God's grace is this: you can't buy it, earn it, or bargain for it. None of us *deserve* it, but because of God's great love for man, He extends it freely! God's grace and mercy is not for sale!

Don't Do All the Talking

Behold, the Lord passed by . . . but the Lord was not in the wind; and after the wind an earthquake, but the Lord was not in the earthquake; and after the earthquake a fire, but the Lord was not in the fire; and after the fire a still small voice.

1 Kings 19:11-12 (NKJV)

This busy world that we live in feels like a roller coaster ride that keeps going faster and faster! That's why it's important to take time to slow down and become quiet so that we can hear God's voice, to sense His leading. The Bible says in Psalm 46:10 (NKJV), "Be still, and know that I am God." So many of us pray—but it is a one-sided prayer. We do all the talking and don't take the time to listen for God's answer. It's important to spend time in God's Word because that's another way for Him to speak to us.

Pray and ask God to guide you during your worship time. Ask Him to lead you as you spend time reading His Holy Word. And don't forget to ask for discernment and understanding. You'll be surprised how much more enjoyable your worship time will be and how much clearer your understanding of the Scriptures. Best of all, you will experience a closer walk with your Lord and Savior!

Struggle Against Hypocrisy

*"Be careful not to practice your righteousness in front
of others to be seen by them. If you do, you will have no
reward from your Father in heaven."*

Matthew 6:1 (NIV)

No one likes a hypocrite, and in fact, most people can spot a *phony* a mile away! Of course, there are others who are just so good at pretending to be something they're not that they deceive others as well. And when the truth does come out, people are devastated. None of us are perfect, and if we are trying to convince others that we are, then we are hypocrites!

It's also important to be careful not to inwardly feel self-righteous; for example, people can talk about how terrible it is for a friend to go to a theater to watch a violent movie, but then they'll watch that same movie in their own living rooms! It is a dangerous game of pretense! We don't see our own sin of *judging*. It's a form of deception that undermines trust in relationships and hurts our relationship with God most of all!

We need to stop deceiving ourselves that we are better than others. As the Bible says in Matthew 7:3 (NKJV), "And why do you look at the speck in your brother's eye, but do not consider the plank in your own eye?" We need to carefully examine our own lives before criticizing others. In the struggle against hypocrisy, remember this: God does not expect us to be perfect, but He does expect us to rely on Him to overcome our sinful natures. Remember—with God, "all things are possible!"

Live for Jesus

*But this is what I commanded them, saying,
"Obey My voice, and I will be your God, and you shall be
My people. And walk in all the ways that I have
commanded you, that it may be well with you."*

Jeremiah 7:23 (NKJV)

Our time here on earth is short, and the way we live our lives is how we will be remembered long after we are gone. We will be defined by the choices we make. If we are selfish, mean, and nasty, there probably won't be very many people that will miss us. On the other hand, Mother Teresa is remembered for her unselfish years of service helping the poor. Her kindness for others will be talked about until Jesus comes!

Living a self-centered life won't bring happiness. Only what is done for Christ will last. We need to ask ourselves: *How do we want to be remembered?* There's no greater way to be remembered than to be someone who has glorified God! Now is the time to make our mark in the world by being obedient to whatever God has called us to do. He wants us to be humble, compassionate servants, unselfishly thinking of others!

When we feed the poor, help the brokenhearted, and show grace and mercy toward our enemies, we are reflecting the character of Christ! Oh, that we would all strive to please our heavenly Father and accomplish all that He wants us to do. In other words, let us all make the decision to *live for Jesus*!

About the Details

*For by Him all things were created that are in heaven
and that are on earth, visible and invisible, whether
thrones or dominions or principalities or powers.
All things were created through Him and for Him.*

Colossians 1:16 (NKJV)

Have you ever wondered if God cares about *details*? If so, then consider examining the world around you. God's attention to detail is demonstrated in every tiny flower, plant, tree, and shrub. Even the weeds are uniquely designed. Every creature He created with distinct characteristics, from the long nose of an elephant to the multiple legs on a centipede. And we haven't even talked about humans and how uniquely different each one of us are. Even *identical twins* are not truly *identical*! Yes, God definitely cares about the details!

When you wonder if God cares about the little things going on in your life, the answer is a resounding—*yes*! No matter how inconsequential your problems may seem to those around you, they matter to God because *you* matter to God! He created you and considered every detail, from the color of your eyes to the shape of your toes to the dimple in your cheek—He loves you . . . just the way you are!

Pursue Joy

But let all who take refuge in you be glad; let them ever
sing for joy. Spread your protection over them, that those
who love Your name may rejoice in you.

Psalm 5:11 (NIV)

It seems that people around the world are in *pursuit of happiness*! But in this life, happiness comes and goes like the wind. It's here one moment and gone the next. That's because it's an emotion that is based on circumstances.

Instead of chasing the elusive *happiness*, it's much more rewarding to pursue *joy* instead. Joy is a permanent condition that automatically comes with a heart that is right with God! It's not based on what happens today or tomorrow or what we think will happen in the future. It's based on our relationship with our Lord and Savior!

Joy is present regardless of the ugliness of this world, because of the known outcome—eternity with Jesus! It's hard to be mad, depressed, or angry when you have a song in your heart, praising Jesus! So whatever trial you are facing, pain you are feeling, or tears you are crying . . . embrace God's gift of joy. It is available to you even in your darkest hour!

Real Reason for Prayer

You do not have because you do not ask God.
When you ask, you do not receive, because you ask
with wrong motives, that you may spend what
you get on your pleasures.

James 4:2-3 (NIV)

Many Christians claim to believe in God, yet they don't spend time talking to Him. When they first met Jesus, their prayer life was vibrant and active—but over time dwindled down to nothing. They justify this by saying they *don't have time*, but the most common reason they no longer pray is because they don't really believe God *hears* or *answers* their prayers.

Some even feel that because their prayers were not answered *when* and *how* that they wanted that God was punishing them. When prayer is not answered in the way and in the time frame that is asked, hands are thrown up in the air with frustration and prayer is viewed as a meaningless exercise. Some even get angry with God! How sad that prayer is used as a tool to get what they want.

The real purpose for prayer is to experience an intimate relationship with Jesus and to know Him as our personal Savior—*not just to ask for things*. Prayer is our direct connection to the only One who can give us real joy and happiness. Some may ask, "Why pray if God already knows our thoughts?" And the answer is this: yes, God *knows* our thoughts, but He *responds* to our prayers!

Life of Humility

But He gives more grace. Therefore
He says: "God resists the proud, but gives
grace to the humble."

James 4:6 (NKJV)

Humility is a character trait that is absolutely required in the life of a Christian! Some people will stand up in church and pray long, beautiful prayers as if wanting others to think highly of them. However, no matter how beautifully worded, a *prideful prayer* goes no higher than the ceiling. *Pride will always separate us from Jesus*!

Christ's life here on earth is a wonderful example of how we should live. He didn't seek attention, demand the best accommodations, or walk around with an attitude of being better than everyone else. No, not at all! He slept in humble dwellings, kept company with the sick, poor, and needy, and had genuine warmth and compassion for man. As Christians, we strive to *be like Jesus*, but that's not even remotely possible without humility!

The Bible says in Proverbs 16:18 (NKJV), "Pride goes before destruction, and a haughty spirit before a fall." There's no need to be *high and mighty* for we are all sinners and have come short of the glory of God, and if it were not for God's grace and mercy—we all would be lost. Let us determine today to live a life of humility—our salvation depends on it!

If You Love Me

*In fact, this is love for God: to keep his commands.
And his commands are not burdensome.*

1 John 5:3 (NIV)

When we begin to understand Christ's sacrifice on Calvary, we can't help but want to spend the rest of our lives showing Him just how much we love Him, and one of the best ways we can do that is by keeping His commandments. The Bible says in John 14:15 (NKJV), "If you love Me, keep My commandments." God has given us the Bible to help guide us through our journey here on earth, and the Ten Commandments are our treasure map to heaven! Only if we follow God's commands will we find our way.

It's not enough to *know right from wrong*; we need to *know our Savior*. We need to develop a personal relationship with God by spending time with Him in prayer and the study of His Word. Through Christ, we can gain the victory over sin! God gives us the power to change our lives when we claim Philippians 4:13 (NKJV), "I can do all things through Christ who strengthens me." Choose today to live a life fully surrendered to God and start experiencing the real joy of living!

Appointment with God

Everyone who goes on ahead and does not abide in the teaching of Christ, does not have God. Whoever abides in the teaching has both the Father and the Son.

2 John 9 (ESV)

There is nothing more important on our calendars than our daily *appointment with God*. We need that special *One-on-one* time with Him every morning for wisdom, guidance, and direction. Some skip prayer altogether, rationalizing that they simply don't have the time, but that excuse just doesn't make sense. Without communicating with our heavenly Father, we would not have a clue how to even go about our day and accomplish everything we need to do! We wouldn't know the first step to take!

We simply cannot live a Holy Spirit led life—without prayer! Think for a moment about Daniel, who held a very high position in the king's court. He was extremely busy, yet he believed in the importance of prayer. He *made time* to pray . . . not once, not twice, but three times a day, and God blessed him abundantly for his faithfulness! Just like He did for Daniel, God stands willing to guide us too—but the key to real joy and contentment is to never miss our daily *appointment with God*!

I Belong to Jesus

*God has made us what we are. In Christ Jesus,
God made us to do good works, which God planned in
advance for us to live our lives doing.*

Ephesians 2:10 (NCV)

God has blessed each of us with special talents and gifts. Some He gives more than others, but not because He loves them more than anyone else. He has a specific purpose for each of our lives, and He gives us the talents we need to accomplish His tasks. Some gifts are more obvious, while others seem to go unnoticed, under the radar. But all are equally important.

Take time to think about the gifts God has given you and then count your blessings! Pray the prayer of Jabez in 1 Chronicles 4:10 and ask for your territory to be expanded. In other words, ask God to bless the talents He gave you so that you might have an even greater impact for Him!

So anytime the devil tempts you to believe you are worthless, there's nothing you can do, you have no talents, etc.—push those evil thoughts out of your mind and say out loud, "I belong to Jesus! I'm a child of the King of the universe, and He loves *me*!"

God Lights the Way

Blessed is that man who makes the LORD his trust, and does not respect the proud, nor such as turn aside to lies.

Psalm 40:4 (NKJV)

God has a very good reason why He doesn't reveal the future. Think for a moment: if we knew what would happen tomorrow, next week, or next year, we would not be leaning on Jesus to light the path before us. The choices on how we live our lives would be based on what we *know* and not our *faith* in our heavenly Father.

God lights the way, but only one step at a time. He doesn't shine the light ten miles down the road ahead of us. He wants us to fully trust Him! He shows us when and where to take each step, and when He does, we need to listen—not walk the other way. Simply be obedient to God's will! Trust that He knows exactly where we need to go and how to get there safely.

There are times when following Jesus that we'll face difficult and challenging trials—but we won't be facing them alone. God is with us always! When the enemy tempts us to disobey His voice, we can resist the devil by calling upon God for an army of angels to surround us and keep us faithful! We can cling to this promise in Psalm 119:105 (KJV), "Thy word is a lamp unto my feet, and a light unto my path."

The Bible Sinners Read

*When you are around people who do not know God,
be careful how you act. Even if they talk against you as
wrong-doers, in the end they will give thanks to God for
your good works when Christ comes again.*

1 Peter 2:12 (NLV)

The world judges you by how you live—not by what the Bible says. Christians are the *Bible* that sinners read. Thus, it is critically important that you live each day totally depending on the Holy Spirit to guide and direct. When tempted to lose your temper and respond in anger, stop a second and ask yourself, "What would Jesus do?" Live your life for Jesus—knowing that you are a constant example and witness to others!

And don't forget to pray for guidance. Prayer is vitally important to God and provides direct communication with Him. As a follower of Christ, you need to live your life in such a way that the world may see Jesus in you. Strive to live a more *holy life*. You can achieve this goal by maintaining a constant connection with your Lord and Savior, the Giver of eternal life! Choose today to *be like Jesus*!

Living a Godly Life

*The fear of the LORD adds length to life, but the
years of the wicked are cut short.*

Proverbs 10:27 (NIV)

There's no doubt about it, when you love the Lord with all your heart, it affects every aspect of your life. How you think, speak, and act are completely different when you are walking with Jesus. A close connection with God gives you the strength to overcome sin and the ability to live each and every day to the fullest!

Ask God to direct your every thought and action. When you live a Godly life, you have nothing to fear—not even death! A life truly surrendered to God is the most fulfilling life you can live.

Instead of focusing on *self*, live every minute, every hour, and every day to glorify our heavenly Father. In Romans 6:23 (NIV), the Bible makes it very clear how God feels about sin: "For the wages of sin is death, but the gift of God is eternal life in Christ Jesus our Lord." Jesus paid the price for our salvation, and through Him, we *can* overcome evil. Through Jesus Christ, we *can* have victory! What an awesome God we serve!

Only Jesus Heals Hearts

*He tends his flock like a shepherd: He gathers the
lambs in his arms and carries them close to his heart;
he gently leads those that have young.*

Isaiah 40:11 (NIV)

When our hearts hurt more than we can bear, it's human nature to seek comfort. Having peace and happiness in our lives is as necessary as breathing, and we will keep searching for it until we find some kind of relief! Satan loves to see us suffer, and he is quite clever, enticing us to seek comfort in worldly pleasures such as gambling, sex, alcohol, or drugs.

Where we go to for comfort depends entirely on how close we are to God. Some learn the hard way that none of the things in this world can bring the peace we are seeking! Only Jesus can heal hearts! He should be our *first* resort, not our *last* one!

God doesn't want any of His children to suffer, but as long as we live on this sinful earth, there will be pain and heartache. The good news is . . . we don't have to carry our burdens or try and face our problems alone! Jesus pleads with us to come to Him, and He will give us rest. The Bible says in Jeremiah 31:13 (NIV), "I will turn their mourning into gladness; I will give them comfort and joy instead of sorrow." When we give our heartaches to Jesus, we will find sweet comfort in His arms of love.

Keep Looking Up

Who shall separate us from the love of Christ?
Shall tribulation, or distress, or persecution, or
famine, or nakedness, or peril, or sword?

Romans 8:35 (NKJV)

People will disappoint you, but Jesus never will. Brother will turn against brother, friend against friend. Even the most loyal employee could turn on you in a moment's notice. One of the main reasons that Christians stop going to church is because of disagreements with other members. Someone makes a snide remark, and they get offended. The next thing you know, they stop coming to church, and after a while, it gets harder and harder to come back. Before long, they've turned their back on God completely!

That's why it's so important that you keep your eyes on Jesus. Don't look to other people as mentors or examples, because your only true example is God! Don't place others on a pedestal—not even your pastor, for pastors are human and makes mistakes too!

There's only one true friend that you can count on to never disappoint you or let you down, and that is your Best Friend, Jesus. Cling to Him and cherish your friendship with Him! He's there to fight your battles, guide you through life's ups and downs, and be there for you when you start to fall. He'll give you strength to face each day and *love* you through all your heartaches! When a friend or loved one lets you down, don't get discouraged, angry, or blame God . . . just look up . . . and keep looking up!

Nothing to Fear

Yet I am always with you; you hold me by my right hand. You guide me with your counsel, and afterward you will take me into glory.

Psalm 73:23-24 (NIV)

———◆———

Some people are afraid to try new things because they don't want to fail. In fact they're so terrified that it becomes, well . . . downright paralyzing! They'd rather not try at all . . . than risk failure!

Fear prevents us from achieving our goals and, even more importantly, from accomplishing all God has planned for us. Most successful people are not afraid to fail. They are willing to take risks and throw pride out the window. After all, does it really matter if someone knows that something didn't quite turn out the way we expected? What is the worst that could happen? Someone gossiping about us? What's most important is what God thinks, not what our neighbors are saying!

We need to be careful what we say to others. A person that is told they will *never amount to anything* can be crippled by those words their whole life. Instead, we should encourage each other. Think positive! Have faith! Have trust in God! Fortunately, God views our successes and failures much differently than man does. He wants us to trust Him and go forward with confidence that He will guide and direct each step of the way. With God . . . all things are possible; we have nothing to fear!

Not the End

Consider it pure joy, my brothers and sisters, whenever
you face trials of many kinds, because you know that the
testing of your faith produces perseverance.

James 1:2-3 (NIV)

 decorative divider

We were not thrown on this earth as if we didn't matter, like dust flying through the air. No, not at all! God has deliberately and lovingly placed us here. He has given us a purpose for our existence and a reason to go on, even in the midst of the worst storm where the dark clouds of discouragement threaten to overtake us.

But we have no cause for worry. When we experience pain and suffering, we not only become more dependent on God, but our love for Him grows as well. We develop a deeper trust knowing He has everything under control; and best of all, those who have committed their lives to Jesus have been promised a bright future—*eternity with Him in heaven.*

So we can smile through the pain, and there's no need for tears because the Bible says in Romans 8:18 (NIV), "I consider that our present sufferings are not worth comparing with the glory that will be revealed in us." Praise the Lord! We can rejoice through times of trouble and take comfort in the knowledge that, as a Christian, what we're going through isn't the end of the story . . . it's simply the rough journey that leads to our heavenly home!

Turn to Jesus First

*In my trouble I called to the LORD. I cried out to my God
for help. From his temple he heard my voice;
my call for help reached his ears.*

Psalm 18:6 (NCV)

When our bank account is empty, our loved one just died,
loneliness and depression is all-consuming, or we're
lost and seeking purpose in life . . . whom do we turn to? It's
during the darkest times in our lives that we really need an
understanding friend that we trust.

It's not easy to find someone we can tell our intimate
thoughts and feelings to and have confidence that what we told
them won't end up on Twitter or Facebook! We need someone
who will understand us, provide the advice and answers we are
seeking, and has the power to change our circumstances. There
is only One who can do all that, and that friend is Jesus, our
Lord and Savior! He is the *best Friend* we could ever have!

When we need help, God is the *first* place we should go!
Take the time to study His Word, and you'll find answers, peace,
and comfort. No matter what struggle we are facing, turn to
Jesus—*first*!

Choose to Shine

Be joyful in hope, patient in affliction, faithful in prayer.
Romans 12:12 (NIV)

As Christians, when we are faced with unexpected hardships, we have a choice to make. We can pout, complain, and be bitter or we can choose to shine for Jesus no matter what life throws our way. Some people react to whatever is around them. If the situation is tense, they are grouchy and irritable. If it's stormy, they worry and fret. If everything is going smoothly, they are calm and happy.

But then there are those who really stand out! They may have every reason in the world to feel sorry for themselves, but instead, they smile through the pain and are loving and kind. No matter the circumstance, they radiate the joy of Jesus. They are so filled with the Holy Spirit that they don't let the situation dictate their mood. They walk so closely with God that they lean on Him completely. They have no need to worry, because there's complete trust! They have absolute faith that whatever storm comes along, there's no need to panic, because . . . Jesus is in the boat with them!

True Christians have this blessed peace. When we have a close connection with God, we can truly experience joy . . . no matter what kind of *bad day* may arise. Even on your worst day, choose to shine for Jesus!

The Waiting Game

*Wait for the LORD; be strong, and let your heart take
courage; wait for the LORD!*

Psalm 27:14 (ESV)

It seems that so often in this life we find ourselves waiting. We
stand in line at grocery stores, at the post office, or boarding
a plane. And then there's the seemingly endless wait at the
doctor's office, and the more pain we're in, the longer the wait
seems! The time becomes even longer outside a surgical unit
or emergency room when waiting to hear of a loved one's fate.

The secret to playing the *waiting game* is to stay close to
Jesus. Clasp His hand and never let go! Pray for patience,
endurance, and more faith and trust in God! Ask for a clean
heart and a right spirit—that all impatience, worry, and anger
be removed and replaced with God's sweet peace.

In this world, it is inevitable that we will be *waiting* for one
thing or another. That's just life! But the most important *wait* of
all is for Jesus' second coming, and because we are so miserable
on this earth, the *wait* for this marvelous day will be the most
challenging of all!

We need to be careful when we pray not to *demand* that
Jesus come *now*! Remember, God has it all worked out, and He
knows what He is doing. So instead of fretting or being mad
at God for not answering our prayers the way we want Him to
and in the time frame we want . . . in all things—trust in *God's
perfect timing*!

Character Assassination

*A gossip betrays a confidence; so avoid
anyone who talks too much.*

Proverbs 20:19 (NIV)

Christians would never dream of stealing, committing adultery, or killing someone. However, gossip seems to be *acceptable* even though the Bible is very clear that destroying someone's reputation is a sin!

Making it even easier today is *high-tech gossip*. As soon as something comes in your email and you push the send button to forward to all your friends, you have effectively spread *gossip*! The Bible says in Psalm 141:3 (KJV), "Set a watch, O LORD, before my mouth; . . ." so when someone starts to give you *the inside scoop* on a Christian brother or sister, friend, family member, or anyone else—stop and walk away before you are tempted to listen to even one *juicy detail* that would make you a part of the character assassination!

There's an old but wise expression: "If you can't say anything good about someone—don't say anything at all!" Not a bad policy, wouldn't you say? Pray for a *clean heart and a right spirit* and ask God to fill you with so much love that you'll only speak kindly of others!

Holy Spirit Hugs

The Spirit of the LORD will rest on him—the Spirit of wisdom and of understanding, the Spirit of counsel and of might, the Spirit of the knowledge and fear of the LORD—and he will delight in the fear of the LORD. He will not judge by what he sees with his eyes, or decide by what he hears with his ears.

Isaiah 11:2-3 (NIV)

When you are willing to allow God to use you however *He* wants to use you, it's the most humbling, joyous, and exhilarating experience you could possibly imagine! Don't be afraid to give up control and let God call the shots because, the truth is, if you're witnessing without God's divine direction, you're not really serving *God* . . . you are serving *self*! It's not until you are willing to do it *God's way*, and not *your way,* that you are truly working for Jesus. When you submit fully and completely to His will, you'll see firsthand the awesome life-transforming power of the Holy Spirit!

The greatest feeling in the world is knowing you are surrendered and following God's plan for your life. Every time your heart responds to the calling of the Holy Spirit, you are flooded with His love. I call this *Holy Spirit hugs*! There's really nothing quite like it this side of Heaven!

That's God's Job

*Humble yourselves, therefore, under God's mighty
hand, that he may lift you up in due time. Cast all your
anxiety on Him because he cares for you.*

1 Peter 5:6-7 (NIV)

God didn't create our human minds to look into the future. Instead, He wants us to be in constant communication with Him so that He can direct our every step! If our minds are spinning out of control trying to figure out what to do next, we will never be at peace. Just when we think we have it all planned out, the enemy causes something unexpected to happen, throwing us into a crisis!

Sometimes, because of our own foolish pride or just plain stubbornness, we fall over and over again until we are so discouraged, we just want to give up! We need to trust Jesus with our past, present, and future! That includes every aspect of our lives—especially what we do for Him.

God has a special plan for each of us, so there is no need for us to try and *figure it out*! That's *God's job*! Our job is to bring Him all our needs, hopes, and fears, committing everything into His care. Happiness and real joy will come when we stop worrying about what will happen tomorrow and trust God with our past, present, and future!

No Excuses

*But each one is tempted when he is drawn away
by his own desires and enticed. Then, when desire has
conceived, it gives birth to sin; and sin,
when it is full-grown, brings forth death.*

James 1:14-15 (NKJV)

It's much easier to please God rather than man. For one thing, God won't judge us falsely or hold us up to unreasonable standards. And, the best part—He will never ask us to do anything by ourselves! He will be with us each step of the way and provide all the tools necessary to do the job, including strength, courage, and talent.

That doesn't mean that God doesn't have high expectations! It just means that He makes it one hundred percent possible for us to reach His goals. This includes keeping His commandments—*all of them*! In fact, when we disobey His commandments, it's a denial of God's authority. When we rebel against God, it is the very essence of sin!

If we truly love God, then it won't be a drudgery for we'll *want* to obey Him. When we are weak and fall, all we need to do is reach out to Jesus, and He'll pick us up, dust us off, and encourage us to keep holding His hand. All who go to God seeking His forgiveness will receive it! We are given the ability to obey—through Christ who strengthens us. We have no excuse for disobedience, for God promises us victory in Him—all we need to do is *trust and obey*!

Can't Buy Happiness

For the love of money is a root of all kinds of evil.
Some people, eager for money, have wandered from the
faith and pierced themselves with many griefs.

1 Timothy 6:10 (NIV)

Many people strive their whole lives to be rich, thinking that if they have financial success that all their problems will go away! However, we should never measure joy and contentment . . . by the balances in our bank accounts. Simply put—*money can't buy happiness*! Yes, it takes money to pay our bills, put food on our tables, and provide roofs over our heads. And God does want us to do our part by working hard and being good stewards. But only a close relationship with our Lord and Savior will bring true joy and peace.

When our lives are fully committed to God, we can rest safely in His arms of love, claiming His wonderful promises of care and protection as in Psalm 34:9-10 (NKJV), "Oh, fear the LORD, you His saints! There is no want to those who fear Him. The young lions lack and suffer hunger; but those who seek the LORD shall not lack any good thing."

Even when the rent is due, cupboards are bare, and wallets are empty, *keep trusting in God!* Jesus will never fail us—not ever! Claim His promise in Philippians 4:19 (NIV), "And my God will meet all your needs according to the riches of His glory in Christ Jesus," and that's more satisfying than all the money in the world!

Wonderfully Made

For you created my inmost being; you knit me
together in my mother's womb.

Psalm 139:13 (NIV)

———◆———

Jesus doesn't just love *all the people in the world* like we were one connected mass of people. No, Jesus loves each of us individually—*it's personal*! Our heavenly Father created us and knows each one of us intimately, inside and out! Yes, He knows our name, likes, dislikes, the way we twist our hair when we are nervous, the way our lip quivers when we are sad, and every other single detail about us.

The Bible tells us in Psalm 139:1-3 (ISV), "LORD, you have examined me; you have known me. You know when I rest and when I am active. You understand what I am thinking when I am distant from you. You scrutinize my life and my rest; you are familiar with all of my ways." And in Matthew 10:30 (NIV) we are told, "And even the very hairs of your head are all numbered." So if you think God doesn't *really* know you . . . *you couldn't be more wrong*!

Jeremiah 1:5 (ISV) says, "I knew you before I formed you in the womb; I set you apart for me before you were born." So the next time you are feeling unloved, worthless, and that you really don't matter in the grand scheme of life, think again! You matter to God . . . and that's what matters most! God didn't leave out one single detail! You are the person He created you to be . . . and God doesn't make mistakes!

Green-Eyed Monster

*Peace of mind means a healthy body, but
jealousy will rot your bones.*

Proverbs 14:30 (NCV)

Jealousy is a real problem that causes trouble in any relationship. It's generally motivated by fear—fear of losing what you have, not getting what you want, not being good enough, and on and on. The truth is—*jealousy destroys lives* and separates you from Jesus! It also causes you to act in ways that are hurtful to yourself and to others. It causes pain, hurt, anger, and bitterness. If jealousy is allowed to be present in your life, it will destroy you. It is often referred to as the *ugly, green-eyed monster*, and you need to recognize when it is present in your heart—then deal with it in a healthy way.

It's not possible to have jealousy in your heart and maintain a close walk with Jesus. The Bible says in Proverbs 27:4 (NLT), "Anger is cruel, and wrath is like a flood, but jealousy is even more dangerous." So, here's the good news! There is a way to rid your heart of envy. Bring it to Jesus and ask Him to take it from you, removing all jealousy from your heart and mind and replacing it with love for others. When your heart is filled with *God's love*, there's no room for jealousy!

Ticket to Heaven

*Behold, I stand at the door and knock. If anyone
hears My voice and opens the door, I will come in to
him and dine with him, and he with Me. To him
who overcomes I will grant to sit with Me on
My throne, as I also overcame and sat down
with My Father on His throne.*

Revelation 3:20-21 (NKJV)

No one, no matter how successful they are in life, can *buy* their way to Heaven! No one can claim victory over death. You may be educated with the highest degree possible, be the richest person on earth, the best athlete on the team, a musician with the most hit records, a businessman with the highest integrity, even a person with the highest moral standards . . . but *only through the blood of Jesus* do you have the blessed hope of eternal life! And it is through faith in Christ that you can claim your ticket to heaven. He is there, hand outstretched, longing for you to come—waiting for you to give your heart to Him.

The time is fast nearing for the train to pull out of the station. Jesus stands at your heart's door, pleading for you to *get on board*. Won't you surrender your heart and soul to Jesus today? He loves you so much—He can't imagine heaven without you!

Feeling God's Presence

On that day you will realize that I am in my Father,
and you are in me, and I am in you.

John 14:20 (NIV)

Some people struggle with *feeling* close to God! They go through all the motions of going to church, talking about the Lord, and even praying, but inside feel *spiritually dead*. There's no big secret on *how* to be close to God. The Bible says in James 4:8 (NKJV), "Draw near to God and He will draw near to you." You see, God wants you to come before Him with a *clean and pure heart* that is open to hear His voice.

Sin will always separate you from Jesus, so if you're harboring unforgiven sins, confess them and ask for forgiveness. Don't let anything stand between you and your heavenly Father.

When you pray, talk to God as you would your best friend. Tell Him what is on your heart and then take time to listen. Open the Scriptures and read what He is saying to you. God knows you intimately, inside and out, and you can trust Him with every thought or secret you've ever had.

There's no one better to trust your heart to! The more time you spend in Bible study and prayer, the closer you will be drawn to God, and it won't be long until you will feel a *oneness* with Him. He will become the center of your motivations, your dreams, aspirations, and the *reason you live*!

Love People to Jesus

Therefore, as we have opportunity, let us do good to all,
especially to those who are of the household of faith.

Galatians 6:10 (NKJV)

———◆———

Church should be a warm and friendly place we can go to feel God's presence and experience His love. A kind word, hug, or *pat on the back* from a fellow believer may be just what we need to help us through a trial or heartache. God wants us to *gather together* to worship Him and also to encourage and strengthen each other. Far too often though, church becomes a place where people *dread* to go for fear of criticism and reproach. Those already discouraged leave church with even heavier hearts until, eventually, they stop coming altogether!

Self-righteous attitudes have no place in the life of a Christian. God created us all *equal*—He *loves* the *sinner,* but *hates the sin*, so let us remember . . . *we are all sinners!* We need to strive in our hearts to be loving, kind, and generous to our fellowman. Sometimes we are so focused on *soul winning* in the world that we forget about the *soul winning* needed right in our own churches. There's an old but true expression: *churches are hospitals for sinners—not hotels for saints!* Let God remove all pride and *better-than-thou* attitudes from our hearts, filling us with His Holy Spirit so that we may *love people to Jesus!*

Willing to Obey

*He replied, "Blessed rather are those who hear
the word of God and obey it."*

Luke 11:28 (NIV)

Obedience is very important to God, so much so that the Bible tells us in John 14:15 (NKJV), "If you love Me, keep My commandments." Our willingness to obey God shows Him how much we love Him.

Many Christians will pray and ask God to answer their prayers, and at the very same time, they are disobedient to God by doing things that they know to be wrong. This can't possibly be pleasing to God! When you fall in love with Jesus, you want to show Him just how much you love Him! And the *best* way to do that is by *obeying Him*! Of course, God doesn't require *perfect obedience* before He responds to our prayers, but if we really want to experience the power of Jesus' name, then we will cheerfully obey Him.

God will give us the strength, courage, and yes, even *make us* willing to obey if we but ask Him. Obedience to God requires that we put our own selfish wants and desires aside and be willing to do whatever He wants us to do! God promises in Jeremiah 7:23 (ISV), "Obey me and I'll be your God, and you will be my people. Walk in all the ways that I command you so it will go well with you."

The Panic Button

Then they remembered that God was their rock, and the
Most High God their Redeemer.

Psalm 78:35 (NKJV)

———◆———

When everything seems to be going wrong, and you're in the midst of the worst possible storm in your life, don't spend even one minute being anxious or worried. As a Christian, you have no reason to fear for you serve a great big God who is powerful and has promised to never leave you or forsake you. And the good news—no matter what, God *always* keeps His promises!

Pray for strength to overcome any burden or heartache. God will command His angels to watch over you and protect you from danger. Do not fear or spend sleepless nights tossing and turning, worrying about what will happen the next day. Trust your problems to God for He is able and trustworthy!

The Bible is full of stories where God performed miracles to save His children, and He is the same God of miracles yesterday, today, and tomorrow! There's no circumstance too small or too big for Him to handle and no prayer will remain unheard or unanswered! Before pushing the *panic button*, hold on to God's promises, place your trust and faith in Him, and through His precious blood, you *will* overcome every trial, struggle, and fear!

Judge Less, Love More

*There is only one Lawgiver and Judge, the one
who is able to save and destroy. But you—who are
you to judge your neighbor?*

James 4:12 (NIV)

———◈———

Oh, what a better world this would be if we judged each other less—and loved each other more! We often overlook our own sins, but expect everyone else to be perfect. Even if we are not so bold to confront someone with their *sin*, we judge them in our hearts, or worse—talk about it with others. We have no idea how sad this makes our heavenly Father. We are all sinners who have *come short of the glory of God,* and the Bible tells us that one sin is *not any better* than any other! *Sin—is sin!*

We all want *grace and mercy*, and in fact, pray for it fervently—but few are willing to extend that same *grace and mercy* to others. We can be harsh, cruel, and unmerciful, convicting others before knowing all the facts. The Bible makes it very clear we are walking on dangerous ground when we judge others, for in Matthew 7:1 (NKJV), Jesus says, "Judge not, that you be not judged."

Clearly, we need to leave the judging to God and pray for even more love in our hearts—so much so that it overflows to everyone we meet! Remember that Jesus loves each of us so much, He can't imagine heaven without us, and yes, that means our enemies too!

Higher Education

*Do your best to present yourself to God as one
approved, a worker who does not need to be ashamed
and who correctly handles the word of truth.*

2 Timothy 2:15 (NIV)

The most valuable education we can receive doesn't come from fancy colleges, universities, or Ivy League schools, but rather from prayerful study of God's Holy Word. This doesn't mean that obtaining traditional education is not important, because it is. But an even *higher education* is possible through a close relationship with our heavenly Father! We should eagerly study Scripture and pray for divine wisdom that we might understand the messages God is giving us.

Most Christians own a Bible, but few actually spend time reading it. However, to be a *follower of Christ*, we must first have a personal relationship with Him. In order to understand what God's plan is for our lives, we need a *closeness* with our Lord and Savior—so close that we can understand His instructions—and this comes as a result of both prayer and Bible study!

God honors our desires to be close to Him, and He gives clarity, discernment, and greater wisdom when we prayerfully seek His truth! Pray for *self-discipline* to faithfully make time every day to spend with God—striving for *higher education*!

Holy Boldness

*He who did not spare His own Son, but
delivered Him over for us all, how will He not
also with Him freely give us all things?*

Romans 8:32 (NASB)

W e need to present our needs before God humbly, but
without shame or fear. Approach His throne room with
holy boldness! There's no need to be shy and bashful. We can
confidently pray to our Lord and Savior, sharing our deepest
desires, pain, and heartache. God loves each of us with an
everlasting love and longs to hear from His children. He doesn't
ask us to be *politically correct* when we pray. Nor does He want
to hear the same recited prayer over and over again. He wants
to hear what is on our hearts!

Which one of us would still be friends with the person
who told us the same thing every time we spoke? I'm sure a
friendship like that would not last very long! So it is with our
Best Friend—Jesus! Sometimes people are afraid to pray boldly
because they feel sinful and unworthy. They are looking at *what
they have done wrong*—instead of what *Jesus has done right*!

The Bible tells us in Hebrews 4:16 that because we are
righteous in Him, we can approach the throne of grace boldly
with our needs. Start each day—praying with *holy boldness*!

Guard Your Thoughts

*Whatever is true, whatever is noble, whatever
is right, whatever is pure, whatever is lovely,
whatever is admirable—if anything is excellent or
praiseworthy—think about such things.*

Philippians 4:8 (NIV)

The Bible tells us to direct our thoughts toward things that are pure, honest, true, virtuous, and of good report. There's a reason that God wants us to control our thoughts. It's because what we think controls our attitudes, which then affects our behavior and actions. If we fill our minds with evil and negative thoughts, the devil uses that against us. He wants us to believe his lies that we are filthy and worthless and that *God couldn't possibly love us*. And when Satan has successfully turned our thoughts away from Jesus, *then he has won*! We will be lost!

It's a dangerous game the devil can play with our minds. We need to *guard our thoughts*. We need to pray for God to fill our minds with only pure thoughts, and when we are tempted to believe the devil's lies, pray out loud for Jesus to come to the rescue! The Bible says in Romans 12:2 (NIV), "Be transformed by the renewing of your mind. Then you will be able to test and approve what God's will is—his good, pleasing and perfect will."

We can claim God's promise in Philippians 4:13 (NKJV), "I can do all things through Christ who strengthens me," to help us have only *good thoughts*—and then God can use us in a powerful way to witness for Him!

God of Peace

May God himself, the God of peace, sanctify you through and through. May your whole spirit, soul and body be kept blameless at the coming of our Lord Jesus Christ.

1 Thessalonians 5:23 (NIV)

Whenever you stop trusting Jesus—the *weeds of worry* grow rapidly! If you're tired of sleepless nights, tossing and turning about what *might happen* . . . it's time to *get on your knees*! Leave your burdens with the Lord and enjoy the comforting blessing of God's peace.

When you're facing an important decision and you just don't know what to do, take it to the Lord in prayer and ask for divine guidance. You will know when you've made the right decision because *God's peace* will be your answer! If something just doesn't *feel right* and you keep mulling it over and over again in your mind—the *absence of peace* is a good indicator that *it's not the right decision*!

Pray about *everything* and wait upon the Lord for your answer. Don't get pushy with God and try to answer your own prayers! When you are afraid to move forward through a difficult trial—put your trust in Jesus. His peace will sustain you! There's no room for God in a heart full of worry, turmoil, hatred, or anger. One of the most obvious signs of a Christian who walks with Jesus is *peace*, because God . . . is *a God of peace*!

Prayer Changes Everything

*"Then call on me when you are in trouble, and I will
rescue you, and you will give me glory."*

Psalm 50:15 (NLT)

———◆◆◆———

Only God can move a mountain, but *prayer and faith . . .*
move God! It's our communication with our heavenly
Father that sustains us on this difficult journey of life, and
thankfully, we don't have to travel this road alone. God has given
us a direct line to His throne room—day or night. He hears us
when we pray and responds to the cries of His children. Pray
believing! Pray sincerely! Pray with complete devotion to our
Lord and Savior!

We cannot expect God to answer our prayers when our
allegiance is divided. In other words, we can't have each leg
in two different canoes. And when we pray, we need to pray
knowing with absolute certainty that our God hears and
answers! Many times we pray and ask God to take away our
troubles, but we pray *hoping*, not *believing*.

Life would be so much simpler if we accepted the fact that we
can't solve our own problems. Only God can see the big picture,
so He alone knows the solution. There's no problem too big for
God to solve, and there's no tear that prayer cannot wipe away!
There is no sadness that God cannot erase! Prayer brings God
to the rescue—so instead of waiting until the problem becomes
so large that we are swallowed up in the pit of depression, go to
God *first*. Prayer changes everything!

God's Beauty

Do not let your adornment be merely outward . . .

1 Peter 3:3 (NKJV)

———◆———

In today's world, everyone is focused on beauty and trying to look younger. A tremendous amount of money is spent on makeup, hair products, clothes, etc. Now there's nothing wrong with wanting to look good, but when it becomes your highest priority and all the attention is on *self*—then it becomes a problem! Your priorities are out of balance. Real beauty comes from within. There is nothing more beautiful than the light of Jesus shining on the face of a Christian, because God's beauty shines through on even the plainest outward appearance.

I love the words to this song: "Jesus loves the little children, all the children of the world; red and yellow black and white, all are precious in His sight!" It doesn't matter what color our skin is or the amount of hair on our heads, we are all beautiful when we allow Jesus into our hearts and lives!

The Bible says in Proverbs 31:30 (NIV), "Charm is deceptive, and beauty is fleeting; but a woman who fears the LORD is to be praised." Sooner or later, even the most gorgeous beauty queen will lose her good looks. Her flawless skin will grow wrinkled and old! We need to concern ourselves with inner beauty by growing closer to Jesus each day, because God's beauty . . . lasts for eternity!

Jesus Our Best Friend

*Jesus said to him, "Today salvation has come
to this house, because this man, too, is a son of Abraham.
For the Son of Man came to seek and to save the lost."*

Luke 19:9-10 (NIV)

We have all heard the expression, "God loves the sinner, but hates the sin." No matter what . . . God loves us! The Bible says in John 3:16 (NKJV), "For God so loved the world that He gave His only begotten Son, that whoever believes in Him should not perish but have everlasting life." God may hate what we are doing, but He will *always* love us. What an incredible, loving God we serve! He will not refuse any sinner that comes to Him with a repentant heart. Instead, He will open His arms of love and say, "Come, all ye who are burdened, and I will give you rest" (see Matthew 11:28).

God turns away no one. He will not slam the door and walk away, deaf to our cries for help. We can come to Jesus as the worst of sinners, and He will never cast us out! We can claim His promise in Isaiah 54:10 (NIV), "Though the mountains be shaken and the hills be removed, yet my unfailing love for you will not be shaken nor my covenant of peace be removed." Jesus is our real Friend who *knows us* and loves us in spite of all our insecurities, weakness, brokenness, and fear! He is our *Best Friend* forever, and He loves us more than we could possibly know! Why not commit your heart and life to Him today?

God Never Promised

*God is our refuge and strength, an ever-present
help in trouble. Therefore we will not fear, though the
earth give way and the mountains
fall into the heart of the sea.*

Psalm 46:1-2 (NIV)

G od's love for us was proven beyond a shadow of a doubt
when He gave His only Son, Jesus, to die on a cross that
we might have eternal life. That is why in every situation, we
can put our faith and trust in the wisdom and goodness of our
heavenly Father. When we face trouble and heartache, we need
not panic, because we are in the safety of God's arms, and there
is no safer place to be!

Most of us have experienced trials, heartache, and pain. We
could be having a normal, peaceful day and one devastating
phone call could turn our world upside down in an instant!
Regardless of these unexpected and unplanned events in our
lives, we have the assurance of God's unfailing love. No matter
how dismal our circumstances, we must never lose sight of the
fact that Jesus loves us with an everlasting, perfect love!

God never promised us a pain-free life here on earth, but
He has promised that we will never go through our trials alone.
He will always be there—supporting, comforting, guiding, and
loving us—each step of the way!

Weeds in Your Garden

*You can trust what your friend says, even
when it hurts. But your enemies want to hurt
you, even when they act nice.*

Proverbs 27:6 (ERV)

A real friend loves at all times—not just when things are going well—but in the bad times too! There are some *friends* who are just there because they want something from us, and the minute they don't need us anymore, they're gone! Those kind of people are weeds in our *friendship garden*—and need to be weeded out.

But friends who are fiercely loyal, dependable, loving, and trustworthy are to be cherished and treasured. They know us so well that they can communicate with us through a quick glance, they can finish our sentences, and even silence between us is comfortable. We can all have this special relationship with our Best Friend, Jesus, who has all these qualities and more!

Jesus tells us In Matthew 16:24 (KJV), "If any man will come after me, let him deny himself . . . and follow me." He pleads with us to accept His friendship, give up our sinful life, and follow Him. Friendship with our Lord and Savior is more than a luxury—it is the key that unlocks the door to heaven! If only every Christian could honestly say, "Jesus and I are friends!"

Only Two Choices

Elijah went before the people and said, "How long will you waver between two opinions? If the LORD is God, follow him; but if Baal is God, follow him."

1 Kings 18:21 (NIV)

Have you stopped praying and can feel your relationship with God drifting away? Perhaps your prayer wasn't answered just the way you wanted or your life hasn't turned out according to how you dreamed it would be. You start grumbling, get discouraged, and begin to blame God. All too soon you become infected with the *poor-me-itis* disease! That is a dangerous state of mind and leaves you vulnerable to Satan's attacks. Stop thinking, *I can make it without God in my life*—because you can't! That is Satan's lie.

You have two choices and only two. You can choose to serve God or Satan, but you can't *walk the line* and choose both. If you choose Satan, you will lose out on eternal life with Jesus and will be lost forever!

Whatever has caused you to drift away can't be important enough to miss out on heaven. Fall on your knees today and pray, "Jesus, save me!" Your heavenly Father loves you with an everlasting love and is waiting and longing to hear those words. Remember, there's nothing you've done that God can't forgive. Surrender your heart and life to Him today!

Why-Me Syndrome

*In everything give thanks; for this is the will of God in
Christ Jesus for you.*

1 Thessalonians 5:18 (NKJV)

———◆———

When you give your burdens to God, even the heaviest burden becomes as light as a feather. The sweet joy of forgiveness allows you to breathe easier, sleep better, and smile more! Sometimes God calls you to bear your burden—and if this happens, do not fear, for *God is with you*. He *will* sustain you. He will give you the strength and courage you need to get through every trial—so much so that, in the end, your burden will become a blessing!

Don't go through your trial with drooping shoulders because of the heavy load you are struggling with. If you do, it will weigh you down until it destroys you with anger, resentment, bitterness, and pain! Instead of crumbling under the weight of the *why-me syndrome*, reach out to Jesus! No one is stronger or more capable to bear your burdens than our Lord and Savior.

Even in your darkest hour, when your grief is so heavy it hurts to breathe, He is there for you! Hand Him your burden . . . and don't take it back! Allow yourself to find comfort in the arms of your heavenly Father. Feel His warm embrace, take a deep breath, and say . . . "Thank You, Jesus!"

Jesus, Save Me

For He will command his angels concerning you to guard you in all your ways.

Psalm 91:11 (NIV)

It's difficult sometimes to have faith when the storms of life are raging out of control. We forget that God has promised to *never leave us or forsake us*. But instead of trusting Him, we become like the disciples with Jesus sleeping on the boat during the midst of the storm. Jesus was right there with them . . . and yet they began to panic! Although they had witnessed Him performing miracles all day long, when the first sign of trouble arose, they had no faith. If the disciples had no faith when their Savior was there *physically* with them, it's easier to have an understanding of the weakness of our human nature.

It takes faith to step out onto the water, knowing with absolute certainty that Jesus will save us! God is patient and lovingly works with our insecurities. He pleads for us to trust Him more! The Bible tells us in Ephesians 2:8-9 (NIV), "For it is by grace you have been saved, through faith—and this is not from yourselves, it is the gift of God—not by works, so that no one can boast."

We need to pray for more faith. When we are in the *eye of the storm* and tempted to panic, we need to just take a deep breath, look toward heaven, and pray the most powerful prayer we can pray: "Jesus, save me!" He has tens of thousands of angels to send to our sides . . . at the minute we need Him most!

Think Big

*Now to Him who is able to do exceedingly abundantly
above all that we ask or think, according to the power
that works in us, to Him be glory in the church by Christ
Jesus to all generations, forever and ever. Amen.*

Ephesians 3:20-21 (NKJV)

God wants you to think *big*! He wants you to have life—and have it more abundantly! There's a common expression: "Ask little, and you'll get little." Well, it's true. Be brave and ask God for the desires of your heart; He wants to give them to you! The Bible says in Psalm 37:4 (NKJV), "Delight yourself also in the LORD, and He shall give you the desires of your heart." You might want something but are too shy to ask because you may feel it is way beyond your reach—but remember, "With God *all* things are possible!" Pray with *holy boldness*!

It's also important to always pray for God's will to be done. He alone knows what is best and will answer accordingly. So share your heart with Jesus. Ask Him to use you to the utmost, stretching your abilities so far that you will have no other choice but to lean totally on Him. You will experience amazing results that will leave you totally blown away by God's greatness! Start today. Dream big! Plan big! Think big!

Embracing Change

Guide me in your truth and teach me, for you are God
my Savior, and my hope is in you all day long.

Psalm 25:5 (NIV)

Sometimes changes in our lives can be scary and, well . . . downright terrifying. When we move out of our familiar home, change jobs, have a baby, get married, or make any other major lifestyle change, it can be one of the most insecure times we ever face in our lives. It's the *dark unknown* that is unsettling. Sadly, we can get so comfortable that, even in a bad situation, we are willing to stay and put up with it rather than face the fear of change. Perhaps we are afraid that the change might not turn out to be as good as we hoped it would, or maybe we'll be even more miserable than we currently are.

As long as we have prayed for divine direction, then we have nothing to be afraid of. When we have the blessed assurance that God is with us, we can go forward with *holy boldness* and joy in our hearts, with absolute confidence that He is guiding each step of the way!

We need to pray without ceasing and *listen* for God to impress upon us the changes He wants us to make! When we are *Holy Spirit led*, we can embrace change with excited anticipation, knowing that our heavenly Father has something awesome planned!

Freedom of Forgiveness

*"But if you do not forgive, neither will your Father in
heaven forgive your trespasses."*

Mark 11:26 (NKJV)

One of the biggest reasons that prayers are not answered
is because of *unforgiveness*. Jesus says that if we will not
forgive others . . . He will not forgive us! It was a lesson that
His own disciples struggled with greatly. Peter demanded to
know how often he should forgive, and Jesus told him, "Seventy
times seven." Wow! Can it get any plainer than that? Even if our
neighbor keeps doing the same mean, hurtful thing over and
over again, Jesus wants us to keep forgiving.

That's because any bitterness or unforgiveness in our hearts
will separate us from Him. Is there really *anything* worth
missing out on heaven? We must stop making excuses for all
the reasons we deserve to be hurt and angry and stop justifying
our anger! Whatever someone else has done to hurt us . . . we
can give it to Jesus! It doesn't matter what that is or how badly
it hurts or even how many times we've been wronged, Jesus can
take away the pain—but we cannot be witnesses for Him if we
have unforgiving hearts.

All we need to do is give our pain to Jesus—then let it go!
Really . . . let it go! It is then, and only then, that we will feel the
full measure of God's love and the freedom of forgiveness—it's
the best feeling in the world!

Prayer Is a Privilege

"For whoever is ashamed of Me and My words, of him the Son of Man will be ashamed when He comes in His own glory, and in His Father's, and of the holy angels."

Luke 9:26 (NKJV)

Prayer is a two-way street that involves both talking and listening. It's having a conversation with your Best Friend, although it's more than mere words. Prayer is reverent and respectful because you are talking to the King of the universe, your heavenly Father, Lord, and Savior.

You can talk to God about anything and everything—anytime and anywhere! Some people are uncomfortable with this, especially when praying in public. At a restaurant, they mutter under their breath a quick prayer or they omit the blessing altogether. Perhaps they are embarrassed for others to know that they are a Christian, or perhaps it just makes them feel uneasy. But Jesus says in Mark 8:38 that if we are ashamed of Him, He will be ashamed of us.

Prayer is not just for church, the privacy of your bedroom, or a specific time or place, so pray about everything wherever you are! Tell God your fears, hopes, and dreams, and don't forget to tell Him how much you love Him! Make time for worship and praise where you don't ask for anything at all. Most of all, remember, *prayer is a privilege that is always ours . . . but the power of prayer is always God's!*

Our Darkest Hour

*For when he has stood the test he will
receive the crown of life, which God has promised
to those who love him.*

James 1:12 (ESV)

Many times we pray and plead with God for healing and demand that God answer instantly, and if that doesn't happen, we think God just doesn't hear us, or worse, that He doesn't care. But that couldn't be further from the truth! Don't get discouraged and stop praying—start trusting *God's perfect timing and His perfect plan.*

There are times He allows the healing to happen *overnight,* but most often, it takes place *over time.* We can take comfort knowing that we're not going through the darkness alone; Jesus is right there, comforting, guiding, leading, and giving us strength to face each day. He wants us to lean on Him and is creating a future for us based on *joy,* not heartache!

The Bible tells us in James 1:2 that we can actually *be joyful* for our trials, for it's during our *darkest hour* that we find ourselves even closer to our Lord and Savior. As Christians, we have nothing to fear—not even death, because Jesus loves us with an everlasting love, and He has promised to *restore us to health and heal our wounds*! We may have to wait until we get to heaven for healing—but we can trust God to do what is *best* for us and to *always keep His promises*!

Imprisoned Minds

To be spiritually minded is life and peace.

Romans 8:6 (KJV)

When we allow our minds to dwell on negative things, our thoughts can completely take over our lives. Focusing on the hurt and pain, mistreatment, hatred, bitterness, or envy only leads to depression and soon we can't see *the light at the end of the tunnel* because we are completely in a *mental fog*! All that negativity soon eats away at our hearts and clouds our judgment. Our imaginations run away with us, and soon we think the whole world is against us! We are even more devastated when we send out invitations to our *pity party* and no one shows up!

Instead of *wallowing in misery*, God wants us to think positive—to focus on what we *do* have instead of what we *wish* we had! Whenever the enemy tries to dredge up the past, call out the name of Jesus, and *the devil will flee*! Allow the Holy Spirit to fill our hearts and lives with an extra measure of God's joy so that we can share it wherever we go!

And we can't forget to take time for faithful Bible study and prayer. It is through communion with our Lord and Savior that we'll receive the inspiration and strength needed to maintain a positive, Christlike attitude throughout our lives! Let us petition God to set us free and guard our minds to think only pure, positive thoughts that we might be dynamic sons and daughters of God!

Making Good Choices

*"The one who sent me is with me; He has not left me
alone, for I always do what pleases him."*

John 8:29 (NIV)

God doesn't force you to love Him, nor does He insist that you serve Him. He wants you to *choose* to serve Him because *you love Him!* Each day you're presented with choices, and whether or not you spend eternity with Jesus will be determined by the decisions you make.

Without God to lead and guide, you can easily lose your way, so pray about everything! Ask Him for advice on the big things and the little things. He is always there to lead and direct, but He won't force His will upon you—you must ask for help and seek His guidance.

It's a sinful, dangerous world we live in, but there's no need to fear or *go it alone.* The only way to survive in this sinful world is by having a close relationship with our Lord and Savior. Never forget that God created you, knows everything about you, and wants what's best for you! He will never lead you down a wrong path or ignore your cries for help. He is always there to show you the way! Remember, God's gift of *choice* comes with a huge responsibility to make *the right* choices—so hold tightly to God's hand, for your salvation depends on it!

One-Day Christians

"Whoever acknowledges me before others,
I will also acknowledge before my Father in heaven."
Matthew 10:32 (NIV)

There are many people in this world who are *one-day Christians*! They go to church each week, sing, pray, listen to the sermon, and then go home until the next Sabbath—only to do it all over again, week after week, year after year. The sad thing is that all throughout the week, they go about their business without even once sharing their faith with a coworker, family member, friend, or stranger on the street—almost as if they forgot they were Christians until the weekend!

Weeks turn into months and months turn into years, and before they realize it, they are nearing the end of their lives and have missed so many opportunities to shine for Jesus. They have merely *gone through the motions* of being a follower of Christ. Far worse, they are *spiritually dead*!

The truth is, a Christian that does not witness is not growing spiritually! When you truly fall in love with Jesus, you want to share Him with others. In fact, *it's impossible to keep Him to yourself!* Whenever you help someone else find Christ, it's the most wonderful feeling in the world! Not only does it place you on a spiritual high—but your own relationship with Him grows even stronger—so shine for Jesus . . . today and every day!

No Welcome Mat

"Peace I leave with you; my peace I give you.
I do not give to you as the world gives. Do not let your
hearts be troubled and do not be afraid."

John 14:27 (NIV)

Whenever *worry* comes knocking at your door—don't invite it in! Lock the door and immediately call for help on your *royal telephone*! Instantly, heavenly angels will be by your side to give you the faith that you need to commit your *worry* to Jesus.

You can be sure that *worry* is one of Satan's favorite weapons to discourage followers of Christ. But don't fall in that trap for even a second! There's no better recipe for faith than walking hand in hand with your Lord and Savior. Throughout the Bible, there are examples of people who were close to Jesus, and yet, they suffered trials and heartache. But it was through these hard times that they became increasingly more committed to God.

So it is with Christians today. It is the difficulties you face that keep you leaning on Jesus! So don't roll out the welcome mat for *worry*. God will give you the strength you need to face any fear. In the darkest hours, you can praise God and, yes, even thank Him for your struggles!

Prayer-Powered Choices

*"To God belong wisdom and power; counsel
and understanding are His."*

Job 12:13 (NIV)

Every day we make dozens of choices, from things as simple as what to eat, which clothes to wear, what to say on the phone, which bill to pay first, and the list goes on and on. How we choose to live today will determine how we live tomorrow.

The choices we made in the past influenced the person we are today. It's so important to make decisions based on what God wants instead of what we want! To do this, we need Holy Spirit guidance. We need to pray and ask for wisdom to know God's plan for our lives . . . and then don't forget to ask for strength and courage to carry it out! Open the Bible and let God's Word be a filter for making better choices. And have patience. In this *I-want-it-now* generation, we sometimes forget that God's timing is perfect!

Jesus wants to give us the desires of our hearts, and He wants us to be happy! We need to trust God to guide our decision-making and then make prayer-powered choices!

The Big Picture

"I make known the end from the beginning, from ancient times, what is still to come. I say, 'My purpose will stand, and I will do all that I please.'"

Isaiah 46:10 (NIV)

Too often when we pray, we're anxiously waiting for the answer that *we* want. In fact, we demand it! But we can't expect God to always answer our prayers just the way we want Him to, as if ordering something from the Internet. What we *can* expect . . . is that God will *always* answer! Our prayers do not fall on deaf ears.

Jesus not only hears and answers our prayers, but He loves us so much that *His answers* are always with our best interest in mind. He wants us to be happy and longs to give us the desires of our hearts! God knows the end from the beginning and looks at *the big picture.* He sees what we cannot. Often, in our *shortsightedness*, we make demands of God, but if He always gave us what we asked for, it wouldn't be the best for us—or make us happy. It may even be disastrous!

We need to trust God for the answers. Our God *is* faithful and trustworthy! He loves us so much that He is preparing our hearts for Heaven so that we can live with Him forever! What a glorious day that will be!

Stressed-Out World

*"Take my yoke upon you and learn from me,
for I am gentle and humble in heart, and you will find
rest for your souls. For my yoke is easy
and my burden is light."*

Matthew 11:29-30 (NIV)

When you feel frustrated, flustered, and all stressed out, don't get upset and start beating yourself up about it. You're only human, and this high-speed, high-tech rat race of a life can be downright overwhelming for anyone. This world is a stressful one, and it's not going to slow down until Jesus comes! Rather than scold yourself for your humanness, remind yourself that God is with you at all times—encouraging and supporting—but *not* condemning!

Slow down your pace by spending *alone time* with God! Talk to Him about every aspect of your life and pour out your heart to Him. Tell Him your deepest fears, challenges, and heartaches as well as your goals and dreams. Ask God to help you prioritize your day, making time for the things He wants you to do. Then, don't forget to *listen* for His answer. Prayer is a *two-way street*, but *sometimes* it's easy to forget that!

Jesus is eager and ready to give you wisdom, discernment, and direction. The Bible says in Matthew 11:28 (NIV), "Come to me, all you who are weary and burdened, and I will give you rest." He's *always* there for you and longs to take the stress away and give you His sweet peace!

True Victory in Jesus

But thanks be to God, who gives us the victory through our Lord Jesus Christ.

1 Corinthians 15:57 (NKJV)

When you invite Jesus to live in your heart, you don't have to wait until Heaven to begin living the abundant life that He promises in John 10:10. In other words, through *passionate prayer*, you can have *victory in Jesus*! You can experience joy regardless of what the devil is trying to throw your way, because Jesus paid the price, and the battle has already been won! Don't let the devil get you down and don't listen to his lies about how *unfair* God is treating you.

When life isn't turning out the way you planned, instead of being bitter and angry about the injustices of life, turn your hurt over to your Lord and Savior, and He will fill you up with His peace and joy, and all resentment will melt away! *Life isn't fair, that's true—but God is always fair!*

When you're willing to surrender to Christ and allow Him to fight your battles, an incredible peace washes over you, and it's the best feeling in the world. It is then and only then that you will experience true *victory in Jesus!*

Think Before You Speak

Death and life are in the power of the tongue,
and those who love it will eat its fruit.

Proverbs 18:21 (NASB)

—◆—

The Bible has quite a bit to say about how we use our words. In Ephesians 4:29 (NIV) we're told, "Do not let any unwholesome talk come out of your mouths, but only what is helpful for building others up." We need to be aware of how powerful our words can be. What we say can be more lethal than a gun and, once spoken, can never be taken back. The old saying, "Sticks and stones may break my bones, but words will never hurt me," is simply not true! Unkind words hurt deeply and may even destroy someone's self-esteem for life!

The Bible is filled with stories of people who God sustained through His words of encouragement. How we speak reflects Christ's character within us. We need to be generous with words of encouragement, and when tempted to give an angered response, stop and ask ourselves, *What would Jesus say?* God will give us the victory. We need only to pray David's prayer in Psalm 141:3 (KJV), "Set a watch, O LORD, before my mouth; keep the door of my lips."

Learning to Trust

*Trust in him at all times, you people; pour out your
hearts to him, for God is our refuge.*

Psalm 62:8 (NIV)

It takes experience to develop trust in God and truly not *worry* when going through difficult times. We all have weaknesses and emotions that are put to the test over and over again. Every time we go through hard times—and God intervenes, our faith increases significantly! If we really want to overcome the habits of *fretting, worry, and fear* . . . there must be a *blind trust* in God that's so strong, we know beyond a shadow of a doubt that He will do what's best!

It starts with a firm commitment of faith in our hearts, and it is then—that *worry* is replaced with the sweet peace of resting in our Savior's arms! We must resist the temptation to give up while in the midst of tribulation because it is through our trials that our characters are being prepared for heaven. Instead of stressing out, trust God who has everything under control. Don't pace the floor with worry—kneel on the floor and pray!

The Bible says in Philippians 4:11-12 (NIV), "I have learned to be content whatever the circumstances. I know what it is to be in need, and I know what it is to have plenty. I have learned the secret of being content in any and every situation." In our darkest hour, we learn patience, endurance, and real faith in God, so don't give up because soon we will develop the habits of being joyful and confident—and trusting in God!

God's Unfailing Love

*Behold what manner of love the Father has
bestowed on us, that we should be called children of God!
Therefore the world does not know us, because
it did not know Him.*

1 John 3:1 (NKJV)

Jesus loves you regardless of how well you are performing, how talented you are, how good you are at your job, how rich or poor you are, or how many friends you have! Sometimes you may question yourself, wondering if you are doing enough to be worthy of God's love. No matter how successful you are, the answer to that question . . . will always be *no*! Your *performance* and *God's love* are two totally different issues that you need to sort out.

Jesus loves you with an everlasting love that flows out from eternity without limits or conditions. God has clothed you in *His* robe of righteousness—*nothing and no one can reverse it!* Not even the enemy himself! Therefore, your accomplishments have no bearing on God's love for you.

Bring your fears of unworthiness to Jesus and receive an extra measure of God's unfailing love! Remember that God is always with you and has promised to never leave you or forsake you. Allow Him to lead, guide, and direct your every thought, deed, and action, because you are *worthy of God's love*!

Run to Jesus

*Therefore confess your sins to each other and pray
for each other so that you may be healed. The prayer of a
righteous person is powerful and effective.*

James 5:16 (NIV)

Running from a difficult situation doesn't make things better or make your problems disappear. It only prolongs the inevitable and usually makes the situation worse. Before you know it, the *molehill* soon becomes a *mountain* and much harder to climb!

When there's conflict between you and someone else—always look inward *first*. Sometimes you don't see the situation clearly because you're blinded by your own self-righteousness. Ask yourself, *Did I act in a Christ-like way? Would God be proud of how I acted? Do others see Jesus in me?*

If you have wronged someone—ask for forgiveness. If someone has wronged you—ask God to put forgiveness in *your* heart. Yes, *even* if that person hasn't asked you to forgive them! But don't stop there—start praying for the person who wronged you, asking God to put more love in your heart for them. You'll find it difficult to have hard feelings toward someone that you're praying for! So the next time trouble strikes and you get the urge to get angry and stomp off . . . *run to Jesus*!

Obey God's Commands

*See, I am setting before you today a blessing . . . if you
obey the commands of the Lord your God.*

Deuteronomy 11:26-27 (NIV)

God's love for us never changes, and we can always count on Him to guide us through every storm. Even though we have bad days and good days, one thing we can always count on is—*God never changes*. He is the same yesterday, today, tomorrow, and forever.

We could avoid a lot of heartache if we would just learn to lean on Jesus for everything! Even though God wants to give us the *desires of our hearts*, poor choices can prevent us from receiving the wonderful life that He wants to give us. For instance, overeating is harmful to our bodies, even if the food we eat is healthy. Good friends can add meaning to our lives, but the wrong relationships can destroy our very souls. A good job can be satisfying, but if turned into a race to climb the corporate ladder, it causes stress and burnout! Heart-to-heart talks with friends can be rewarding, but gossip and careless words cause pain for a lifetime.

Fortunately, we don't have to go it alone! God doesn't leave us to wander aimlessly through life by ourselves. He gives us direction and guidance. When we pray and ask Jesus to come into our hearts and lives, we become changed. Through prayer and the study of God's Holy Word, we can blindly go forward, having complete faith that with Jesus as our Guide, we are safe in His care!

Trusting God's Forgiveness

Therefore, there is now no condemnation for those who are in Christ Jesus.

Romans 8:1 (NIV)

———◆———

Do you lie in bed at night tossing and turning because you are overcome with guilt? You've asked God to forgive you but you just don't *feel* forgiven? Well thankfully, freedom from sin is not based on *feeling*! The Bible says in 1 John 1:9 (NKJV), when we confess our sin, "He is faithful and just to forgive our sin and cleanse us from all unrighteousness."

To keep feeling guilty after asking for forgiveness is really a lack of trust in Jesus! It's like saying, "God, I don't believe You!" What you need is more faith. Ask God to help you trust Him more, and He will. You can be assured that Jesus paid the price on Calvary for sin, and He alone has the power to forgive. John 3:16 (KJV) tells us, "For God so loved the world, that he gave his only begotten Son, that whosoever believeth in him should not perish, but have everlasting life."

When Jesus forgives, you can trust completely and fully that you are forgiven. And the best part—He doesn't keep bringing it up and throwing it in your face! Once they are forgiven—they are gone forever, as if they never happened. You are free from the burden of sin because Jesus paid the price! What amazing love! The best way to thank Jesus for His incredible sacrifice is by living each day for Him!

Don't Steal God's Glory

"But whoever would be great among you must be your servant, and whoever would be first among you must be your slave, even as the Son of Man came not to be served but to serve, and to give his life as a ransom for many."

Matthew 20:26-28 (ESV)

God has called each of us to be *ministers*; however, many have a false sense of what that means. To some, it's being in control—being *popular*, *dynamic*, *prestigious,* or the *authority figure* people go to for answers. But ministry is none of those things! Ministry is the act of serving—doing whatever God asks us to do. It doesn't matter if He is using us to minister to tens of thousands or a single lowly beggar on the street—ministry and humility go hand in hand!

A heart filled with pride will destroy the very essence of who God made us to be! The minute we start stealing God's glory and accepting all the praise and adoration as our own—we fall! We may have won thousands to Jesus, but will lose our own souls! The Bible says in Psalm 51:17 (ESV), "The sacrifices of God are a broken spirit; a broken and a contrite heart, O God, you will not despise." God welcomes us with open arms when we humbly come before Him with tender and humble hearts. His mercy is overflowing, and when we are completely humble and surrendered, God can fully use us to minister for Him!

Bitter Taste of Revenge

For it is written, "Vengeance is Mine,
I will repay," says the Lord.

Romans 12:19 (NKJV)

When we've been *wronged*, the human response is—*revenge!* We want to get even and make that person *pay* for what they have done. All throughout time—yes, even in the Bible—there are stories of people wanting vengeance. We have all heard the expression, "Revenge is sweet," but the truth is . . . revenge leaves a bitter taste in our mouths! The initial euphoric feeling of *victory* quickly dissolves into a feeling of emptiness. That sweet taste we were hoping for isn't so sweet after all! The only way to experience the comforting, soul-refreshing peace we long for—is to *forgive!*

Real forgiveness does not harbor any hatred in our hearts. If we hear news of something terrible that happened to an enemy and we gloat or even get a smile on our face—then we truly haven't forgiven! With true forgiveness, there will be nothing inside our hearts that wants to hurt the person who has done us wrong!

Some people have been hurt so deeply that it is humanly impossible to forgive—but not impossible with God's power. Pray and claim Philippians 4:13 for strength, asking God to remove all hatred and bitterness from your heart and replace it with His sweet forgiveness!

God's Mighty Right Hand

"See, I have engraved you on the palms of my hands;
your walls are ever before me."

Isaiah 49:16 (NIV)

God's hand is powerful and can save to the utmost! David acknowledged the strength of God's hand in Psalm 89:13 (KJV), "Thou hast a mighty arm: strong is thy hand, and high is thy right hand." You may notice that God's *right hand* is referred to quite a bit in the Bible, and that's because it represents strength, might, and power.

Even Jesus sits on the *right hand of God*, a place of power and authority. God's hand is able to lead you, uphold you, and save you! And *no one* has the power to take you out of *God's hand* . . . not even the devil himself! You alone are given that choice. But God won't force you to stay with Him! It is totally *your decision* to abide in the safety of His almighty hand.

Jesus loves you more than anyone else ever could, and He longs for you to come to Him. Reach out today and put your hand in His, where He eagerly waits to heal you, comfort you, encourage you, bless you, and lift you up! God's right hand is outstretched, willing and ready to meet your every need. Run to Him today!

It's Not About Stuff

*And He said to them, "Take heed and beware
of covetousness, for one's life does not consist in the
abundance of the things he possesses."*

Luke 12:15 (NKJV)

———◆———

So many people spend their whole lives working for material goods—you know, just *stuff* that they think they *have to have* in order to be happy! After college, they move into a tiny little apartment and work hard filling it up with *stuff* until they get so much that they move into a house, filling it with more *stuff*; then they move into a bigger house, working overtime to have enough money to buy even more *stuff*, until they reach middle age and decide it's time to downsize, so they give away most of the *stuff* they worked so hard for. By the time they reach their retirement years, they are living back in a tiny little apartment, and all that *stuff* they worked so hard for was given or thrown away, and they look back over their life and say, "Was my whole life spent working for *stuff*?"

Life goes by so quickly, and there is no time to waste! We must decide now how we want to use this life that God has given us. The Bible tells us in Matthew 6:19-21 (NIV), "Do not store up for yourselves treasures on earth, where moths and vermin destroy. For where your treasure is, there your heart will be also."

A Silent Witness

For I am not ashamed of the gospel of Christ, for it is the power of God to salvation for everyone who believes.

Romans 1:16 (NKJV)

Going to church each week is not what demonstrates the depth of our Christian faith to the world; it is our actions and how we live our daily lives that speak volumes about our relationship with Christ. When we give our hearts to God, our old selfish natures go away and the light of God's love shines through in everything we do! We treat coworkers with respect and show kindness to everyone, including our families, neighbors, or just strangers on the street.

If someone were to ask the person who works alongside you, under you, or over you about your Christianity, you can pretty much guarantee that person will not be talking about how you act at church. But they will talk about what you are like to work with day after day, all week long. What would your coworker say about you? Do they even know you are a Christian? Have you ever asked God for an opportunity to witness to them? In most cases, talking about religion at work is not allowed; however, you'll be surprised at how many opportunities will appear if you're willing to ask God for them!

Never be ashamed to stand up for Jesus! Luke 9:26 (NKJV) says, "For whoever is ashamed of Me and My words, of him the Son of Man will be ashamed when He comes in His own glory." Why not ask God for your *divine appointment* today? And don't forget to be a *silent witness* every day!

Bitter or Better

*Happy are the people who know how to praise you.
Lord, let them live in the light of Your presence.*

Psalm 89:15 (NCV)

Whether we like it or not, there will be times in our lives that we will face trouble, sorrow, and disappointments. The fact is, we live in a sinful world that will never be free of heartache and pain until Jesus comes! We will never live a perfect life here on earth. But here's what defines us—we can choose to let our problems make us *bitter* or *better*; the choice is ours.

If we allow ourselves to be resentful or angry, before we know it, we start feeling sorry for ourselves and even put the blame on God. But this is a *pity party* that no one wants to attend. Instead of being angry, we need to see life from God's perspective. Viewed from above, the problem that frustrated us is only like a speck of sand on the beach.

Once our perspective is from above, we can look away from our troubles altogether and turn our eyes upon Jesus, our Savior, and choose to be better—not bitter!

Is Prayer Necessary?

*Devote yourselves to prayer with an alert
mind and a thankful heart.*

Colossians 4:2 (NLT)

Why is it that Christians pray? After all, God already knows everything we are thinking! And this is true—God does know our *thoughts*, but He *responds* to our prayers! Prayer is a gift and powerful privilege that God gives each one of us. There's no need for a pastor, priest, or anyone else to pray on our behalf because God wants us to talk to Him directly! He's interested in every aspect of our lives! When we are facing a difficult decision or going through a dark valley, it is prayer that sustains us.

Don't be afraid to take that step into humility and ask others to pray too. In the Bible, there are countless examples of people who asked for prayer from fellow believers. When we pray for each other, our hearts are connected in new and loving ways. We're not only drawn closer to our heavenly Father, but also to our brothers and sisters in Christ.

We need to choose wisely and carefully with whom we share our private concerns, but we can ask other Christians to pray for us without giving them all the specific details because God knows *every* detail! It's rather selfish to pray only for our own needs, wants, and desires. God longs for us not only to love each other, but to pray for one another too!

Because We Love Him

*For we are God's fellow workers; you are
God's field, you are God's building.*

1 Corinthians 3:9 (NKJV)

If we truly believed Jesus was coming soon, would we live our lives the same way? If we believed He was coming next month, next week, or even tomorrow, would it make a difference in what we do today? It's far too easy to get so caught up in the every day hustle and bustle of our lives that we place *work for God* on the back burner.

Some feel that as long as they go to church each week, then they've purchased their ticket to heaven. But we can't *earn our way to eternal life*! No amount of duties performed or offerings given—will pay our way! Jesus said in John 14:6 (NKJV), "I am the way, the truth, and the life. No one comes to the Father except through Me." Jesus already paid the price on Calvary! Our salvation is assured when we surrender completely to Him.

You see, God doesn't need us to finish His work—He allows us the *privilege* to work for Him. When we fall in love with Jesus, we just can't help but want to serve Him and do whatever He asks *because* we love Him! It's all about the *love!* Our motivation for serving God should never be to guarantee our place in heaven. The real reason we choose to dedicate our lives to God is because we love Him so much we want to spend our whole lives pleasing Him!

Nothing but the Truth

*"You shall not steal, nor deal falsely,
nor lie to one another."*

Leviticus 19:11(NKJV)

Truth is always better than a lie! Although many Christians feel it is acceptable to tell a *little white lie*, there's really no such thing in God's eyes. In fact, the Bible has quite a bit to say about how God values honesty! In Proverbs 24:26 (NIV) we're told, "An honest answer is like a kiss on the lips." And in Isaiah 33:15 (CEV), "But there will be rewards for those who live right and tell the truth." God says in Proverbs 16:8 (NLT), "Better to have little, with godliness, than to be rich and dishonest." Even in the Ten Commandments, God says, "Thou shalt not bear false witness."

To be a *Christian* means to be *Christlike*, and that means living a life of integrity and honesty! When we make ourselves look better on a resume, *fudge* a little on our taxes, exaggerate our accomplishments to people we want to impress, or even lie about our age, it is being dishonest! In this sinful world we live in, deceit is almost expected and considered normal, but there's no room in Heaven for dishonesty! More than ever, we need to pray and ask God to guard our lips that we may always speak truth, the whole truth, and nothing but the truth!

Kill with Kindness

*If your enemy is hungry, give him bread to eat; and if he
is thirsty, give him water to drink; for so you will heap
coals of fire on his head, and the LORD will reward you.*

Proverbs 25:21-22 (NKJV)

———◈———

Most of us have enemies, and although we don't go out and try to make enemies—there's always someone who just doesn't like us. And no matter what we do or say, they are determined to be antagonistic toward us—as if they feel it is their mission in life to make our lives miserable!

Jealousy is a huge motivating factor that generates enemies. Of course, there are other reasons, but almost always—*selfishness* is involved. And of course, we need to be on the alert for our biggest enemy of all . . . Satan! He is by far the most dangerous!

There is only one way to fight our enemies, and that is to put on the whole armor of God and shield ourselves with His armor of truth. We need to shower our enemies with love and kill them with kindness. It's easy to love people who are good to us, but much more difficult to love those who are evil! Yet God commands us to love our enemies—and if we don't, we won't spend eternity with Jesus! It's that simple. So instead of striking back in anger, let's pray and ask God to put an extra measure of love in our hearts for our enemies—so much in fact, that we couldn't imagine heaven without them!

Perfecting Our Characters

*I will praise You, for I am fearfully and
wonderfully made; marvelous are Your works,
and that my soul knows very well.*

Psalm 139:14 (NKJV)

———❖———

God has created each of us uniquely different. In fact, not
even identical twins are exactly the same. Some people
are weak and some are strong—but everyone faces their own
individual challenges. There are those who deal with frail
health, chronic pain, or physical impairments—but that doesn't
mean God doesn't love them. Those who are weak need not feel
as though it's a *punishment*. On the contrary, everyone needs to
lean on Jesus, but the weak are less tempted to walk alone. They
must lean on Him even more and depend totally on Jesus to
make it through their day!

God is perfecting each of our characters and wants us to
develop such closeness with Him that we'll trust Him more
and lean on Him for everything! Instead of relying on our own
power, He wants us to depend totally on Him. We don't need
perfect bodies, the most outgoing personality, or even the best
of health to shine for Jesus. We need only surrender our lives to
our Creator and embrace who He made us to be. When we trust
God to strengthen, lead, and guide, we can enjoy the abundant
life He has given us, and best of all, instead of moaning and
groaning about all the things we wished we had, or how we
should have been taller, thinner, wiser, or healthier—we'll be
praising Jesus for making us just the way we are!

One Day at a Time

Let us hold fast the confession of our hope without wavering, for he who promised is faithful.

Hebrews 10:23 (ESV)

If you are constantly worrying about what will happen tomorrow, you'll not only be living a stressful life, but you'll miss the joy that God wants to give you. There's a familiar song that goes like this: "I don't know about tomorrow . . . and I know who holds my hand." The words are so comforting knowing it doesn't matter what the future holds as long as you allow God to *hold your hand*. Your life will be a whole lot happier if you trust Jesus and throw worry out the window.

As you face difficult times, instead of trying to solve your own problems, ask God to take over! Remember, *with God, all things are possible*! So stop worrying about *tomorrow* and take one day at a time. Jesus is your strength, and He will empower you to handle whatever challenge comes your way. And here's the good news: because Jesus is your *strength and joy*, He will give you a song in your heart even on your darkest day! No need to walk with a frown when you can choose to walk joyfully by faith . . . *one day at a time*!

God-Pleasing Life

*I will put My Spirit within you and cause you
to walk in My statutes, and you will keep
My judgments and do them.*

Ezekiel 36:27 (NKJV)

———◆———

People who have accomplished much in their lives tend to be goal-oriented. They have specific goals in mind and then work very hard to reach them. Some goals are driven by selfish motives, but the goals of a Christian are different than others. When you surrender your dreams and goals to God, He will accomplish great things in you and through you. Before choosing your goal, ask for wisdom by praying, "Lord, is this what You have in mind for me? Is this the path You want me to follow?" As long as you are following God's plan for your life— you just can't go wrong! The Bible says in Psalm 37:23 (NKJV), "The steps of a good man are ordered by the LORD, and He delights in his way."

Choose the goal of living a *God-pleasing* life! It is only when you are following *God's goals* that you will be truly happy and experience the abundant life God wants you to have. Ask Jesus for *divine appointments* throughout your day and then listen to the Holy Spirit's leading as He guides and directs. You will experience incredible joy when you turn your life over to Him. Keep your eyes on the *heavenly goal* and receive the ultimate reward of eternal life with your Lord and Savior!

Cure for Stress

Delight yourself also in the LORD, *and He shall give you the desires of your heart.*

Psalm 37:4 (NKJV)

———◆———

Doctors' offices are filled with people suffering from all types of illnesses brought on by stress! Nothing seems to be effective in eliminating it from our lives, even though stress is a very real killer. It affects every aspect of our lives, including family, work, and most importantly, our connection with God. Some try to decrease their anxiety by going to the gym every day, seeing a therapist, or taking medications, while still others change jobs, end relationships, or sink into depression. Millions of dollars are spent trying to find ways to de-stress, but the one and only real cure for stress—doesn't cost a thing. *Jesus is the answer*! When we put our faith in God and surrender our hearts to Him—we have no stress!

Allowing God to lead and guide each moment of our lives takes the stress completely away. The pressure of making the right decisions or accomplishing everything on our *to-do lists* no longer exists because God is in charge of our calendars. With Jesus in charge—we have nothing to fear. We can have the abundant, stress-free lives that God wants for us. We need only to put our full faith and trust in our Lord and Savior!

Don't Wait Any Longer

" 'Rejoice with me, for I have found my sheep which was lost!' I say to you that likewise there will be more joy in heaven over one sinner who repents than over ninety-nine just persons who need no repentance."

Luke 15:6-7 (NKJV)

Just like a good shepherd looking for his sheep, Jesus is looking for us! We often acknowledge the need for us to seek out our Savior, but rarely do we consider the fact that God is actively seeking us. He loves us so much that He can't imagine Heaven without us! In Luke 19:10 (NKJV) we're told, "For the Son of Man has come to seek and to save that which was lost," and in John 4:23 (NKJV), "But the hour is coming, and now is, when the true worshipers will worship the Father in spirit and truth; for the Father is seeking such to worship Him."

Jesus loves us so much that He doesn't want any one of us to perish! Even when we turn our backs on Him—He never turns His back on us. He keeps whispering in His still, small voice, "I love you. Please come home." Time is short, and *Jesus is coming soon*! He's tenderly reaching out—why wait any longer?

Time is short for no one is promised tomorrow. Whatever or whoever is standing between you and God—surrender it today, for there's no sin too big for God to forgive, and nothing is worth missing out on eternity with Jesus!

Perfection Not Required

*And He said to me, "My grace is sufficient for you,
for My strength is made perfect in weakness."
Therefore most gladly I will rather boast in my
infirmities, that the power of Christ may rest upon me.*

2 Corinthians 12:9 (NKJV)

We all have weaknesses! Even the person who seems confident and has it all together has an area in their life that they struggle with. No one in this world is strong enough to handle all situations with confidence and ease.

Most people fight the feeling of *not being good enough*. And is it really any wonder, when we live in a world that demands perfection? We are expected to be the wealthiest, the smartest, the most beautiful, and the list goes on and on. It's not really surprising that people feel they need to be perfect to *come to Jesus*! But Jesus accepts us just as we are. He invites us to come to Him, and He will cover all our imperfections with His robe of righteousness!

God doesn't expect us to be perfect . . . because He makes us perfect! The Bible says in Ecclesiastes 7:20 (KJV), "For there is not a just man upon earth, that doeth good, and sinneth not." Perfection doesn't happen overnight and is not a one time cure. It is a work of a lifetime—every hour of every day, striving to be more like Jesus.

Ask God to give you the strength to face each day—He will! Once you accept Jesus as your personal Savior, you can face your day with confidence, knowing that God's grace is sufficient.

My Hope Is Built

*Some trust in chariots and some in horses, but we trust
in the name of the LORD our God.*

Psalm 20:7 (NIV)

The word *hope* means different things to different people. Many put their *hope* in all the wrong places, such as money, power, fame, status, their own strength, and even other people. But they will be sorely disappointed! Only God has the power to sustain hope! Your bank account can be wiped out in a moment's notice. Power, fame, and status are remarkably fragile. Your own strength and even your health will be gone someday. People will fail you, but God never will.

There's a song that describes *hope* with these words: "My hope is built on nothing less, than Jesus' blood and righteousness. I dare not trust the sweetest frame, but wholly lean on Jesus name!" Without *hope,* we would all give up. There would be no reason to get out of bed in the morning. It is *hope* that motivates us to keep moving, keep trying, and to keep *breathing*!

No one loves you more than God! No one! He created you. He knows you. He loves you so much He sent His only Son to this earth to die for you that you might have eternal life. It doesn't get better than that. What more assurance do you need? Seal this truth in your heart and know that . . . Jesus *never* fails. No, not ever! Place your *hope* and trust in Him!

Love One Another

*If someone says, "I love God," and hates his brother, he is
a liar; for he who does not love his brother whom he has
seen, how can he love God whom he has not seen?*

1 John 4:20 (NKJV)

This world would be such a better place if we could just
take away all the *hate* and love each other more! Once the
seed of hatred is planted, it spreads faster than a wildfire and
soon burns out all happiness because everyone is consumed
with *hate*. Bottom line—hatred destroys all *joy*! The two simply
cannot coexist! It takes much more energy to *hate*, and you can
accomplish so much more with kindness and love.

But the best reason not to hate is because *it is a sin*. The
Bible says in 1 John 3:15 (NIV), "Anyone who hates his brother
or sister is a murderer," which breaks the sixth commandment!
Breaking the commandments is a *sin*! Throughout the Bible,
we're told to *love each other*. We need to accept and, yes,
embrace each other's differences. Imagine how different our
world would be if we stopped hating others because of their
race, ethnic background, or religion!

We can only remove hatred by surrendering our hearts to
God, for when we do, there's no room in our hearts for anything
but God's love! When we learn to hate the sins in our own lives
more than we hate the sins of others—this world will be a better
place, and we'll enjoy an even closer walk with God!

Just the Perfect Time

Because the foolishness of God is wiser than men, and the weakness of God is stronger than men.

1 Corinthians 1:25 (NKJV)

God is such a patient God—for even when we are acting like spoiled children, selfishly demanding what we want—He still loves us. Oh, if only we could trust Him more. But all too often, we think we know better than God. We demand that our prayers be answered instantly—and in the way that we want. What a wonderful God we serve, who sees *the big picture*—the end from the beginning—and knows better than we do what is good for us.

What we don't realize is that *if* God granted our pleas, we would be miserable! We would discover the hard way that it wasn't what we wanted after all! The fact is, we are human and too shortsighted to even know what to pray for. But God knows us inside and out, and in answering our prayers, He gives us what is *best* for us—*not everything we want* or *ask for*! The Bible says in Philippians 4:19 (NKJV), "And my God shall supply all your need according to His riches in glory by Christ Jesus."

God loves us more than we could possibly comprehend, and because of His great love, He is willing to perform miracles and pour out His grace and mercy . . . at *just the perfect time*!

Our Heavenly Father

*"I am the good shepherd. I know my own and my own
know me, just as the Father knows me and I know the
Father; and I lay down my life for the sheep."*

John 10:14-15 (ESV)

Jesus watches over us—like a mother who watches her toddler on a busy playground. At any moment, should her precious little one start to wander in a wrong direction, she gently guides her child out of danger's way! A *good mother* knows where her child is at all times. She loves her child so much that, if needed, she would lay down her own life to protect her little one. So it is with our heavenly Father, who *did* lay down His life for us! He loves us so much that He tenderly watches over us—willing to jump in and save us whenever we're headed in a wrong direction! His deepest desire is to keep us close to Him, safe from harm and danger.

Jesus doesn't watch over us because it's His job—something He *has* to do. No! He is motivated by His deep and intense love for us. God knows each one of us by name. He knows our good points *and* our bad ones and loves us anyway. No parent could love their child as much or more than God loves us! He knows our every need! He knows our exact location, our exact circumstances, and the exact problems we are facing! And best of all—God knows how to handle every situation. We need only to answer His call and run into His outstretched arms! He is waiting for us right now!

Not a Total Mess-Up

"Therefore do not worry about tomorrow,
for tomorrow will worry about itself. Each day has
enough trouble of its own."

Matthew 6:34 (NIV)

You shouldn't fret about all the things that have happened in your past, nor should you worry about your future! You can look ahead and drive yourself crazy wondering and obsessing about tomorrow, or you can choose to put your trust in Jesus!

Satan loves to make you feel like a failure—afraid and unworthy of God's love! He wants to keep you in a constant state of discouragement and hopelessness. And let's not forget the *guilt game*—his favorite tool to separate you from God! But don't allow anything to come between you and Jesus. Even though the situation looks impossible and the future never seemed bleaker, *trust God anyway*!

When you are weak, pray for strength. Claim Philippians 4:13 (NKJV), "I can do all things through Christ who strengthens me." And when you feel like your sin is too great to forgive, pray anyway! God will forgive you and wrap His arms around you. He alone has the power to change your life! Bottom line—you are not a failure, a mistake, or a total mess-up! You are *not* a lost cause. Never forget that you are a child of the King of the Universe and your heavenly Father loves you more than anyone else possibly could!

Smell the Roses

*He restores my soul; He leads me in the paths of
righteousness for His name's sake.*

Psalm 23:3 (NKJV)

Every year, every day, every minute you live is a *gift from
God*. What you do with that gift is entirely up to you. God
has also given you the *gift of choice*, so you can use your time to
glorify God or yourself. You live by the consequences of your
actions—both good and bad.

God wants you to be kind and helpful to others, but having
said that, He also wants you to be kind to yourself. Living an
abundant life with Jesus is a balance! God doesn't expect you
to spend every waking moment working—even if your work is
ministering to others. He wants you to enjoy life and experience
the fullness of His joy. There is a difference between being *selfish*
and taking care of *you*! What a sad life you would have if you
never stopped to appreciate all the wonderful things that God
created for you. Take time to enjoy your family, your friends,
and don't forget to take time for you as well!

That old familiar expression is not bad advice: *take time to
smell the roses!* After all, God created them for you to enjoy!
Be kind to yourself for God wants you to be happy! You'll be
surprised at how much more productive your day will be and
how much happier you'll be too. God loves you and wants you
to enjoy a little heaven on earth!

Forgiveness Brings Peace

*Then I confessed my sins to you and didn't hide
my guilt. I said, "I will confess my sins to the LORD,"
and you forgave my guilt.*

Psalm 32:5 (NCV)

When your conscience is killing you from the weight of sin, seek forgiveness from the only One who has the power to forgive—Jesus Christ! Forgiveness is the only thing that will bring you peace. Don't wallow in self-pity or self-righteousness. Don't try and *justify* the reasons you sinned or place the blame on someone else. Sinning does not kill God's love for you. He hates the sin . . . but loves the sinner!

Humble yourself before God, confessing your sin and ask for forgiveness with a truly repentant heart. Jesus stands ready to forgive you and cleanse you from all unrighteousness!

When you are walking with Jesus, nothing can separate you from Him, so never leave the safety of His presence. Allow God to heal your heart and enjoy the comfort and joy of His sweet forgiveness. The safest place you can be is in the arms of Jesus! Claim Him today as your Lord and Savior and reach out and accept His gift of unconditional love!

Going Through the Motions

*"These people come near to me with their
mouth and honor me with their lips, but their
hearts are far from me."*

Isaiah 29:13 (NIV)

———◆———

Jesus longs for us to give Him our *whole hearts*! He wants us to have true devotion and love for Him—the kind of devotion where we love Him so much, we can't wait to spend quiet time alone with Him. Unfortunately, many people are just *going through the motions* of being a Christian. Church membership becomes a false sense of *being saved*, with no real praise in worship. They attend church every week out of habit, sing without joy, and listen to the sermon while their minds are thinking about everything but what the pastor is preaching about, looking at their watches, and breathing a sigh of relief when it is finally time for the benediction!

Church becomes a dreaded event instead of precious time spent with God—and what a missed opportunity to receive a special blessing! *Playing church* or pretending to be a Christian makes for an empty and meaningless life and, even worse, results in missing out on eternity in Heaven.

Are you going through the motions of being a Christian? Is church boring to you? Do you need a spiritual awakening? Ask God to search your heart today and pray, "Lord, please give me so much love for You that I will long to be with You, not just in church, but every moment of every day!"

Be Like Jesus

Do not love the world or anything in the world.
If anyone loves the world, love for the Father is not
in them. For everything in the world—the lust
of the flesh, the lust of the eyes, and the pride of life—
comes not from the Father but from the world.

1 John 2:15-16 (NIV)

We've often heard the expression, "By beholding, we become," and that is definitely true! If we're in an environment long enough, we begin to imitate what is around us. We become what we see. If we fill our minds with things of this world, soon all interest in spiritual things disappear. But when we keep our eyes on Jesus, we soon become just like Him.

Christ's every thought, deed, and action reflected His intimate relationship with His Father. He made time for worship, memorized scripture, prayed, and took His instruction from God. Jesus had a *godly* heart!

There's a song that expresses so beautifully just how to live a godly life called "Be Like Jesus," and the words go like this: "Earthly pleasures vainly call me, I would be like Jesus; nothing worldly shall enthrall me, I would be like Jesus. Be like Jesus, this my song, in the home and in the throng; be like Jesus, all day long! I would be like Jesus." Ask God today to give you a burning desire to be more like Jesus!

Don't Give Up

I can do all things through Christ who strengthens me.

Philippians 4:13 (NKJV)

No matter how challenging your life struggles are, don't give up! Keep trying! Keep putting one foot in front of the other and keep on going. It doesn't matter how dark your problems may seem—nothing is impossible with God! When the enemy tempts you to question, *Why me? Is it worth it? Does anyone even care?* shove those thoughts right out of your mind! The Bible promises over and over again that your determination will be rewarded.

Remember that even when it seems like no one else cares, God does! He not only cares, He loves you more than anyone else ever could and longs for you to run to Him for help. Stop trying to solve your own problems. Take your burdens to Jesus. He understands and sees the whole picture. He has *all* the answers. He knows and feels your pain and is pleading for you to let Him take control and carry you to the finish line.

Call out to Jesus right now! Don't wait till you are exhausted, weak, and so discouraged that you are an easy target for Satan. Remember, a call to God is toll-free, and His line is never busy!

God Does Not Gloat

I will hear what God the LORD will speak,
for He will speak peace to His people and to His saints;
but let them not turn back to folly.

Psalm 85:8 (NKJV)

No matter what crisis you're facing, God is there, giving words of wisdom to guide, comfort, and encourage. Listen carefully, and you will hear His voice, gently guiding and directing your every step. Some think of God as this stern, ridged, powerful presence, but God is not like that at all. He loves us so much that He tenderly watches over us! He *wants* us to be with Him for all eternity and is definitely not gloating when we choose to sin and separate ourselves from Him!

When God sees that we are falling, He tries even harder to save us! There are so many negative voices trying to drown out what God is saying to us, which is why the Bible tells us in Psalm 46:10 (NKJV), "Be still, and know that I am God." We need to spend quiet time alone with Him in worship and Bible study so we can hear and obey His voice. God is tenderly calling to all His children, "This is the way, walk ye in it" (see Isaiah 30:21). All we need to do is stay close to our Best Friend, Jesus!

Prison of Fear

My foes have trampled upon me all day long, for they are many who fight proudly against me. When I am afraid, I will put my trust in You. In God, whose word I praise, in God I have put my trust; I shall not be afraid. What can mere man do to me?

Psalm 56:2-4 (NASB)

———— ◈ ————

Fear is crippling and deadly and can affect every aspect of your life. It keeps people from reaching their goals or becoming successful in life. Those who are afraid to talk to a stranger, go for a job interview, ask for help, or even take a church office will never really experience the true joy of living because they are trapped in the *prison of fear*! But there is One who holds the key to prison—and that person is your Best Friend, Jesus! He longs to set you free!

When you're too devastated by fear to face your problems, give them to your heavenly Father! The Bible says in Isaiah 41:10 (NKJV), "Fear not, for I am with you; . . . I will uphold you with My righteous right hand." And in Psalm 27:1 (NKJV), we're told, "The LORD is the strength of my life; of whom shall I be afraid?" God gives all an open invitation to come to Him— all who are weak and heavy-laden—and He will give His sweet peace and rest! He will give you the courage, strength, and confidence to face each day.

No matter the circumstance or how big the problem, there is no need to panic and get all stressed out! Just remember, there's *nothing* that you and Jesus can't handle together!

Thank God for Family

Why, then, do you criticize your brother? Or why do you despise your brother? For all of us will stand before the judgment seat of God.

Romans 14:10 (ISV)

Families are one of God's precious gifts! They come in all different combinations, but the purpose is the same—so that we can love and support each other through this difficult journey of life. How sad it is when there's fighting and jealousy inside the family. Oh so much joy is missed because of selfishness and pride.

Some people may not have family that is *blood related*, but you still belong to a family—the best family ever: *the family of God!* This forever family is made up of believers who are connected through faith. Brothers and sisters in your church should be there to encourage, help, and spiritually uplift each other! Pray and ask God to make you the brother or sister He wants you to be!

Throw criticism, jealousy, and hatred out the window and replace them with an extra measure of God's love for your fellowmen! The result will be a much more rewarding, uplifting, and happy life, filled to overflowing with God's gift of joy!

Hang on to Jesus

*That He would grant you, according to the riches
of His glory, to be strengthened with might through His
Spirit in the inner man . . . to know the love of
Christ which passes knowledge; that you may be
filled with all the fullness of God.*

Ephesians 3:16, 19 (NKJV)

It's easy to have faith when everything is going smoothly in your life. But when trouble strikes, how you react reveals how strong your faith actually is! Disappointments and even trials that shake you to the core come with living in this sinful world! No one is exempt from pain and heartache, but never lose faith in Jesus! It's not His fault that you suffer—the devil gets all the blame for that!

Jesus is preparing a place in heaven where you can live with Him forever, where there will be no more tears, pain, suffering, or death, but each day will be more glorious than the day before! Human minds can't possibly comprehend the glory of meeting Jesus face to face! You must not lose sight of the heavenly goal! No matter what the devil throws at you—hang on to Jesus!

When you increase your prayer time, worship, and study of God's Word, you'll discover peace such as you have never known! Ask Him to give you more faith! He will! And, He will also give you the strength to overcome any trial you could possibly encounter!

Sweet Forgiveness

"For I will be merciful toward their iniquities, and I will remember their sins no more."

Hebrews 8:12 (ESV)

It's so peaceful watching clouds form beautiful scenes in the sky. But as quickly as they come, they are gone—*never to be seen again*. Not ever! God's sweet forgiveness is even more beautiful . . . and just like the disappearing clouds, once you have confessed your sin and asked for forgiveness, God's grace wipes that sin away . . . forever! Your *forgiven sin* is gone for eternity! God won't throw it in your face the next day, the next month, or years down the road. He doesn't expect or want you to keep begging for forgiveness over and over again for that same sin! No need—because that sin has disappeared and will never be brought up again! God has erased it just as surely as if it had never happened.

Sometimes your remorse and guilt is so great that you just can't stop pleading with God. But this only reveals lack of trust in His power to forgive. God's Word is trustworthy! You can know with absolute certainty that when He forgives . . . He forgives completely! No need for sleepless nights worrying about that transgression. You can sleep peacefully wrapped in the love and comfort of God's sweet forgiveness—the best blanket ever!

Focus on Jesus

Looking unto Jesus, the author and finisher of our faith, who for the joy that was set before Him endured the cross, despising the shame, and has sat down at the right hand of the throne of God.

Hebrews 12:2 (NKJV)

When your world crumbles all around you, don't focus on the crisis—focus on Jesus! As long as you focus on Him, you have nothing to worry about! This sinful world is full of roadblocks and pitfalls, all orchestrated by Satan to keep you from the only one who can save you. But don't let the devil deceive you for one moment!

Whatever difficulties your day may bring, don't spend time regurgitating every depressing detail in your mind. Nor does it help to keep telling anyone who will listen until the actual experience becomes so dismal, all just seems hopeless. This does nothing to fix your problem, and it won't make you feel any better either!

Instead, talk to God as earnestly as you would tell your best friend, and once you've shared your troubles, then relax, take a deep breath, and trust God to take care of you. He is the only one who can give you the strength to face each day and the confidence to go forward without fear! Every day is a beautiful day—when your Best Friend is Jesus!

Instant to His Will

I will hasten and not delay to obey your commands.
Psalm 119:60 (NIV)

When praying and waiting for God's answer, it's important to listen for the clear, gentle voice of the Holy Spirit. Don't be deceived by the enemy. Satan will tempt you to think God doesn't care about you and that He doesn't *really* answer prayers. He wants you to believe God has forsaken you. But don't allow the devil's lies to enter your heart for even one single moment!

Know God's voice! There are many ways you can know He is speaking to you. One that you can always count on is this: the Holy Spirit will never impress you to do anything that goes against God's Holy Word! And, the Holy Spirit is perfectly aligned with the will of God the Father and His Son, Jesus.

When the Holy Spirit speaks to you, act on it! Don't hesitate, rationalize, or allow Satan to talk you out of doing what God is directing you to do. Pray that God will make you *instant to His will* and respond as young Samuel did in 1 Samuel 3:10 (KJV), "Speak; for thy servant heareth."

Be Generous

*Whoever brings blessing will be enriched, and one
who waters will himself be watered.*

Proverbs 11:25 (ESV)

If you want *more*—give *more*! It's that simple! Jesus said in Luke 6:38 (NIV), "Give, and it will be given to you. A good measure, pressed down, shaken together and running over, will be poured into your lap. For with the measure you use, it will be measured to you." Wow! You just can't *out-give* the Lord!

That goes not only for your finances but for your time as well. God promises to bless abundantly when you are generous in sharing the talents, abilities, and resources He gives you. But many times it's easy to forget that everything you have belongs to God. In fact, He is the very reason that you have talents, and how you use them—determines the blessings you'll receive.

There's no room in your heart for God if you're filled with selfishness. Throughout the Bible, there are warnings about the evil of selfishness. Philippians 2:3 (NIV) reads, "Do nothing out of selfish ambition or vain conceit. Rather, in humility value others above yourselves." Giving is an important aspect of a Christian's life.

Pray and ask God to guide and direct your giving, and when you give, do so with a pure heart—*not expecting something in return*! God will honor you by blessing you abundantly more than you could ever ask or think!

We Can't Fool God

My eyes are on all their ways; they are not hidden from me, nor is their sin concealed from my eyes.

Jeremiah 16:17 (NIV)

Some people think that if they are Christians, their lives will be perfect without any temptation to sin. But that's simply not true. Everyone struggles with their own individual human weaknesses. We do our best to hide our struggles, trials, and evil desires in the deepest, darkest corners of our hearts where no one else can possibly see. That's because there are things that cannot be trusted to even our closest earthly friends. Why? Because we know that if people knew the truth about us, they wouldn't understand, and it would change how they feel and think about us.

But, the blessed hope is this: God does understand, and He is the only One who truly can. There's nothing we can hide from our Lord and Savior! We may be able to fool our friends and even our family, but we will never fool God. He alone sees our hearts, knows our weaknesses, and yet, He still loves us with an everlasting love! He longs to help, guide, comfort, and heal us! He stands ready to give us the victory and deliver us from falling into the darkness of sin.

No matter what you are facing or going through, remember . . . you can trust your deepest secrets, even your darkest thoughts to Jesus, and He will give you the strength to overcome temptation and be victorious in Him!

Surrender

*For none of us lives for ourselves alone, and none
of us dies for ourselves alone.*

Romans 14:7 (NIV)

O ur biggest battle here on earth is with *self.* We tell ourselves
we'll be happy when we find the perfect mate, get married,
have children, get that big promotion, buy a new house, have
money in the bank, and get rid of all our enemies! But none of
that will bring happiness. True joy in life is only achieved when
we *die to self* and surrender completely and totally to Jesus! It's
only when we are in God's plan for our lives that we can be
happy. It doesn't matter what the devil throws at us—as long as
our lives are in harmony with God—we can rejoice.

Paul tells us in Philippians 4:11 (KJV), "Not that I speak in
respect of want: for I have learned, in whatsoever state I am,
therewith to be content." That's a pretty powerful statement!
God wants us to be content with whatever path *He* chooses for
us, which brings us back to that ole battle with self. We *must*
win this battle, and we *can . . . with God's help*! All we need to
do is pray and ask Him to take control of our lives and then stay
surrendered! This is not a one-time action. We need to die *daily*
to self.

Surrender is based on love. When we truly love Jesus, we
joyfully surrender our wants, plans, and desires and do that
which honors and pleases God. The result is true happiness and
incredible joy!

Go to Jesus First

*"I have seen his ways, and will heal him;
I will also lead him, and restore comforts to
him and to his mourners."*

Isaiah 57:18 (NKJV)

There are times when faced with a difficult situation, you may try and fix things yourself, only to end up making it ten times worse! Instead of making God your last resort—make Him your *first* resort! Jesus is the only one who knows the end from the beginning, and He's the only one you can trust your problems with. Best of all, He loves you more than anyone else ever could! He wants what is best for you, with no hidden agenda—and *that's truth* you can count on!

You can find peace and strength in Jesus because He knows you inside and out, and He is the only one who fully understands. When your heart is heavy, and you don't know where to turn, remember that Jesus is waiting for you with open arms. Pour your heart out to Him, asking for wisdom, guidance, and direction. Then, experience the amazing peace, joy, and contentment that only God can give.

There's no need to freak out and prepare for the worst when you choose to allow God to take control. Walking hand in hand with Jesus is the only safe way to venture on life's journey, and it's the only road that leads to true joy and happiness!

Pray for Prosperity

Beloved, I pray that you may prosper in all things and be in health, just as your soul prospers.

3 John 2 (NKJV)

God wants us to be successful and to prosper! He tells us in Jeremiah 29:11 (NIV), "For I know the plans I have for you . . . plans to prosper you and not to harm you, plans to give you hope and a future." Although God wants us to be prosperous, that doesn't mean that we will all live a life of luxury. What it does mean is that God wants us to have everything we need to accomplish the tasks He has given us to do. That includes having the funds, the material goods, the opportunities, and the grace and mercy needed to be a blessing to others! It does not mean that God wants us to be prosperous just so we can be rich and selfish!

In 1 Peter 4:10 (KJV) we're told, "As every man hath received the gift, even so minister the same one to another, as good stewards of the manifold grace of God." All good gifts come from above! It's very clear in James 1:17 (KJV): "Every good gift and every perfect gift is from above, and cometh down from the Father of lights, with whom is no variableness, neither shadow of turning." We need to pray for *good gifts*, and ask God to prosper us for the purpose of blessing others in carrying out His plan for our lives.

On Your Knees

*"For the LORD your God is living among you. He is a
mighty savior. He will take delight in you with gladness.
With his love, he will calm all your fears. He will
rejoice over you with joyful songs."*

Zephaniah 3:17 (NLT)

One way you can please your heavenly Father is to trust Him—fully and completely! Instead of biting your nails, pacing the floor, and crying in despair—give your troubles to the only One who can help you—Jesus Christ, our Lord God and Savior!

When tempted to worry and fret, cry out to God, "Lord, this is Your battle, for surely it is too large for me to bear! Please give me more faith in You. Help me to trust You more and not try to fix things myself. Lord, give me patience to wait upon You for Your answer." And when you get off your knees, if tempted to pick those burdens up again, ask God to give you the strength you need to leave them at the cross.

Claim Philippians 4:13 (NKJV), "I can do all things through Christ who strengthens me," and then ask God to give you an extra measure of faith! Choose this very day to begin trusting *God* fully and completely!

You Can't Buy Heaven

*For the wages of sin is death, but the gift of God is
eternal life in Christ Jesus our Lord.*

Romans 6:23 (NKJV)

———◆———

Salvation is a gift from God that is absolutely *free*! Because
God sacrificed His only Son to come to earth and die on
Calvary—eternal life is now available to everyone. All we have
to do is surrender our hearts and lives to Him! Many have
difficulty comprehending how such a gift could actually be *free*.
So, they try to *earn* salvation by doing good things, working
hard in the church, giving bigger offerings . . . but the truth is,
you can't *buy your way to heaven*!

The only way we can receive God's gift of salvation is by
giving our lives totally to Him! The act of surrender enables
us to be brought into a personal relationship with God and
experience His amazing love. When we understand His love,
our gratitude motivates us to show our appreciation and gives
us an incredible desire to do even more for our Lord and Savior!

We need to thank God daily for His deep and abiding love.
If it were not for Calvary, where Jesus paid the ultimate price
for our sins, our eternal life would not be possible! He gave
His life willingly, not because we deserved it, but because of
His unfathomable, unending, amazing love for us. What an
awesome God we serve!

Friend or Foe

"You are My friends if you do whatever I command you."
John 15:14 (NKJV)

———◆———

We can only serve one master, and there are only two choices: God or Satan. It's not possible to serve both. Our highest priority should be pleasing God because, if we are following God's plan for our lives, we don't have to worry about anything else! We can't let what other people think determine our actions.

Most of us want to look good in the eyes of our friends and family. So much so that some will exaggerate on their resumes or embellish their accomplishments, but God is our Creator, and He doesn't want us to pretend to be someone we're not. He made us, and He knows more than anyone else the *best* plan for our lives.

In fact, He already has our entire lives all mapped out—all we need to do is allow Him to lead and guide. It's impossible to be pretentious when we are listening to God's voice and following His lead—so choose today, are you a friend or a foe?

Forgiving Our Family

*"Lord, how often shall my brother sin against
me, and I forgive him? Up to seven times?" Jesus said to
him, "I do not say to you, up to seven times,
but up to seventy times seven."*

Matthew 18:21-22 (NKJV)

This journey here on earth is difficult, and God created *family* to help and support each other along the way. Having said that, no family is perfect because humans are not perfect! Unfortunately, nearly everyone at some point will betray, hurt, or disappoint a family member. In some cases, for your mental health, it becomes necessary to distance yourself from them. But in all cases, God requires you to forgive!

Now that doesn't mean that He expects you to be best friends and hang out—but the Bible does say that unless we forgive others, He will not forgive us! It's very clear that without forgiveness, there is no hope of eternal life! Is anger and *revenge* really worth missing out on Heaven?

Instead of harboring bitterness, ask God to put forgiveness in your heart, and let Him judge the ones who caused your pain. When you release the anger and *truly forgive*, you will no longer be dragged down by the weight of guilt. Instead, you'll feel as if you are walking on air, and your heart will be rejoicing, singing praises to God!

Fully Satisfied

*The LORD will guide you continually, and satisfy
your soul in drought, and strengthen your bones; you
shall be like a watered garden, and like a spring
of water, whose waters do not fail.*

Isaiah 58:11 (NKJV)

God loves to bless His children. He wants for us to bring our requests to Him and tell Him the desires of our hearts. However, many times if we actually received what we *think* we want—it wouldn't be good for us at all! In fact, we would be quite miserable. The Bible tells us in Psalm 37:4 (NKJV), "Delight yourself also in the LORD, and He shall give you the desires of your heart." Only God knows the end from the beginning and what is best for us! We can trust Him to guide us in all our decisions—whether large, small, or seemingly insignificant.

When we fall in love with Jesus, everything changes, including the things we want—we no longer are focused on *selfish* and *material things*! Our desires become the things that will *draw us closer to our Savior*! God doesn't promise to give us everything on our *want list*, but He does promise to *supply our every need*.

Here's a promise we can claim in Proverbs 13:4 (NIV), "The desires of the diligent are fully satisfied." When we live our lives in full surrender to God, we can be assured that we will absolutely, positively, and most definitely . . . be *fully satisfied!*

Spiritual Laziness

*Do not love sleep, lest you come to poverty; open your
eyes, and you will be satisfied with bread.*

Proverbs 20:13 (NKJV)

One of the biggest reasons for laziness is lack of passion.
When there is nothing that excites or *motivates* us, we
tend to just go through the motions of living. Coworkers don't
like laziness because they have to work extra hard to make up
for the one who is slacking! Family members get frustrated for
the same reason! The Bible has quite a bit to say about how God
feels about laziness. Ecclesiastes 9:10 (NKJV) reads, "Whatever
your hand finds to do, do it with all your might."

God wants us to work hard and do a good job. Unfortunately,
laziness carries over in our Christian lives, too. There are
those who suffer with the deadly disease of *spiritual laziness.*
Fortunately, our heavenly Father has a cure! All we need to do
is pray and ask Him to take away all laziness from within us!

Why not pray today: "Dear God, thank You for opening my
eyes to my spiritual laziness. Forgive me for the times I have
ignored Your Holy Spirit's *wake-up call.* Remove all laziness
within me. Help me to get up early to spend time with You.
Fill me with energy so that You can use me in a powerful way. I
claim Your promise in Matthew 10:22 (NKJV), 'He who endures
to the end will be saved.' O Lord, mold me and make me into
a worker who will endure to the end that I might receive Your
heavenly reward. In Jesus' precious name. Amen."

Get Thee Behind Me

*Be clear-minded and alert. Your opponent, the Devil, is
prowling around like a roaring lion, looking for someone
to devour. Resist him and be firm in the faith.*

1 Peter 5:8-9 (ISV)

Many of us have an unrealistic idea of just *who* Satan is. Artists often sketch him with a red demon face and a pitchfork in his hand or make him look like a funny cartoon character that's not real. But nothing could be further from the truth because Satan is very *real* and *extremely dangerous*!

Satan has done an amazing job confusing us about his *real* identity through movies, TV shows, video games, music, websites, and so much more! He cleverly disguises himself to make us think *he is harmless.* Our kids are singing songs with sexual meanings, watching satanic movies, practicing witchcraft, using profanity . . . and parents think nothing of it! Yes, the devil is doing a wonderful job at making us immune to his evil ways—all of which lead to separating us from God!

Satan's goal is to confuse and disarm us, and it is when we underestimate his power that we become most vulnerable to his deceptions. Our only protection is staying close to Jesus! When we are under *enemy attack,* say these words out loud: "In the name of Jesus, get thee behind me, Satan," and the mere mention of Christ's name will cause him to flee in terror!

Keep Holding His Hand

"I come to you in the name of the LORD of hosts. . . .
This day the LORD will deliver you into my hand. . . .
Then all this assembly shall know that the LORD does not
save with sword and spear; for the battle is the LORD's,
and He will give you into our hands."

1 Samuel 17:45-47 (NKJV)

As Christians, there will be times when our faith is really *put to the test*! It could be a boss who asks us to compromise our beliefs or, even though wanting a life-saving miracle for a dying loved one, choosing to pray, "God's will be done." We might have empty bank accounts and bill collectors calling every day, but we decide not to cheat on our taxes even though we need the money! When we're tempted to break our commitments to God—stop and listen. He is right there beside us. Listen to His still small voice! He has given us His strength through the power of the Holy Spirit to resist temptation!

The Bible says in James 4:7 (NIV), "Submit yourselves, then, to God. Resist the devil, and he will flee from you." The provision Christ gives will be sufficient for any temptation the enemy throws at us, whether we are at work, home, or on vacation!

When our faith is weak, we can call out to Jesus and He will give us strength. Claim His promise in Isaiah 40:29 (NIV), "He gives strength to the weary and increases the power of the weak." If we keep holding God's hand, He will fight our enemies for us!

No Mistakes

*Being confident of this very thing, that He
who has begun a good work in you will complete it
until the day of Jesus Christ.*

Philippians 1:6 (NKJV)

Jesus loves you! Yes, He *really* loves you! It's God's unending, amazing, miraculous love that gives you the desire to surrender your heart and life to Him. There is so much freedom when you follow Jesus. Burdens are lifted—because they are no longer *your* burdens, they are His! No more worrying about what you should do or what direction to take. God will direct your path! You only get in trouble when you start doubting God and walk away.

It's important to realize that *you* are special to Jesus! He made you uniquely different from everyone else—with your own set of talents and gifts. So, never compare yourself to others! When you focus on other people's expectations and not what God wants you to do, you will surely stumble and fall! Don't compare your journey to anyone else's. God has a special plan . . . just for you! But don't get all puffed up with pride thinking you are more important than others—because you are not better or worse than anyone else.

God made everyone equal, but with individual differences. He created *you . . . to be you!* He has a purpose for your life, and He will give you everything you need to accomplish His plan for you. Best of all, God doesn't make mistakes. He intentionally made you and loves you more than you could possibly know!

Worthy of Love

But God, being rich in mercy, because of His great love with which He loved us, even when we were dead in our transgressions, made us alive together with Christ (by grace you have been saved), and raised us up with Him, and seated us with Him in the heavenly places in Christ Jesus.

Ephesians 2:4-6 (NASB)

God wants you to experience the joy of being loved constantly and perfectly! But sometimes, it's easy to start judging yourself based on how you look or behave or feel. If you like what you see in the mirror, you feel a bit more worthy of God's love. When things are going smoothly, and it's been awhile since you've made any major mistakes, then you find it easier to believe that Jesus loves you!

However, when you feel discouraged from weakness and failure, you tend to punish yourself and question how anyone could possibly find you worthy of love. Instead of spending all your energy on self-loathing and regret, turn to Jesus. God has a special way of taking the ugliness of your life and turning it into something beautiful that will glorify Him.

No matter how badly you've messed up or how awful you feel about yourself, give all that pain to Jesus and allow Him to wash it all away—forever! Remember, you are God's cherished and beloved child, whom He gave His life for. He believes you are worth saving and *worthy of love*!

Not Ashamed

Because Your lovingkindness is better than life,
my lips shall praise You. Thus I will bless You while I live;
I will lift up my hands in Your name.

Psalm 63:3–4 (NKJV)

The world sometimes views Christians as *weak, strange,* or just plain *weird.* Perhaps that's one reason so many Christians try to *blend in* with the world, hoping no one will notice. But the truth is . . . there's nothing *weak, strange, or weird* about Jesus Christ. He was both human and divine. He was firm, yet tender; courageous, yet humble. Even in His weakest moment, He was strong.

When Satan tried to tempt Jesus on the mountaintop, although He was exhausted, weary, and hungry, He resisted temptation. He was a man of utmost integrity at all times. And above all, His love for mankind, as well as for His heavenly Father, shone through His every word, deed, and action!

Jesus set an amazing example for all Christians to follow. We have no reason to fear or be ashamed of our Leader. Our *God is worthy of praise*! We need not be ashamed to call ourselves *Christians*—followers of Jesus!

Nothing Between

*Let us throw off everything that hinders
and the sin that so easily entangles. And let us run with
perseverance the race marked out for us.*

Hebrews 12:1 (NIV)

There are many Christians who truly desire a closer walk with Jesus, but they can't seem to obtain the joy that loving our Lord and Savior brings. They leave the church feeling empty, disillusioned, and lost, not knowing why they don't feel connected to God!

Some try to work their way to heaven by spending hours in ministry, but never achieving that intimacy with Jesus that they are longing for. Others avoid all church duties and are content to be *pew-warmers*, not realizing that they are dying spiritually. Week after week goes by, year after year, and the distance grows as they *go through the motions* of living Christian lives. However, God longs to bring us into a oneness with Him! He wants to jump-start our lives so that we can enjoy the abundant life that He has planned.

There is absolutely nothing worth hanging on to if it separates us from God! Cut it out like a cancer! Then ask God to create a clean heart and a right spirit within and don't forget to increase prayer time—that special *alone time with Jesus* that brings the intimacy that we long for. We should search our hearts and get rid of anything that is separating us from Jesus— leaving nothing between our Lord and our Savior!

Worth Saving

In a desert land he found him, in a barren and howling waste. He shielded him and cared for him; he guarded him as the apple of his eye, like an eagle that stirs up its nest and hovers over its young, that spreads its wings to catch them and carries them aloft.

Deuteronomy 32:10-11 (NIV)

God does not abandon people; rather it is people . . . who abandon God! He stands ready to help, but won't force Himself into our lives. We must invite Him in. He wants to take our burdens and make them light. He longs to lift us up out of the dark pit of despair and fill our hearts with joy.

Contrary to what the devil would have us believe, He is not an angry, stern God who waits with eager anticipation to bring down His wrath and fury the second we mess up. No, not at all! He is a loving God who waits patiently for us to come to Him.

Even though we are stubborn, selfish, and filthy with sin . . . Jesus loves us. In fact, He loves us so much—that He died on a cross so that we might have eternal life with Him! God never gives up on us because He believes . . . we are *worth saving*!

Strive for Holiness

*More than that, I count all things to be loss in view
of the surpassing value of knowing Christ Jesus my Lord,
for whom I have suffered the loss of all things, and count
them but rubbish so that I may gain Christ.*

Philippians 3:8 (NASB)

———— ❖ ————

When we pray, it's important to trust God to know what is best and to trust His perfect will. When we have a close relationship with our heavenly Father, we would never be comfortable just going through the motions of *playing church*. In fact, it is quite the opposite because the closer we are to God, the more we long to remain in His presence!

Prayer warriors know, believe, and have seen answers to prayer, and the more we pray, the stronger our connections are to Christ! Prayer brings us into a *oneness* with Him, and in that closeness, we have a deeper desire for more of God's Holy Spirit! We yearn to be saved and delivered from not just one sin, but from *all* sin, and from its power and corruption. We do not want even one sin to separate us from our Lord and Savior!

That's why we need to increase our prayer time and strive for holiness in our hearts and lives! Never settle for a mundane, compromising life of *living as the world lives*. Instead, focus on a richer life with Christ—our salvation depends on it!

Victory Is Ours

In all circumstances take up the shield of faith . . .

Ephesians 6:16 (ESV)

W e don't have to fear destruction at the hand of the devil, because the battle has already been won! Christ paid the ultimate price on Calvary, and the blood of Jesus has purchased our salvation! But that doesn't mean Satan has given up trying to separate us from the only One who can save us! In fact, the devil knows his time on earth is short, and he's trying harder than ever to tempt us to sin.

He's quite clever and, oh, so cunning at making worldly pleasure seem enticing. He's an expert at disguising the evils of this world—making them seem like *it's not so bad* and easier to say, "Well, just this once," or "I'll have some fun for awhile and *then* give my heart to Jesus." But it really doesn't work that way! If we yield to temptation, before we know it, we are weighed down with the guilt of sin and sink deeper and deeper into the enemy's trap!

Don't be deceived into thinking the devil is not a threat— and don't underestimate his evil power. Satan is dangerous and we should never play on his playground! We are cautioned in 1 Peter 5:8 (NKJV), "Be sober, be vigilant; because your adversary the devil walks about like a roaring lion, seeking whom he may devour." Stay close to Jesus—resist the devil, and he will flee from us. With God at our side—*victory is ours*!

God of Miracles

"For the Father loves the Son and shows him all he does.
Yes, and he will show him even greater works than these,
so that you will be amazed."

John 5:20 (NIV)

———◇———

Miracles happen every day! Yes, God didn't just perform miracles in Bible times, but He continues to work miracles today! Some are more obvious than others, but all are faith-building and evidence that our God is real, all-knowing, all-powerful, and in charge of the entire universe!

It's important to remember that God is not the only one who can perform miracles. It is also in Satan's power to do so whenever it suits his purposes. The devil is quite clever at using *supernatural happenings* to deceive us. That's why it's so important that we stay closely connected with our heavenly Father for His divine direction.

It doesn't matter how much money we have, how educated we are, how rich or famous we are, the color of our skin, or anything else—God can and will perform miracles in our lives. They are evidence of His power and amazing love for us. We need only surrender our hearts to Him and *believe* in His power! If we are struggling with *unbelief*, all we need to do is pray and ask God to give us more faith and trust in Him . . . and He surely will!

Bad Things Happen

*"The thief does not come except to steal, and to kill,
and to destroy. I have come that they may have life, and that
they may have it more abundantly."*

John 10:10 (NKJV)

Many people ask the question, "Why do bad things happen to good people?" and wonder why God allows such horrible things to happen to *His* children! Some even blame God for their troubles and want to know, "*If* God is in control of the universe, then *why* does He allow pain and heartache?" And the answer is this: because of that first sin in the Garden of Eden, we live in a sinful world, and until Jesus comes, there will be pain and suffering.

There's a battle going on right now between good and evil, and yes, God *is* in control as the King of the universe, but He has given each of us the *gift of choice*. When we make wrong choices, we reap the consequences. God is not a dictator. He's not going to *make us do the right thing* or prevent us from sinning. The Bible tells us we cannot serve two masters, so we must choose God or Satan. Jesus does not want us to serve Him because we are *afraid* of Him—He wants us to give our hearts to Him *because we love Him*!

It's because of Jesus' death on the cross that our salvation is even possible. We would have no hope of eternal life except that God made the ultimate sacrifice by giving His only Son to die so that we might live with Him forever. He loves each of us that much! Won't you recommit your life to Jesus today? He is waiting for you with outstretched arms!

Do Your Best

*Bondservants, obey in everything those who
are your earthly masters, not by way of eye-service, as
people-pleasers, but with sincerity of heart, fearing
the Lord. Whatever you do, work heartily, as for the Lord
and not for men, knowing that from the Lord you
will receive the inheritance as your reward.
You are serving the Lord Christ.*

Colossians 3:22-24 (ESV)

There's a common expression: "If a job is worth doing at all, it is worth doing well!" Unfortunately, many people today don't live by this standard, choosing instead to *settle* for *good enough*! Companies are having a harder and harder time finding employees who want to exceed expectations instead of just skimping by. Workers want to do as little as possible, not caring if it is done right or in a timely manner!

The difference between something *good* and something *great* is attention to detail! This is true of fixing a delicious meal, growing a beautiful garden, or even having a well-run church! Consistently bad sermons week after week—lead to empty pews! We need to make a commitment to always do our best, aim for high quality, and strive for perfection . . . then God will do the rest!

Never Forget Calvary

But He was wounded for our transgressions, He was bruised for our iniquities; the chastisement for our peace was upon Him, and by His stripes we are healed.

Isaiah 53:5 (NKJV)

God loves each one of us so much that He gave His only Son to come to this earth and die for our sins—giving us the gift of eternal life! It's a gift that none of us deserve, but because of His great and unimaginable love for us, He gave it freely. As Christians, we have heard the story of what happened at Calvary over and over again, but for some, it has lost its meaning. There are those who claim to love God, but at the first sign of trouble, blame Him for everything! Instead of relying on Him to help them through the storm, they turn on Him, forgetting all about the depth of His love. Oh, how that must break God's heart! What a wonderful and loving Lord and Savior we serve who never turns His back on us—even when we forsake Him, He does not forsake us. Our God is patient, tenderly and lovingly guiding each step of the way.

Whatever difficult times we face here on earth, they fade in comparison with what Jesus did for us! Our daily prayer should be, "Thank You, Jesus, for loving us so much that You gave Your life to save us. Forgive us when we fail You and help us to trust and love you more. What an awesome God You are!"

'Tis So Sweet

*And those who know Your name will put
their trust in You; for You, LORD, have not
forsaken those who seek You.*

Psalm 9:10 (NKJV)

As a Christian, you hear a lot about *faith* and the importance of *trusting in Jesus*. This beautiful song, " 'Tis So Sweet to Trust in Jesus," by Louisa M.R. Stead, expresses so beautifully the peace of having real faith in our Lord and Savior.

" 'Tis so sweet to trust in Jesus, just to take Him at His Word; just to rest upon His promise, just to know thus saith the Lord." Oh, that we could all sing and rejoice in this chorus: "Jesus, Jesus, how I trust Him! How I've proved Him o'er and o'er; Jesus, Jesus, precious Jesus! O for grace, to trust Him more!" These words express just how rewarding it is to have a deep and meaningful relationship with our Lord.

Pray and ask God to give you more faith—the kind of faith that will not waver when faced with heavy trials and that will keep you trusting in Jesus even when every fiber of your being is screaming for proof that there *is* a God! When you have an unshakable faith in Jesus, you can be at peace not only during the good times, but in the darkest, most difficult times as well. Start exercising your faith today by taking hold of your Savior's outstretched hand and *trust in Jesus*!

Treasured Sins

Who executes justice for the oppressed; who gives food to the hungry. The Lord sets the prisoners free. The Lord opens the eyes of the blind; the Lord raises up those who are bowed down; the Lord loves the righteous.

Psalm 146:7-8 (NASB)

Many run from God because they want to hang on to their *treasured sins*. They fear that a Christian's life is boring, and they'll miss out on all the things they *can't* do—you know, the usual list of *cant's*: *can't smoke, can't drink, can't swear*, and so on. But just the opposite is true.

When you accept Jesus as your personal Savior, you will experience freedom such as you have never known! You won't be weighed down by selfishness, resentment, fear, and anger. You'll feel like a prisoner that has just been set free! Your heart will be filled with joy and your shoulders light as a feather because you are no longer trying to carry your heavy burdens!

Choose *freedom* today! Ask God to forgive you for your sins, and commit your life fully to Him. There's nothing you have done that is too great for God to forgive. Surrendering your heart and life to Jesus is the most liberating feeling in the world, and it is the *only* road to true happiness!

Wake Up

But I press on to take hold of that for which
Christ Jesus took hold of me.

Philippians 3:12 (NIV)

Many Christians claim to love the Lord with all their heart and soul, but their actions speak differently. They would never consider getting actively involved—taking a church office, helping out at the local food bank, or going on a mission trip. No, they are quite satisfied to *love the Lord* just going to church once a week and then going about their weekly routine, until time to go to church again the next week! Week after week turns into year after year, until they are ready for retirement and their bodies are too weak to give service to anyone!

Sadly, too many are blindly going through the motions of *being a Christian*—and truly do not realize they are *not* connected to our Savior. Going to church will not *save* anyone! We need to *know* our Savior! And the more we get to know Jesus, the more we love Him and *want* to serve Him! We need to *wake up* from our *spiritual slumber* and allow God to use us—however He wants to use us.

Ask yourself the questions: *Do I love Jesus so much that I am willing to give of my time, my finances, and my whole heart? Do I love Him more than my comfortable lifestyle, more than my career, more than financial success?* Honestly examine your heart and answer the question that Jesus asked Peter in John 21:15 (NKJV), "Do you love Me more than these?"

Prescription for Peace

Even before there is a word on my tongue,
behold, O LORD, You know it all. You have enclosed me
behind and before, and laid Your hand upon me.
Such knowledge is too wonderful for me; it is
too high, I cannot attain to it.

Psalm 139:4-6 (NASB)

If you truly want to feel relaxed and at peace, there's no need to fly to some exotic location or check into a month long spa that guarantees to take away your stress. No, the only *real cure* for anxiety and worry is fully trusting in Jesus! Give your problems to Him!

You don't have to figure out the solution to your troubles or lay awake at night worrying about what the future holds. God already has it all figured out, and His plan is always *perfect!* When you have complete faith that God is in control of your life, then it's easy to give up your worries and cares to Him. And it's only then that you can experience real peace and joy.

God wants you to not only outwardly serve Him, but inwardly as well. He wants you to have His sweet peace in your heart and soul! If you find yourself with a heart full of *panic, anxiety,* and *worry*, Jesus has the cure and the prescription is free. Just take two doses of *faith* and *call your Great Physician*! P.S. God makes house calls!

Key to Heaven

*Jesus said to him, "I am the way, the truth, and the life.
No one comes to the Father except through Me."*

John 14:6 (NKJV)

Is your relationship with God *close and personal? Distant and aloof? Or something in between?* Take time to really examine your friendship with God and ask yourself, *How often do I pray or study the Bible? Do I only turn to God when I'm in trouble?* There's no better time than right now to renew your commitment with God! It is only by having a close and personal relationship with Him that His plan for your life is revealed!

There are those who have been *Christians* all their lives, but have no idea who God really is! They don't read their Bibles on a regular basis, and many don't pray at all because they have no real faith that God even *hears* or *cares*. But God does hear and answer every prayer. Jesus says in Jeremiah 33:3 (NKJV), "Call to Me, and I will answer you, and show you great and mighty things, which you do not know."

Without God as Lord of your life, you can't possibly experience the true joy of living, and you'll never know the incredible plan He has for you! There's no time for anyone to be going through the motions of *playing church*. It's time to *get serious about surrender*! Make a decision right now to strengthen your walk with God. Spend time each day talking with Him in prayer and reading His Holy Word! Surrender your whole heart to God—holding nothing back. Remember, *Jesus is the key to heaven—and faith unlocks the door!*

Price of Earthly Pleasures

Now I know that the LORD saves His anointed;
He will answer him from His holy heaven with the
saving strength of His right hand.

Psalm 20:6 (NKJV)

Some people run from God because they're afraid of what He will ask them to do. They don't want to give Him control and be forced into a strict religion full of rules. But losing out on eternity with Jesus is a high price to pay for earthly pleasures—which won't last and cannot give everlasting peace and happiness.

God has given each of us the gift of choice. We can choose a life of sin or a life surrendered to Jesus—but we can't have both! Before we can enter the kingdom of heaven, we must allow God to remove sin from our lives. Fortunately, God is in the soul-winning business and stands by eager and ready for the task. All we need to do is surrender our hearts to Him and ask for His forgiveness. Jesus promised to save us *from* our sin, but He doesn't say *in* our sin.

Allow God to separate you from your sinful desires and ask Him to give you a hatred for your own sin. The three most powerful words you can pray are "Jesus, save me!"

God Has Your Back

*Do you not know that if you present yourselves
to anyone as obedient slaves, you are slaves of the one
whom you obey, either of sin, which leads to death, or of
obedience, which leads to righteousness?*

Romans 6:16 (ESV)

With Jesus in your life, there is absolutely no reason to fear! You are empowered to accomplish anything God asks you to do. There's no need to get all upset about the things the devil throws your way, although that's exactly what he wants. Satan loves to see you lose faith in God and become discouraged!

When you're leaning on Jesus to take care of your problems, you don't have to worry about a thing! God has your back! No need to waste a moment of your day trying to figure out how to overcome the challenges, because you only need to follow God's directions, and He will lead, guide, and direct each step of the way. But, you do need to be careful not to tell God *how* to answer your prayers. It's easy to become weighed down and frustrated trying to do it yourself, struggling to solve your own problems, but that never works!

Remember, there's nothing you can't do as long as you hand over the control to God! You can go forward in *holy boldness* with Jesus as your Guide—trusting in His perfect plan!

Forgive, Forget, Move On

*Put on tender mercies, kindness, humility, meekness,
longsuffering; bearing with one another, and forgiving
one another, if anyone has a complaint against another;
even as Christ forgave you, so you also must do.*

Colossians 3:12-13 (NKJV)

Our human hearts have a difficult time understanding *forgiveness.* We all want forgiveness and pray for *grace and mercy*—even begging God for it—but few are willing to give it themselves! Forgiveness is about making a decision to move forward and allowing God to release us from the past.

Holding grudges only causes pain and bitterness, and contrary to what we may think, *revenge does not bring happiness.* We can't change the past, but we can change how we respond to it. We can choose to hang on to *justified anger* or we can choose God's gift of joy! But we can't have both. We must choose! If we hang on to all that hurt, pain, and anger, we will miss out on any hope of happiness on this earth and in the new earth to come—*because we won't be there!* God says that if we won't forgive others, then He won't forgive us! Is there any hurt in our lives that is really worth missing out on eternity with Jesus?

Sometimes the pain is so deep that forgiving doesn't seem humanly possible. But *all* things are possible with God! He can put *love* in our hearts and even when we cannot love with our *human love* . . . we can love that person with *God's love.* Ask God to put forgiveness in our hearts—and then *forgive, forget, and move on*!

Fear Nothing

*The angel of the LORD encamps all around those who
fear Him, and delivers them.*

Psalm 34:7 (NKJV)

We could avoid a lot of heartache and worry if we learned to put our trust in God. Instead of living in *fear*, we would enjoy the sweet peace that He gives to all who believe and trust Him. But God's peace cannot be present in a heart consumed with fear. This battle against the enemy must be won! Fear cannot be *wished away*, it must be *prayed away* and confronted with God's Holy Word.

The Bible says in Deuteronomy 31:6-8 (KJV), "Be strong and of a good courage, fear not, nor be afraid of them: for the LORD thy God . . . he will be with thee, he will not fail thee, neither forsake thee: fear not, neither be dismayed." What a blessed promise! When you are tempted to retreat in fear's closet of darkness—stop and pray. Claim God's promises! God's Word will give you power to fight the enemy, and Satan will retreat in an instant!

We know that fear does not come from God because in 2 Timothy 1:7 (KJV) we are told, "For God hath not given us the spirit of fear; but of power, and of love, and of a sound mind." When God is with us, we have absolutely no reason to fear! So the answer to obtaining God's wonderful, life-sustaining sweet peace is this: trust Jesus! Pray about everything . . . fear nothing!

Faith and Obedience

Let us hear the conclusion of the whole matter: fear God and keep His commandments, for this is man's all. For God will bring every work into judgment, including every secret thing, whether good or evil.

Ecclesiastes 12:13-14 (NKJV)

The Bible tells us in John 15:7 (KJV), "If ye abide in me, and my words abide in you, ye shall ask what ye will, and it shall be done unto you." Some read this and think, *Great! All I have to do is be a Christian, and God will give me whatever I ask Him for!* But that's not what this text is saying at all. The key phrase is the very first line: "If ye abide in Me . . ." God makes it very clear that He wants our obedience—and faith and obedience go hand in hand!

When we're walking with Jesus, we want what He wants! We no longer desire our own wills. Our faith is in God and His wisdom to know what's best for us. God is calling each of us to serve Him. It doesn't matter whether we made the highest grades in school, have successful careers, or enjoy friendships in high society, God can use anyone who is willing, obedient, and has a surrendered heart.

The important thing is to be willing to serve God in whatever capacity *He* chooses, whether the task be great . . . or small! Pray for more faith and strength to always be obedient to God's will!

I Love You

Love must be sincere. Hate what is evil; cling
to what is good. Be devoted to one another in love.
Honor one another above yourselves.

Romans 12:9-10 (NIV)

The words *I love you* are probably the most popular words ever spoken in any language—and also the most misunderstood. In fact, people use the phrase so casually now that in many cases it has lost its true meaning. So often it becomes just a casual thing to say, like *How are you*? or *Have a nice day*!

The real meaning of the word *love* is impossible to comprehend or understand if you don't know who God is— because God *is* love! When you can grasp the sacrifice made on Calvary—then you can begin to understand the real meaning of *love*! Jesus says in John 15:13 (NASB), "Greater love has no one than this, that one lay down his life for his friends."

True love is putting yourself *last* and others *first*. True love is not selfish, impatient, mean, or unforgiving. True love is being kind, giving, and making sacrifices for the ones you love— without boasting or wanting something in return. True love is demonstrated by your actions when you have Jesus in your heart. *True love* can be summed up in one word—*God*!

Lasting Change

*You were taught to leave your old self—to stop
living the evil way you lived before. That old self becomes
worse, because people are fooled by the
evil things they want to do.*

Ephesians 4:22 (NCV)

Most of us have at least one bad habit! Some of those habits are more annoying to others than to us, such as loudly chewing gum, not cleaning up after ourselves, or talking with our mouths full. Then there are other bad habits more serious in nature, such as abusing drugs, lying, or gossiping.

The Bible says in Psalm 1:1 (NIrV), "Blessed is the person who obeys the law of the LORD. . . . They don't make a habit of doing what sinners do." It's important that we live godly lives and practice good habits that glorify God!

Whatever bad habits we are trying to break, we need *Holy Spirit power* to give us the strength to overcome these destructive patterns. We need to claim Philippians 4:13 (NKJV), "I can do all things through Christ who strengthens me." Jesus is the *only* answer if we want to break bad habits and live godly lives, reflecting real *lasting change*!

September 13

Yield Not to Temptation

*But be doers of the word, and not hearers
only, deceiving yourselves.*

James 1:22 (NKJV)

———◆———

Satan is working overtime to entice Christians to come over to the dark side. He knows his time is short, and he is desperate to win the war between good and evil. And don't be fooled, because he not only uses individuals to tempt us to go astray, he also uses many worldly tools. Some of them come from a cable television channel or the Internet or a magazine or peer pressure from classmates or colleagues at work.

Make no mistake—the devil is real, and he is out there seeking to kill, steal, and destroy. He knows your weaknesses and will attack when you least expect it. He doesn't care how he gets you to fall, just as long as you fall!

Let's be very clear: *a surrendered child of God cannot dabble in the temptations of sin!* The greatest gift you can give to your spouse is your purity and fidelity. The best character trait you can provide your family is moral and ethical self-control.

Stand firm! Resist the devil! Refuse to yield to the traps of temptation that the enemy has set for you. The greatest gifts you can give God are your *integrity*, your *faithfulness*, and your *surrendered heart*!

How to Live a Godly Life

I have set the LORD always before me; because He is at my right hand, I shall not be moved.

Psalm 16:8 (NKJV)

There are those who feel it's not possible to live a *godly life* because we are human and have sinful tendencies which are impossible to avoid. But that's simply not true. After all, the Bible says in Matthew 19:26 (NKJV), "With God all things are possible." The key words here are—*with God*.

The secret to living a *godly life* is to stay close to Jesus, who will lovingly lead us safely through this difficult journey. In doing so, we not only receive strength to overcome sin, but also divine direction on what paths to take and potholes to avoid. He gives us the wisdom to know right from wrong and leads us away from temptation.

When God is ever in our hearts and minds, we have pure thoughts and Christlike characters. We won't be motivated to reach Heaven because of the fear of going to hell, but rather by our deep and abiding love for Jesus. Our greatest desire will be to spend eternity with the One who gave His life to save us.

With Christ as our Guide, we cannot fail! Jesus *is* the answer! He came to this earth and lived His life as a perfect example for all to follow. Trying to make it on our own will lead to failure every time. God and God alone—makes it possible to live a *godly life*!

I'll Pray for You

*For I know that this will turn out for my
deliverance through your prayer and the
supply of the Spirit of Jesus Christ.*

Philippians 1:19 (NKJV)

—◆—

Most people when faced with a crisis reach out to God!
Even those who don't really have a close relationship
with Jesus will ask their family, friends, and even strangers
to pray. But how many people make that commitment and
never follow through? The words, "I'll pray for you," have
become just something to say, like any other common words
of comfort when you feel sorry for someone or sad because of
what trial they are facing. It's almost like saying, "Have a nice
day." But when we tell someone that we will pray for them,
we have made a commitment before God to earnestly lift
that person up in prayer, asking for God's will to be done in
their lives.

If we have no intention of praying, then we should not
make a *commitment* to do so. If at all possible, it's good to stop
what we are doing right then and there and lift them up to our
heavenly Father! There's a world of hurting people all around
us, so why not start praying for them today? And the next time
someone asks for prayer, say sincerely, "I'll be happy to pray for
you. Let's pray now."

Eternal Life with Jesus

The ransom of a man's life is his riches, but the poor does not hear rebuke. The light of the righteous rejoices, but the lamp of the wicked will be put out.

Proverbs 13:8-9 (NKJV)

When you give your life over to Christ, your future couldn't possibly be any brighter or more secure! And the prize of *eternal life with Jesus* is definitely worth waiting for! Although the road of a Christian isn't an easy one, it will be the most joy-filled life you could possibly live and better than anything you could have hoped for. There's no greater joy than serving Jesus!

The highway to heaven is not, however, without struggles and uphill battles. There will be fun times, happy times, and incredible peaceful times, but don't be fooled into thinking you won't have trials and heartache. You will. And don't think for one moment that the enemy won't attack, because he will.

But here's the good news: God has promised never to leave you or forsake you. He is there right beside you, every step of the way, and you are never alone. Your future is safe in the arms of Jesus; you need only to trust in the very One who gave His life to save you . . . Jesus Christ!

Love Your Enemies

"But love your enemies. . . . Therefore be merciful, just as your Father also is merciful."

Luke 6:35-36 (NKJV)

There's no possible way that we could ever repay our Lord and Savior for His incredible sacrifice on Calvary. Oh, what amazing love He has for each one of us! We can, however, show Him how grateful we are by sharing His love with others. God wants us to *love one another as we love ourselves*. We are not capable of passing God's love on unless we are filled with the Holy Spirit, because we cannot give . . . what we do not have! We need to ask God to come into our hearts and lives and fill us with His love!

Becoming *more like Jesus* is the best way that we can show our love for Him, and the more we become like Him, the more His love will flow out to others—and yes, that means our *enemies* too! The Bible tells us in Matthew 5:44 (NKJV), "Love your enemies, bless those who curse you, do good to those who hate you, and pray for those who spitefully use you and persecute you." When we truly *love as Jesus loves* . . . we won't even experience a twinge of satisfaction when we hear something bad has happened to our worst enemies. Instead, we will lift them up in prayer.

Remember Jesus loves our enemies *just as much* as He loves us! He does not want anyone to perish. Resolve today to be more like Jesus! Pray often, love much, and always err on the side of *grace and mercy*!

Repetitive Prayer Rut

*"Then you will call upon Me and go and pray
to Me, and I will listen to you."*

Jeremiah 29:12 (NKJV)

———◆———

Prayer strengthens your connection with your heavenly Father and is your direct line to the King of the universe! What an incredible blessing it is to talk with God directly! You don't need someone to intercede, and you don't need an appointment. God's throne room is open day and night, and He loves to hear the prayers of His children. Tell Him what's on your heart, no matter how trivial or how serious.

You wouldn't want to hear the same thing repeated over and over again every time someone talks to you and neither does God! Stay away from *recited prayers,* and if you find yourself stuck in a *repetitive prayer rut,* ask God to *pull you out*! The Bible tells us in Matthew 6:7 (NIV), "And when you pray, do not keep babbling like pagans, for they think they will be heard because of their many words."

You don't need fancy words—pray with simplicity. All you need to do is remember that Jesus is your Best Friend, and you can confide in Him! Don't hold back—*tell Him everything*! Be sure and ask for wisdom, advice, and most importantly, to *take charge of your life*!

September 19

Strength for the Weary

*You are a hiding place for me; you preserve me from
trouble; you surround me with shouts of deliverance.*

Psalm 32:7 (ESV)

When the world seems to be crashing down all around you, and the devil has done his best to make you miserable, *don't give up*! Instead . . . use God's Holy Word as a sword against the enemy. It's the most powerful weapon you can have! When you are at your weakest, remember that your strength comes from Jesus.

Pick up your Bible and read Isaiah 40:29 (NKJV), "He gives power to the weak, and to those who have no might He increases strength." Keep reading, and in verse 31, He reassures us with, "But those who wait upon the LORD shall renew their strength; they shall mount up with wings like eagles, they shall run and not be weary, they shall walk and not faint." Always remember that God is right there beside you, waiting to lift you up out of the darkness. You're not fighting the battle alone!

Although you might believe otherwise, just because you're a Christian doesn't mean you're immune to enemy attacks. When you give your heart to Jesus, Satan will try even harder to knock you down, discourage you, and try to make you so miserable that you will yield to his temptations of sin. Don't give the devil even one moment to smile. Stay faithful! Stay close to your Savior. God never promised sunshine every day, but He does promise to be with you through every storm!

Living God's Love

Therefore be imitators of God as dear children.
And walk in love, as Christ also has loved us and given
Himself for us, an offering and a sacrifice to God
for a sweet-smelling aroma.

Ephesians 5:1-2 (NKJV)

Sometimes the greatest need for patience is within our own homes. It seems easier to treat a guest or stranger with courtesy and respect than the ones we claim to love the most. If a guest spills milk all over the floor, we are quick to reassure them that it's okay by saying, "Don't worry about it." But when a family member does the exact same thing, the reaction and even tone of our voice is usually quite different. It's more like, "Why did you do that? You are such a klutz! Don't you know you shouldn't bring milk into the living room?"

Everyone desires and needs to be loved, and we should have even more grace and mercy for the people we claim to care about! We need to speak in tones of respect, show kindness, and be tender with each other. Can you imagine how much love would be in our homes if we treated each other as Jesus would? Now that's called *living God's love*!

Help or Hindrance

*Now accept the one who is weak in faith, but not for
the purpose of passing judgment on his opinions. . . . Who
are you to judge the servant of another? To his own
master he stands or falls; and he will stand, for the
Lord is able to make him stand.*

Romans 14:1, 4 (NASB)

Prayer is a powerful tool that God has given not only to help
yourself through this journey of life, but to help others as well.
Unfortunately, Jesus' disciples missed out on the opportunity to
pray for their Master, but all God's children should learn from
that important lesson in Gethsemane. The next time you see a
brother in need—*pray for him*!

Open your heart, and you will hear the silent cries from
those who are depressed, fearful, insecure, or brokenhearted.
Ask God for wisdom and discernment of how to *be a help—not
a hindrance*. Remember that Jesus is the *only Healer of hearts*,
and He alone has the answers. But if you are willing, God will
guide you to discern their need. People who are hurting need
love, acceptance, and prayer that come from a humble heart—
not someone who has a *self-righteous attitude* that is trying to
fix them! So ask God to remove any *spirit of pride* and replace it
with an extra abundance of *His love* for others.

Hating Our Own Sins

*The Lord is not slack concerning His promise,
as some count slackness, but is longsuffering toward us,
not willing that any should perish but that all
should come to repentance.*

2 Peter 3:9 (NKJV)

To truly be *Christlike*, we must love our neighbors as ourselves! There's no room for a *better-than-thou* attitude in the life of a Christian. We must learn to hate the sin in our own lives—*more* than we hate the sins of others! This may be quite a struggle, but when we do, we'll have more love for our fellowman. We'll be less critical, less judgmental, and more patient with everyone we meet. Simply put, we will be more like Jesus!

Studies have shown that people who are quick to find fault with others usually are struggling with that same sin in their own lives! The Bible tells us in Romans 3:23 that we are all sinners and have come short of the glory of God! Instead of pointing fingers at others, let's ask God to point out the sin in our own lives and then ask Him to forgive and give us the strength and power to overcome it. Then pray and ask God for a deeper love for our friends and neighbors and the strength to *help them*—not *condemn them*! God stands willing and ready to replace the judgment in our hearts . . . with His unending, patient, passionate love!

September 23

God of Abundance

*Now may the God of peace . . . make you complete
in every good work to do His will, working in you what is
well pleasing in His sight."*

Hebrews 13:20-21 (NKJV)

———◆———

Ood doesn't do things *halfway*. He doesn't give us a small
portion of grace, forgive just a few of our sins, or listen
to just one or two of our prayers. His heart does not respond
to us in disgust or in tones of annoyance or superiority. No,
our God is always a God of abundance, and He pours out His
immeasurable love to all His children, generously giving His
power, grace, and mercy to all who seek Him! The Bible says
in John 10:10 (NKJV), "I have come that they may have life,
and that they may have it more abundantly." He loves to give us
the desires of our hearts. In Matthew 7:11 (NKJV) we're told,
"If you then, being evil, know how to give good gifts to your
children, how much more will your Father who is in heaven
give good things to those who ask Him!"

We can rest assured that our heavenly Father loves us—with
a deep, abiding, and everlasting love. When we confess our sins,
He forgives fully and completely! He doesn't keep reminding
us of each transgression just to torture us over and over again.
It's a human trait to forgive, but not forget, for when someone
makes us angry, we quickly throw every past mistake back in
their faces.

But that's not the kind of grace and mercy that comes from
God. God forgives abundantly, blesses abundantly, and loves
abundantly, and it is His supreme desire . . . to be like Him!

Walking with Jesus

*And do not be conformed to this world, but
be transformed by the renewing of your mind,
that you may prove what is that good and
acceptable and perfect will of God.*

Romans 12:2 (NKJV)

Walking with Jesus does not mean we are perfect! It means that we are striving to live within the will of God! When we commit our lives to Jesus and are willing to surrender our own sinful wants and desires and live according to the light that we know . . . it is then that we are *walking with Jesus*! This is a lifelong process and requires a daily, hour-by-hour, minute-by-minute commitment.

However, God is not up in heaven just waiting to pound the hammer down to condemn us the minute we make a mistake! God loves us so much that when we fall, He tenderly picks us up, dusts us off, and guides us back on the right road. Spiritual growth takes time, and it's important not to look around the church pews and use others as *measuring sticks*!

We are all on a different rung on the ladder to heaven. The more time we spend with God, the closer we will be to Him. Some are on higher rungs, as they have walked with Jesus longer, while others are baby Christians and are new in their spiritual climb! Instead of judging, we need to love, encourage, and help each other on our journey to heaven! Strive every day to *walk with Jesus*!

Fear of Failure

He shall cover you with His feathers, and
under His wings you shall take refuge; His truth shall
be your shield and buckler.

Psalm 91:4 (NKJV)

There are many people who never achieve their goals or full potential because they are crippled by *fear*. They're afraid of looking foolish, traveling on airplanes, riding on elevators, going to the dentist, and the list goes on and on! However, there's absolutely no reason for fear in a Christian's life because, when we turn our lives over to God, He promises to lead, guide, and protect us. There's no safer place to be than with Jesus! We can blindly follow Him wherever He leads, fully trusting that He will never lead us down the wrong path!

God has a special plan for each of us, but we will never even know what that is unless we trust Him and surrender our wills to Him. Only then will we reach our full potential, becoming all that He wants us to be. With Jesus as our Guide, we will accomplish all the goals He has set for us, and we will live our lives full of joy and happiness.

Only God can deliver us from fear! The Bible says in Psalm 34:4 (NIV), "I sought the LORD, and he answered me; he delivered me from all my fears." Living a life cloaked in fear—is a miserable way to live! Ask God today to take away all fear and replace it with complete trust in Him!

Stop the Rat Race

O God, You are my God; early will I seek You . . .
Psalm 63:1 (NKJV)

———— ◆ ————

It seems our world keeps spinning faster and faster, and everyone is racing just to keep up! From the moment the alarm goes off in the morning, we are racing out the door to face the day, racing through our work, trying to meet every appointment, racing home, and the *racing* doesn't stop until we fall into bed exhausted, only to do the same thing the next day.

Sadly, in all this *racing around*, there is no time carved out for special moments with God. This racing through life is not only empty and unfulfilling, but deadly, because in the end— we will lose out on eternal life! Nothing is worth missing out on Heaven. God wants us to have balance in our lives. We all know the story of Creation, when God created six days to work and play, but the seventh day was for Him; however that doesn't mean we ignore God through the week!

We need to spend quiet time each day with Jesus, studying the Bible, praying, worshiping, and praising Him! When we do, our lives will be richer, fuller, and more rewarding than we could possibly dream! Not because everything is perfect in our lives— but because we are not racing through life alone. Jesus, our *Copilot,* is navigating through all the difficult twists and turns, and He does all the worrying for us! We'll experience a little heaven here on earth once we stop the rat race and increase our prayer and worship time.

Choose Wisely

But Peter and the apostles answered, "We must obey God rather than men."

Acts 5:29 (NASB)

God has given each of us the most amazing gift—*the gift of choice!* We can choose good things or we can choose bad things—but the *privilege to choose* is totally ours! However, what comes with this incredible gift . . . is consequences. Every choice, no matter how insignificant it may seem, has a consequence. One small decision could be fatal and change the entire history of our lives! Unfortunately, Satan wants us to believe that we can do anything we want without consequences and many fall into his trap.

In order to make the *right choices,* we need to ask for Holy Spirit guidance—for our salvation is at stake! The choices we make can lead to eternal life or eternal death, so before making a decision, we should ask ourselves, *If I do this, how will it affect me tomorrow? Next week? Next year?*

The Bible says in Galatians 6:7 (NKJV), "Do not be deceived, God is not mocked; for whatever a man sows, that he will also reap." *If* we pray and ask God to give us wisdom and guidance before making decisions, and then follow His leading, we will not only experience joyful and more abundant lives here on earth, but in heaven as well!

Family of God

*We announce to you what we have seen and
heard, because we want you also to have fellowship with
us. Our fellowship is with God the Father and
with his Son, Jesus Christ.*

1 John 1:3 (NCV)

God created us as human beings who need much more than air, food, and water to survive. We need human contact and love from each other as well. That's why He created *earthly families*. However, for many reasons, not everyone has a *family*. And unfortunately, because we live in a world of sin, not all families are healthy ones. Sometimes it becomes necessary to adopt a family! Friends become the mom or dad, aunt or uncle, or brother or sister in our lives. And these relationships can be just as strong and fulfilling!

We need to stop bickering and fighting, putting jealousy and sibling rivalry behind. Instead, love, uplift, and cherish our families, providing support and encouragement through the good times and the bad. God wants us to enjoy strong, close family bonds.

If for whatever reason you do not have a *family*, pray and ask God to give you people in your life who will be a positive Christian influence and will be there to love, support, and comfort you. Our journeys here on earth are difficult ones, and we all need friendship and love, so if you see someone who is lonely, reach out and welcome them to the *family of God*!

We Won't Remember

For you, LORD, have delivered me from death, my eyes
from tears, my feet from stumbling.

Psalm 116:8 (NIV)

Jesus is the only *Healer of hearts*! And He longs to give us the comfort and healing that we need. He tells us in Psalm 34:18 that when we are brokenhearted, He is close to us. And in Isaiah 40:11, He wants us to know that as a shepherd carries a lamb, He has carried us close to His heart. Wow! It's difficult to even comprehend the depth of God's love! He loves us so much that He wants to bear our burdens and take away our heavy loads.

We don't have to be all stressed out . . . when we can give our problems to Jesus. In 2 Corinthians 1:3-4, He says that He is also the Father who comforts us in all our troubles. And God promises in Revelation 21:4 that one day He will wipe away every tear from our eyes. Best of all, He declares in Romans 8:38-39 that nothing will ever separate us from His love again.

God's promises are true! We can count on His Word. He reassures us again in Revelation 21:4 that He will take away all the pain we have suffered here on earth.

When we get to heaven, the things of this earth will pass away! We won't remember the tears. We will know only true joy and happiness, and each day will be better than the day before. No matter what heartache or pain we have experienced, the first moment of eternity . . . will be worth it all! *Precious Jesus, keep us faithful to the end that we might obtain Your gift of eternal life with You!*

The Holy Spirit

*"How much more will your heavenly Father give the
Holy Spirit to those who ask Him!"*

Luke 11:13 (NKJV)

The reason that we can have the privilege of the Holy Spirit in our lives is because Jesus asked His Father to send Him to us, and this gift is a direct answer to His prayer! It's the gentle pleading of the Holy Spirit that speaks to our hearts and draws us from darkness into truth. The Holy Spirit opens our eyes to the peace and joy that comes from loving our Lord and Savior. Without the guidance of the Holy Spirit, we would be wandering aimlessly in darkness, for it is God who sends the Holy Spirit to light our way and keep us on the right path! He whispers tenderly when He sees us getting ready to make mistakes, and when we listen . . . we can avoid the dark pitfalls of certain destruction.

The Holy Spirit is ever-present to help us understand Scripture, make wise decisions, and open our spirit to feel God's presence that we may more fully comprehend His unconditional, amazing love for us! God counsels us in Ephesians 4:30 (KJV), "And grieve not the Holy Spirit of God, whereby ye are sealed unto the day of redemption."

Wow! That is powerful! God makes very clear the importance of listening to the Holy Spirit. When you are discouraged, facing difficult trials, or responding to a task God has called you to, be sure and pray for an extra anointing of His Holy Spirit!

October 1

When God Calls

*"I am the vine, you are the branches . . . for apart
from Me you can do nothing."*

John 15:5 (NASB)

———◇———

God has a special plan for your life, and you never have to
be afraid to say, "Yes, Lord, I'll do it!" That's because God
will never ask you to do something and then leave you hanging!
He will give you everything you need to accomplish the task,
and He will guide you each step of the way. There are times you
may question God because you feel inadequate, unqualified,
uneducated, or unworthy. But don't forget that with God, *all
things are possible*, and He knows what He is doing. *If* God
only called the *capable*—it would be too easy to steal the glory!
People might even be tempted to think it was their own doing
instead of giving God the praise.

God knows you inside and out—so much more than you
even know yourself! He gives you the talents you need to shine
for Him, and as you use those talents for His glory, He trusts
you with even more talents. Never fear where God is leading
because Jesus never fails and He never makes a mistake.

You can know when it is God calling by communing with
Him in prayer and asking for an outpouring of His Holy Spirit.
Be assured that He will never ask you to do something that is
immoral, sinful, or goes against His Holy Word. So, when God
calls, say sincerely, "Yes, Lord, send me!"

Through God's Eyes

*"Do not judge according to appearance, but judge
with righteous judgment."*

John 7:24 (NKJV)

If we could see others through God's eyes, what a different world this would be! Imagine if we could see the reasons behind the actions of people that are so irritating—that person who just cut in line might not be so annoying . . . if we knew the urgency of why they did so, or we might have more empathy with the postman that never smiles . . . if we knew the personal pain he's suffering. Then there's the grouchy cashier at the grocery store—we wouldn't be so offended if we knew her rent was overdue and she was working three jobs to keep her family fed! The list is endless, but the analogy is obvious.

Instead of criticizing, we need to pray that God will put more love in our hearts for our fellowman! Far too often, we are quick to judge, lay blame, and criticize. We all ask God for *grace and mercy*, but few are willing to extend that same *grace and mercy* to others! If we truly want our fellowman to see Jesus in us—it starts with sharing His love!

The next time someone does something that tempts you to explode in anger—stop and pray, "Lord, give me patience and love for this person. Allow me to see them through Your eyes!" When you look at people with *God's perspective*—the world looks a whole lot clearer!

Be a Leader

*Let no one despise your youth, but be an example
to the believers in word, in conduct, in love, in spirit,
in faith, in purity. Till I come, give attention
to reading, to exhortation, to doctrine.*

1 Timothy 4:12-13 (NKJV)

How we live our lives every day can influence the people around us. Depending on our actions, our influence can be either positive or negative. This is a choice that only we can make. But unless we choose to allow God to be first in our hearts, we can't possibly be the people God wants us to be.

In this sinful world we live in, it's easy to be influenced by others. Smooth-talking business acquaintances, questionable friends, or even captivating church leaders can quickly lead us down a wrong path. That's why it's critical that we keep our eyes on Jesus and stay close to our Lord and Savior. It's too easy to go down the wrong path by allowing others to lead us astray. Instead of the one being led—*be the leader*! God wants us to influence the quality of life for the people around us in a positive way. A kind word, thoughtful gesture, or a reassuring smile can go a long way to brighten someone's day!

Strive to be a true Christian example to everyone you meet by being a person of the utmost integrity, and yes, it *is possible* when Jesus is in full control of your life!

Only God Changes Hearts

*"And why do you look at the speck in your brother's eye,
but do not consider the plank in your own eye?"*

Matthew 7:3 (NKJV)

Many relationships fail because one person is always trying to change the other person—it may be as trivial as a hairstyle change to a whole personality overhaul! But the truth is—only God can change people! You can nag, pout, or demand all you want, but those tactics are never really successful. There might be small changes for a little while, but inside, they will feel rejected or that they're not good enough. Feelings of resentment and anger are sure to follow.

Although you can't change others, you *can* change yourself—*with God's help*! God created you with your very own unique differences, such as looks, talents, and personalities. Instead of trying to make everyone *just like you* . . . embrace your differences! And if a friend or family member annoys you, be a quiet, loving example. It's much more effective than pointing out their faults! When you act in a kind, *Christlike* way, pretty soon that other person's heart begins to soften. The reward of loving like Jesus loves is amazing! The Bible tells us in Romans 15:7 (NIV), "Accept one another, then, just as Christ accepted you, in order to bring praise to God."

Worth the Wait

*But if we hope for what we do not yet have,
we wait for it patiently. In the same way, the Spirit helps
us in our weakness. We do not know what we ought to
pray for, but the Spirit himself intercedes
for us through wordless groans.*

Romans 8:25-26 (NIV)

When our own troubles seem too much to bear, it's easy to start questioning God as to *why* they are happening! *Why is He letting the pain go on and on? Why doesn't He heal me? Why can't He just get rid of my enemies? Why not just fix things right now?* But when you look at the lives of many Bible characters, we can see that God is patient—His timing is perfect!

For instance, think how Joseph must have felt—betrayed by his own brothers, sold into slavery, falsely accused, and thrown into prison. No one would blame him if he got angry and felt like God had forsaken him. However, Joseph trusted God! He stayed faithful. And His reward was great!

Instead of asking God *why*—ask for *strength*! Instead of wallowing in despair—have faith! Instead of *doubting*—*trust in Jesus*! God loves you, gave His only Son to die on a cross to save you, and is looking forward to eternity with you in heaven. Be patient . . . *it's worth the wait*!

Solving Your Problems

*My help comes from the LORD, who
made heaven and earth.*

Psalm 121:2 (NKJV)

———◆———

We should look to our heavenly Father for answers to all our questions—no matter how trivial or how seemingly insurmountable. We can go before His throne room with holy boldness anytime, day or night, with full confidence that we will receive an answer! Believe God's Word and know with absolutely certainty God will fulfill His promises to you!

Look back in biblical times and you will see a history marked by people who repeatedly asked for and received blessings from God! Well, here is the good news: our God is still the same God—yesterday, today, and tomorrow! He stands ready to meet our every need, whether it's comfort, wisdom, guidance, or whatever else is required by our situation. In Philippians 4:19 (NKJV) we're told, "And my God shall supply all your need according to His riches in glory by Christ Jesus."

That's a promise we can count on, and God always keeps His promises! He will give us Holy Spirit power to meet every difficult task or go through any heart-wrenching trial. With Him . . . *all things are possible*—so instead of trying to solve your own problems—go to the best Problem Solver of all—God!

Pray Passionately

*"Ask, and it will be given to you; seek, and you
will find; knock, and it will be opened to you. For
everyone who asks receives, and he who seeks finds,
and to him who knocks it will be opened."*

Matthew 7:7-8 (NKJV)

The reason we pray is not to get rich, move mountains, or find our keys. Our *real reason* for prayer is to get to know Jesus as our *personal Savior* and to fall more deeply in love with Him. It's to become one with our Creator so that *His will* becomes *our will.*

Passionate prayer and God go hand in hand. Jesus didn't just pray mumbling empty words. No, He prayed passionately! He shared His heart with His heavenly Father and so should we! Talking to our Best Friend is a two-way conversation.

Prayer is not just asking for things we *think* we want. True *passionate prayer* is a love relationship with the most awesome God of the universe—trusting Him to answer according to what is best for us! And when we pray, we can be sure that He will never let us down.

Instead of praying *hoping* our prayers will be answered, we need to pray passionately from our hearts *knowing* with absolute certainty that God will answer. Then, trust Him to open the windows of heaven and pour out so many wonderful blessings that we'll be totally amazed by the depth of His love!

Playing the Blame Game

*You keep track of all my sorrows. You have
collected all my tears in your bottle. You have
recorded each one in your book.*

Psalm 56:8 (NLT)

Just because you are a *Christian* does not mean that you are excluded from pain and heartache. As long as you are living on this earth, sorrow is unavoidable. There's a battle going on between *good and evil*, and Satan is not happy with *anyone* who is following Christ. It is his sole mission to separate you from the Savior of the world! He doesn't care *how* he does it—just as long as he succeeds! Pure and simple—the devil wants to make sure that you won't make it to heaven!

Perhaps the death of a loved one has shaken your faith, or your heart was broken by someone you trusted, or you received an unfair sentence . . . it is at your weakest moment that the enemy tempts you to *blame God*! But it's *not* God's fault, nor is it His desire that anyone should suffer. Whatever your trial or pain you are suffering, don't play the *blame game* and tell yourself *it's all God's fault*. It's not!

Pain and heartache are the direct results of sin, and it won't be a perfect world until Jesus comes. Don't allow Satan to rob you of eternity—instead run to the open arms of Jesus for comfort, guidance, and peace. God will walk with you through the valley and replace your tears with His joy!

No Need to Beg

But let him ask in faith, with no doubting . . .
James 1:6 (NKJV)

Passionately praying and begging are two very different things. God does not expect us to *beg* when we pray! He knows what is best for us, and we should always pray, "God's will be done!" But sadly, there are those who selfishly plead with God in prayer for what they want and don't stop to think that what they are praying for might not be the best thing for them. They pray, insisting that God give them exactly what they want, and if He doesn't, they blame Him for not doing what they wanted!

True believers don't *beg God*—they pray trusting in God's perfect plan to answer their prayers how He sees best! In Matthew 21:22, we're told that anything we pray believing, we will receive. And Hebrews 4:16 (KJV) reads, "Let us therefore come boldly unto the throne of grace." Boldly does not mean begging or demanding. It means that we can approach God's throne room with absolute confidence that He loves us and has the power to answer our prayers. He loves to hear from us and delights in giving us good gifts.

No one will ever love us as much as God does. He will never turn His back on His children, and He will *always* do what is best for us! We can trust Him fully and completely. Sincere and humble prayer goes straight to the heart of God. Let us bring our requests before God—remembering to pray *believing* . . . not begging. Our God *is* trustworthy!

Spinning Out of Control

"If you return to the Almighty you'll be restored, as you remove iniquity from your household."

Job 22:23 (ISV)

———◆———

Do you feel yourself *slip-sliding* away from God? Are you finding yourself too busy or too tired to pray? Are you returning to your old sinful habits? Is life overwhelming, and you feel like it's spinning out of control? If so, run to Jesus, fall on your knees, and confess your sins. Tell God how much you love Him and need Him in your life. He is always quick to respond to the cries of His children.

There's no sin too big or too horrible for God to forgive. With deep repentance and sincere faith, you will find the peace and joy in your heart that you are seeking. Don't listen to the devil's lies that *It's too late*, *My sin is too great*, or *God doesn't love me*. The real truth is, Jesus loves you so much that He can't imagine heaven without you! He stands by, eager to hear your confession and forgive your sins.

Decide today to live your life fully surrendered to Jesus, as this is the only way to experience true joy and happiness. Any other option is filled with pain, tears, heartache, and despair! Jesus *is* the answer!

October 11

Jesus Our Sin-Bearer

Seek the LORD while He may be found, call upon Him while He is near. . . . Let him return to the LORD, and He will have mercy on him; and to our God, for He will abundantly pardon.

Isaiah 55:6-7 (NKJV)

Everyone needs the saving grace that God offers, however, it can only be obtained in answer to prayer. It doesn't matter what sin we are drowning in—sin is sin—and Jesus is our *Sin-Bearer*! He is our Savior and the only one who can save us! He provides His sweet saving grace to all that repent and ask for His forgiveness.

God does not just look down on the world, then sprinkle grace from above, letting it land wherever it falls! No! God's grace and mercy is prayed for. Sometimes it's in answer to *intercessory prayers* offered by others—when we are too weak to pray for ourselves. Other times, it is in direct answer to our heartfelt prayer of "Jesus, save me!"

Prayer is not only a privilege—it is our duty. God wants to hear from His children. No one is turned away from the throne room of God. There are no guards holding us back, no waiting, and no long lines before our Lord and Savior! God has given each of us direct access—anytime, day or night! All we need to do is pray! The privilege of prayer is always ours, but the power of prayer is always God's!

Between Good and Evil

*"Today you are on the verge of battle with your
enemies. Do not let your heart faint, do not be afraid,
and do not tremble or be terrified because of them; for
the LORD your God is He who goes with you, to fight for
you against your enemies, to save you."*

Deuteronomy 20:3-4 (NKJV)

There's a vicious war going on between good and evil, and as Christians, we will fight this battle until Jesus comes. Satan will use every method he has to discourage us, and we can be sure, he knows exactly which buttons to push! But no matter how fierce the battle, we can have perfect peace—for God is with us! He will give us the strength and courage to face each day. He gives everlasting, unconditional love to sustain us, and He will give us wisdom and guidance to fight every battle.

God has promised in Joshua 1:5 that He will never leave us nor forsake us, and that's a promise we can count on! Friends may come and go, but Jesus will stand by us always. Best of all, we know and have the blessed assurance that, in the end, God wins! Our Creator God, King of the universe, is more powerful than Satan. The enemy *will* be defeated. We can have blessed peace as long as we keep our eyes focused on Jesus, our Savior, Protector, and Friend!

Believing Is Not Enough

*"For I will set My eyes on them for good, and I
will bring them back to this land; I will build them and
not pull them down, and I will plant them and not pluck
them up. Then I will give them a heart to know Me,
that I am the Lord; and they shall be My people,
and I will be their God, for they shall return
to Me with their whole heart."*

Jeremiah 24:6-7 (NKJV)

Most Christians accept the Bible as truth but ignore it in their daily living. They simply don't realize that it's how we *live* that's important . . . not just what we *believe*. For instance, there are many who *believe* in God and in the Bible, but even though they believe and know what's right, they choose not to obey. Their daily actions don't reflect the life of a person who *knows* God's truth and is fully surrendered to Him!

It is *not* enough to *believe* in God's truth—we must *live* it every day! Just knowing right from wrong won't save us! We must choose to obey God. When Jesus is the focal point of our every thought and action, *God's will* becomes *our will*. The Bible says in Matthew 28:20 (KJV), "Lo, I am with you always, even unto the end of the world." The fact that God is *with us always* makes it possible to live *how we believe*!

Invitation to Live Forever

He has made everything beautiful in its time.
Also He has put eternity in their hearts, except
that no one can find out the work that God
does from beginning to end.

Ecclesiastes 3:11 (NKJV)

God wants us to spend eternity with Him in heaven, but He won't force us to come. He wants us to make the decision based on our love for Him. This choice is positively the most important decision that we will ever make! It can be hard to grasp the concept of living for a limitless amount of time . . . a beginning without end. Just imagine living in a place with no crime, no tears, no death—where only love, joy, and happiness exists. Amazing! Our human minds can't even begin to understand the beauty and splendor of heaven!

Whenever we face any big decision, it is important to find out all the facts before making a commitment. This life-changing decision is no exception. We should research everything we can on *eternity*, and the best resource manual is the Bible. After all, no one knows more about eternity than the One who created it. God's Holy Word makes it crystal clear how to obtain eternal life. Each of us is given the opportunity to live forever, and the only requirement is to give our hearts to Jesus!

Love as Jesus Loves

Dear friends, let us love one another.

1 John 4:7 (NIV)

God is a generous God! He is a loving God! A gracious and forgiving God! When we surrender our hearts to Him, we strive to be more like Him. But why is it so difficult? As Christians who love God and want to be more like Him, we should be generous, loving, gracious, and forgiving too, right? Yet, even in our churches there is bickering, snide remarks, hateful looks, and hearts full of pride.

One of the easiest places to lose your Christian experience can be in church board meetings where tempers are raised as soon as a vote doesn't go our way, and a simple discussion over the color of new carpet in the sanctuary can escalate into fighting. None of this behavior should be exhibited in the heart of someone striving to be like Jesus. But the reason we fail is simple. When we focus on self and take our eyes off Jesus . . . we fall!

We need to daily surrender *self* and keep our eyes on our Savior, asking God to fill our hearts with love for our enemies— yes, even those who have hurt our feelings! When our hearts are overflowing with God's love, we'll have the ability to forgive— truly forgive! If tempted to wallow in self-pity about perceived injustice, remember how Jesus was treated, and yet, through it all, He loved His enemies. May we all *love* as Jesus loved!

Jesus Never Changes

Jesus Christ is the same yesterday, today, and forever.

Hebrews 13:8 (NKJV)

Every day brings some sort of change in our lives. One day we have a job, the next day we don't. One day we have a friend, the next day he's our enemy. One day we're financially stable, the next day we could be out on the street! One day we're married, the next day our spouses are gone.

Change is inevitable. However, not all change is bad. Many times we can be in our darkest hour and the good news we've been hoping for finally arrives that changes the course of our lives, such as: a promotion comes through, a marriage proposal is accepted, a new baby arrives, a soldier returns from war unharmed, and on and on.

But the most important change we could ever make is our decision to give our hearts to Jesus! When we do, our lives become changed in an instant. And the really exciting news is . . . Jesus *never* changes! He is the same yesterday, today, and tomorrow. And His power, His character, His faithfulness, and His love for us will never change. No matter how many times we disappoint Him, He still loves us like no one else ever could!

There's no need to live in fear that one day we'll wake up and find that God doesn't love us anymore. Jesus never changes and He loves us so much He gave His life for us—and there's no greater love than that!

Never Too Late

I have been crucified with Christ; it is no longer
I who live, but Christ lives in me; and the life which I
now live in the flesh I live by faith in the Son of God, who
loved me and gave Himself for me.

Galatians 2:20 (NKJV)

———◁◈▷———

How we choose to live each day determines our future: eternal life or eternal death! Those that live for self, enjoying the sinful pleasures of this world, will never experience the true joy of living, not on this earth or in the earth to come, because they won't be there! When we follow God's plan for our lives, we will experience peace, joy, and happiness that the world cannot give, nor take away.

The secret to a happy life starts with a relationship with God through prayer, Bible study, and surrender. God wants us to love each other, keep ourselves pure, and keep His commandments. Some may feel like it's too late; they've made too many mistakes and are too great a sinner—not worthy of salvation. But the Bible reassures us in Luke 19:10 (NIV), "For the Son of Man came to seek and save the lost." And in Isaiah 59:1 (NKJV), we're promised, "Behold, the LORD's hand is not shortened, that it cannot save; nor His ear heavy, that it cannot hear."

Satan is working overtime trying to separate us from our Savior. But let us not be deceived by the devil's lies for even a moment—for it is never too late to run to Jesus! His loving arms are outstretched, ready and waiting to receive His children!

The Golden Rule

"You shall love the LORD *your God with all your heart, with all your soul, and with all your mind."*

Matthew 22:37 (NKJV)

———❖———

Various versions of the *golden rule* have been passed on for generations. Although each version may be stated a little differently, the message is the same—*everyone has the right to fair and just treatment and a responsibility to treat others the same way*. This has become a *moral* code of ethics that is understood and expected worldwide.

The golden rule is what God expects all Christians to abide by. The Bible says in Matthew 7:12 (NIV), "So in everything, do to others what you would have them do to you, for this sums up the Law and the Prophets." Basically, we need to be more considerate of others and think about how our own actions may affect them. Before responding in anger or with malice in our hearts, we need to think about how the other person is feeling. In other words, put ourselves in their place and ask, *Would I want someone to respond to me in this way?*

Abiding by the golden rule doesn't mean that we only do so if we think that person deserves it! We need to behave in a *Christlike* way, regardless of how the other person is acting! We must give an account to God for our own actions, and we don't want to be responsible for causing another person to fall. When we practice the golden rule, we are allowing Christ to shine through us!

Pray with Faith

*"And when you pray, do not use vain repetitions as
the heathen do. . . . For your Father knows the things you
have need of before you ask Him."*

Matthew 6:7-8 (NKJV)

───────◆───────

Why is it that so many people feel like God has abandoned them? Well, first of all, it's important to know that God *never abandons people—people abandon God!* And the real reason for not sensing God's presence is almost always . . . a *dead prayer life.*

If you're experiencing this same distance from God, then ask yourself some eye-opening questions, such as: *When was the last time I prayed? When I do pray, am I truly sharing my heart with God—or merely going through the motions, reciting the same thing over and over, almost like I'm not even conscious of what I am saying? Does my mind begin to wander during prayer, thinking about other things, forgetting altogether that I am in the midst of prayer?*

God wants to hear from you, and He wants to hear what is on your heart! If you want to make a meaningful change in your prayer life, ask God to *teach you how to pray.*

The Bible is a good place to learn about prayer as there are many examples of *heartfelt prayers* throughout. We're told in James 5:16 (TLB), "The earnest prayer of a righteous man has great power and wonderful results." God wants to hear from our hearts, so pray often, pray sincerely, and pray with faith—because God hears, answers, and is always faithful!

People Pleasers

For am I now seeking the approval of man, or
of God? Or am I trying to please man? If I were still
trying to please man, I would not be a servant of Christ.
For I would have you know, brothers, that the gospel that
was preached by me is not man's gospel.

Galatians 1:10-11 (ESV)

A s much as we all want people to like us, we have to face the fact that we really can't please everyone! There will always be someone that, for whatever reason, will be irritated by our presence! We have to move beyond the naive expectation that if we are nice, people will treat us right. The fact is, they may . . . or . . . they may not!

God doesn't want us to live our lives trying to please other people. But He does want us to live for Him and become more like Him! In other words, don't be *people pleasers,* be *Jesus pleasers*! We can't control the behavior of others, but what we can do. . . is control our own behavior! We can be kind, even when others are not. We can smile when frowned at and be gracious in the most trying situation, choosing not to retaliate or respond in anger.

This is only possible with God's help. We can claim Philippians 4:13 and trust that God *will* give us the strength to respond in a Christlike way. Ask Him to fill our hearts with love for everyone—including our enemies!

Don't Look Back

*Brethren, I do not regard myself as having laid hold
of it yet; but one thing I do: forgetting what lies behind and
reaching forward to what lies ahead, I press on toward the
goal for the prize of the upward call of God in Christ Jesus.*

Philippians 3:13-14 (NASB)

B riefly looking back can sometimes be helpful when reflecting on past experiences as it reminds us not to make the same mistakes. But the key word here is *briefly*, because when we spend too much time in the past, it can prevent us from moving forward.

If we keep wallowing in our misery, content to enjoy our own *pity party*, it can be downright paralyzing! We can easily drown in the *poor-me pool of pain*! Nothing good comes from it, and it will weigh us down like the heaviest anchor around our necks. It doesn't matter whether or not it was our fault that something bad happened. With Jesus, we can push past the pain, keep the past in the past, and change the future!

We should never allow the bad experiences, no matter how horrific, to define *who* we are. The enemy wants to use our past to justify our failures today. When we play the *blame game*, becoming the eternal victim, it prevents us from being the person God wants us to be. If we really want to enjoy an abundant life with Jesus, don't look back . . . move forward!

Best Part of Your Day

*Therefore be careful how you walk, not as
unwise men but as wise, making the most of
your time, because the days are evil.*

Ephesians 5:15-16 (NASB)

There's a common expression, "Spend time wisely." That's because *time* is precious, and it's important how you use it. In fact, on Judgment Day, you'll have to give an account to God for how you spent your time here on earth. Talking with God and asking Him for divine wisdom will help you discern what is important and what is not. Unfortunately, time passes quickly, and before you know it, you realize that you've spent your entire life focused on all the wrong things.

There's nothing in this world that compares to spending *eternity with Jesus*! Absolutely nothing! Time spent with Jesus is the most precious time of all. It is never wasted and will only enrich your life. Ask for God's forgiveness for the time you've wasted and then invite Him to come into your life and guide each step you take.

Increase your praise and worship time each day and allow God to transform you through this time alone with Him. You'll be surprised at how quickly your life will change. You will have renewed energy and strength and a passionate desire to witness and tell others about God! You'll find that this special time with Jesus—will be the best part of your day!

God's Grace and Mercy

*Let the message about Christ, in all its richness,
fill your lives. Teach and counsel each other with all the
wisdom he gives. Sing psalms and hymns and
spiritual songs to God with thankful hearts.*

Colossians 3:16 (NLT)

———— ⤐⬥⤏ ————

God's love is amazing, and He is generous with mercy toward His children. There's no problem that He can't solve and no heart that He can't heal! God's compassion is poured out without measure, bringing relief from our pain, comfort in times of sorrow, and hope during deep despair.

Sometimes God uses people to be His hands to comfort those who are hurting, give a word of encouragement to the brokenhearted, or do a good deed. When we allow God to use us however *He* wants to, there's no end to what God can do *through* us! We will be amazed at how God can use us to bless others! There's no greater joy than to be used by God!

Many have experienced so much pain and heartache in their lives that they lose hope—but God can use us to remind them that *He is their hope*! He is a loving, merciful, and forgiving God! When people realize how much He loves them, and that He's waiting with open arms to receive them . . . it makes all the difference in their decision to accept Him as their personal Lord and Savior!

Attitude Adjustment

*For those who live according to the flesh set their
minds on the things of the flesh, but those who live
according to the Spirit, the things of the Spirit.*

Romans 8:5 (NKJV)

When someone we love *does us wrong*, it seems to hurt much worse than if it were a *mere stranger*. Stung by the injustice of it all, we're quick to put on our protective coat of armor, avoiding all contact with the offending person. Soon the hurt festers, and before we even realize it, our emotions are out of control, affecting our self-esteem and how we feel, think, and act about everything. We take a self-righteous attitude—all the while insisting that we're *okay*. When we fall this low, Satan has us right where he wants us!

There's a reason that God places such a high priority on maintaining pure thoughts. We can't possibly live a joy-filled life with Jesus if we hold grudges or hard feelings toward the ones that hurt us. Instead, we need to do what the Bible has instructed us to do in Psalm 51:10 (NKJV): "Create in me a clean heart, O God, and renew a steadfast spirit within me."

If you are struggling with forgiveness, ask God to give you an *attitude adjustment*, replacing all hurt with an extra measure of God's love! And ask Him to let you see those who hurt you *through His eyes* so that you'll respond with kindness, compassion, and forgiveness. When you do, all anger, hurt, and self-righteousness will melt away, and you'll soon see that forgiveness . . . *erased the pain!*

October 25

Running the Race

. . . so that I may finish my race with joy, and the ministry which I received from the Lord Jesus, to testify to the gospel of the grace of God.

Acts 20:24 (NKJV)

This life's journey is like a race to the finish line that will bring us through the valleys, the hills, the rivers, the deserts, and the plains. Although it can seem like an obstacle course at times, there's no need to get discouraged, grow faint, or give up, because, through it all, God will give us the wisdom, strength, and endurance we need. Instead of focusing on the difficulties of the race, focus on the blessings and faith-building experiences. Hebrews 12:1 (NIV) tells us, "Let us throw off everything that hinders and the sin that so easily entangles. And let us run with perseverance the race marked out for us." God wants us to enjoy the journey—slow down to a steady pace and smell the roses, embracing the fresh air and the beauty around us!

On those dreary days, when the hills seem more like mountains and the storms of life are raging—don't give up, because all we need to do is focus on the goal! Run the race, fight a good fight, and keep our eyes on Jesus! He's waiting with outstretched arms, cheering us on to the very last step as we cross the finish line. And then we will receive our long-awaited prize . . . eternal life with Jesus!

Motivated by Love

*And walk in love, as Christ also has loved us
and given Himself for us, an offering and a sacrifice to
God for a sweet-smelling aroma.*

Ephesians 5:2 (NKJV)

Throughout the Bible, God asks us to love each other *as He loves us*! When Christ was here on earth, He set a wonderful example of how to live our lives—including *how to love.* Jesus loved everyone—the poor widow, the uneducated shepherd, the prostitute on the street, the annoying children, and the richest men in the land. He made no *class* distinctions when He gave a kind word, stopped to listen, or performed miracles, because He loved them all the same.

Every decision God makes is made out of *love.* This should be our policy as well. Before making a decision, we need to ask ourselves, *Is this motivated by love, or am I just wanting to be in control merely because I can?* On Judgment Day, we'll have to answer for every decision we make! The only way to be sure we are making wise choices is to pray and allow *the Holy Spirit to lead and guide.* We need to ask God for more love in our hearts! Decisions motivated by love will not only make us happier, but will be putting into practice God's principles, which draws us even closer to Jesus!

Quicksand of Pain

"Listen, King Jehoshaphat and all who live in Judah and Jerusalem! This is what the LORD says to you: 'Do not be afraid or discouraged because of this vast army. For the battle is not yours, but God's.'"

2 Chronicles 20:15 (NIV)

There may be days when it seems everyone is against us. Our world looks so dark and dreary that we become discouraged, and our faith weakened. Every cell in our body just wants to give up, and God feels like He is a million miles away! But whenever we feel all alone and distant from God, it's usually because we have neglected our daily devotions, Bible study, and prayer time.

When we stop communicating with our heavenly Father, we are vulnerable to the devil's attacks. The enemy is quick to rush in and take advantage of our weakened state. Before we know it, we've allowed Satan's evil influence to take over, and we fall deeper into despair. Instead of being swallowed up in the quicksand of heartache and pain, we need to hold on to God's hand, declaring our loyalty, trust, and love for Him!

Choose to join forces with our all-powerful Lord and Savior, King of the universe, and then nothing can stand against us! When we arm ourselves with the power of God Almighty—we have nothing to fear!

No Need to Fear

Why are you cast down, O my soul, and why are you in turmoil within me? Hope in God; for I shall again praise him, my salvation and my God.

Psalm 42:11 (ESV)

Fear keeps us from becoming who God wants us to be and can be downright crippling, even forcing us to hide who we really are. It's easy to have faith when everything is going our way. But when the chips are down, it's human nature to start doubting. We don't need to be afraid when we are walking with Jesus! With God holding our hands—we cannot fail!

There's no need to be afraid of what we will *look* like or what someone else may say. Why lay awake worrying about what others think? It only matters what *God* thinks! We need not compare our lives to others, as we have no idea what their journey is all about. Instead, we should live our lives for Jesus and allow the Holy Spirit to speak to our hearts and guide our every decision.

Pray and ask God to remove all fear from your life and replace it with faith and trust! And when you are weak and feel like those old fears are trying to creep back in . . . pray for strength, claiming Philippians 4:13. God will give it to you!

Honesty Is the Best Policy

*A deceitful person will not sit in my house; a liar
will not remain in my presence.*

Psalm 101:7 (ISV)

Unfortunately, the society we live in today doesn't always value truthfulness. *Little white lies* are not only considered okay, but often encouraged. Whether it is telling the police officer we were not speeding, breaking a promise, cheating on taxes, or as simple as lying about our age . . . it is all dishonest!

Dishonesty not only displeases God, but it is, in fact . . . a sin! When our hearts are right with God, it is reflected in our characters, and we can't help but want to be like Him. God does not lie; His Word is truth. There's no room for dishonesty in a Christian's life. Telling the truth is so important to God that He even made it one of His Ten Commandments! And the Bible says in Isaiah 33:15-16 that there will be rewards for those who live right and tell the truth.

When you are tempted to *stretch the truth* or intentionally deceive someone, immediately pray for God's Holy Spirit to give you the strength and power to stand up for what you know to be right. If you have already lied, ask God to forgive you and make it right. It isn't always easy or popular to *tell the truth*, but no lie is worth losing out on heaven! Stand up for truth, and allow God's character to shine through you!

God-Given Confidence

*"I know that You can do everything, and that no purpose
of Yours can be withheld from You."*

Job 42:2 (NKJV)

Few people possess true self-confidence. It's human nature to
have feelings of inadequacy. Even those who appear to have
it all together and outwardly appear confident are not immune.
People struggle with self-doubt no matter how old they are,
what country they're from, or how much money is in their
bank accounts. Mothers worry that they're not good enough,
bosses wonder if they're making the right decisions, employees
are stressed that someone else will be better at their job, or a
spouse feels threatened that their mate will find someone new.

The fact is, we are all weak—emotionally, mentally, and
spiritually. We can't even serve God without His assistance.
That's why He allows our lack of confidence. Those feelings force
us to face the truth that we need to rely fully and completely on
God. The good news is that Christ stands willing and ready to
give us His Holy Spirit to sustain us! All we need to do is give
our hearts to Jesus!

When we're a follower of Christ, the Holy Spirit literally
resides within us. The more we yield our lives to Him, the more
His power flows through us! No need to worry and fret about
our lack of self-confidence, for God is ready and waiting to
empower us with *God-given confidence*!

October 31

Love at Home

*"And these words which I command you today shall
be in your heart. You shall teach them diligently to your
children, and shall talk of them when you sit in
your house, when you walk by the way, when
you lie down, and when you rise up."*

Deuteronomy 6:6-7 (NKJV)

———◆———

God has blessed us with the ability to *love,* and when we pray and ask Him to fill us with *His love*—He will. He wants us to share His love with everyone we come in contact with—including our own families. As Christians, too often we are so busy trying to witness to the world that we neglect the needs of those we *love* the most.

In fact, sharing *God's love* should begin at home! How we treat the ones who are closest to us says a lot about our characters and what's really in our hearts. When words are spoken harshly in haste, or we are rude or unkind—this is not only displeasing to God, but we are missing out on an opportunity to shine for Jesus in our own homes!

Even if you are mistreated and live in a house where not everyone loves God—you should always shine for Jesus! Your witness begins at home! The Bible says in Joshua 24:15 (NKJV), "Choose for yourselves this day whom you will serve." Ask God to give you more patience, understanding, and love, not only for others, but for your own family as well—and be a witness for Him . . . starting in your own home!

God Deserves Reverence

The fear of the LORD is the beginning of knowledge, but fools despise wisdom and instruction.

Proverbs 1:7 (NKJV)

———◆———

In our world today, swearing and cussing is so common that no one thinks a thing about it. It used to be considered *bad manners*, and although there are some who still feel that way, they are not the overwhelming majority. People swear for all sorts of reasons. Comedians use God's name to *get a laugh*, while others think it makes them sound *cool*. But it's definitely *not cool* to disrespect God, the King of the Universe.

God deserves and commands our respect and reverence. The Bible says in Exodus 20:7 (NKJV), "You shall not take the name of the LORD your God in vain, for the LORD will not hold him guiltless who takes His name in vain." Wow! That's pretty serious! I don't think it can get any clearer than that. God commands respect!

Today, we have become so desensitized about taking God's name in vain that we often don't even recognize when we're doing it. When we listen to others swear, we are allowing our minds to become immune to the lack of respect shown our heavenly Father. God wants us to *talk to Him* and confide in Him, but He wants us to show respect by the way in which we address Him—not just by speaking His name, but also by our tone of voice and our attitude. We can show God how much we love Him by giving Him the respect that He deserves!

Why Worry?

"Look at the birds of the air; they do not sow or reap or store away in barns, and yet your heavenly Father feeds them. Are you not much more valuable than they? Can any one of you by worrying add a single hour to your life?"

Matthew 6:26-27 (NIV)

The words to this children's chorus really bring to light the importance of trusting in Jesus: "Why worry, when you can pray? Trust Jesus, He'll be your stay. Don't be a doubting Thomas; rest fully on His promise. Why worry, worry, worry, worry when you can pray?" Trusting in Jesus is the only way to experience the real joy of living, and it's a character-building lesson that we all need to learn.

The Bible says in Hebrews 11:1 (NKJV), "Now faith is the substance of things hoped for, the evidence of things not seen." Waiting until we actually see proof—*is not faith*! God wants us to trust Him with our whole hearts, not worry about what the future holds.

When we worry, we focus on the negative—what we *can't* do, problems that *might* arise, bad things that *could* happen, and on and on. But faith focuses on what God *can* do—His power and His wisdom to know what is best! Pray for more trust and leave the worrying to God!

Ticking Time Bomb

"For whoever desires to save his life will lose it, but whoever loses his life for My sake will find it."

Matthew 16:25 (NKJV)

Time seems to go by faster and faster, and it gets harder to fit in all the things we need to do each day, but God wants us to use each moment wisely! In fact, He wants us to consult with Him *before* we commit to do anything. If we always let God make the decisions as to how we will spend our time—our lives would be so much fuller and richer.

The strange thing about *time* is that no matter how busy people are, everyone seems to find the time to do the things *that are important to them*! In fact, we can learn a lot about someone by just looking at their calendars. People book their schedules to the max with appointments, meetings, social events, and things that they are most interested in. But we can accomplish so much more when we allow God to plan our day!

Everyone has the same number of hours per day and how we spend that time is what's important. Once the day is gone—it's gone forever. How many blessings and divine appointments have been missed? We have no excuses to waste even one moment of God's precious time, because He stands by eagerly waiting to set our priorities and book our calendars for us.

Instead of watching day after day go by like a *ticking time bomb*—stop and reevaluate your life! To experience the fullness of God's joy, allow Him to be in complete control of your clock, your calendar, and your life!

He Believes in You

So prepare your minds for action and exercise
self-control. Put all your hope in the gracious salvation
that will come to you when Jesus Christ is revealed to the
world. So you must live as God's obedient children. Don't
slip back into your old ways of living to satisfy your own
desires. You didn't know any better then.

1 Peter 1:13-14 (NLT)

When life seems too much to bear, and everything looks dark and dreary . . . walk by *faith,* not by *sight!* Take each step with confidence in God, rather than by your own feelings. Pray for the gift of *self-control* to keep you from falling into the pits of depression, fear, and darkness. Above all, *don't give in to Satan's lies.* He wants you to believe life is useless, you have no friends, you're a failure, and *you* don't matter! But, don't allow the enemy to control even one second of your thoughts!

You *do* matter to Jesus, and *He is your Best Friend!* He longs to heal your heart and wants you to be happy. Jesus says in Jeremiah 29:11 (NKJV), "For I know the thoughts that I think toward you, says the LORD, thoughts of peace and not of evil, to give you a future and a hope."

Love for God and your commitment to Him is *not* based on feelings! So, when you have a *down day,* keep moving ahead one step at a time and push the devil away! Your Lord and Savior is willing and ready to help you choose self-control! Keep your thoughts on Jesus and believe in Him . . . for He believes in *you*!

Our First Resort

The LORD is near to all who call upon Him, to all who call upon Him in truth. He will fulfill the desire of those who fear Him; He also will hear their cry and save them.

Psalm 145:18-19 (NKJV)

Sometimes it's hard to imagine that our Almighty God, King of the Universe, and Creator of the world takes time to listen to the individual prayers of His children! Imagine someone so powerful, stooping down to hear the cries, complaints, and often, selfish requests from earthly sinners. And yet, He does! He not only listens, He cares and answers each lowly prayer.

He doesn't keep office hours or make us wait for months to get an appointment. He makes Himself available to all who seek Him—24/7! Absolutely amazing! There's only *one reason* God does that, and that's because He loves us with an everlasting, unfathomable love. Oh, how sad that more people don't utilize this direct line to Heaven! How different lives would be if they communicated with the only one who knows the end from the beginning and can help navigate through this sinful world.

Trust God with your heart! The minute you start to pray, faith will begin to grow and soon you will long to stay in His presence. Avoid the pitfalls of life by making prayer your *first resort*, not *the last one*!

Fair-Weather Friends

But may the God of all grace, who called us to His eternal glory by Christ Jesus, after you have suffered a while, perfect, establish, strengthen, and settle you.

1 Peter 5:10 (NKJV)

It is difficult to comprehend the concept of *why bad things happen to good people.* Some people immediately blame God when tragedy strikes. They claim that Jesus is their Best Friend—until something goes wrong in their lives, and then all of a sudden, it's all *God's fault!* I call these people *fair-weather friends,* or those who are only *friends* as long as everything is *going their way.*

God needs children who love and trust Him through thick and thin—not *fair-weather friends.* We all need to understand this very important fact: *God doesn't cause the pain in our lives*—pain is a result of *sin!* He does, however, allow us at times to experience trials in life to perfect our characters so that we can be drawn closer to Him. If everything were easy, we would be leaning on self—*not* Jesus.

There are some who need to hit *rock bottom* before they look up and see their need of a Savior. Whatever struggles we are facing, it's important to remember that it is not for us to ask *why,* but only to *trust . . .* and our God *is* trustworthy!

God's Guidebook

*The precepts of the LORD are right, rejoicing
the heart; the commandment of the LORD is pure,
enlightening the eyes.*

Psalm 19:8 (ESV)

Before reading our Bibles, we need to pray and ask God for wisdom and understanding so that we can hear His voice and not miss out on the blessing He wants to give us. Reading His Word with an *open heart* is essential to understanding the Scriptures. The Bible is God's love letter to us, as well as a guidebook and training manual. It's our step-by-step instruction book to walk this journey here on earth so that we might have life and have it more abundantly!

Every word of Scripture is true, and when we read with a heart full of faith and a burning desire to obey, we will understand God's plan for us. We need to accept the Bible in its entirety—not pick and choose which verses to believe in because they suit our purposes! God's Word is holy—all of it! We should hold it with reverence and treat it as the treasure it is. We should revere it so much that we wouldn't even consider laying anything else on top of it. The Bible says in 2 Timothy 3:16 (KJV), "All scripture is given by inspiration of God."

Savor the time spent in prayer and study of the Scriptures. When we read the Bible with an earnest desire to know its Author, we will be brought into a oneness with our Creator . . . and gain a deeper understanding of God's amazing love!

November 8

Evidence of Transformation

"So they come to you as people do, they sit before you as My people, and they hear your words, but they do not do them; for with their mouth they show much love, but their hearts pursue their own gain."

Ezekiel 33:31 (NKJV)

———◆———

Christianity starts at home! How we treat our family and those we love most speaks volumes about our personal relationship with God. Some professed Christians are looked up to by church members for being kind, considerate, and great workers for Christ, but a glimpse into their homes tells a whole different story! They are critical of their spouses, yell at their children, are selfish, and are basically grouchy to live with.

Living a Christ-centered life does not mean *putting on a show* when people might notice us. God doesn't need *show ponies*! It's not enough to *know* Bible truth—we must live it every day. God not only wants us to be *informed*, He wants us to be *transformed*!

When a life is transformed, there is evidence of transformation. We become changed from the inside out, and God's love shines out of us wherever we are—especially in our homes, around the people that we profess to love the most! We need to strive to live our lives in such a way that everyone we meet will see Jesus in us—starting with our family!

Friends with God

*Greater love has no one than this, than to lay
down one's life for his friends. . . . No longer do I call you
servants, for a servant does not know what his master is
doing; but I have called you friends, for all things that I
heard from My Father I have made known to you.*

John 15:13, 15 (NKJV)

Maintaining a friendship with God is key to having a vibrant and meaningful prayer life! It's human nature to treat *friends* differently than we do casual acquaintances. For instance, when a favor is needed, we usually don't ask a stranger because it would feel awkward and presumptuous. It is much more comfortable to go to a close friend whom we know cares about us and would be sincerely eager and willing to help. We speak differently and guard what we say to someone we don't know. But when talking with a friend, it's more intimate, and we feel at ease saying what we really think!

With friends, we can be shamelessly persistent when asking for a favor or expressing our desires. So it is with our friendship with God. When we are close friends and know God *personally*, there's a comfort level that supersedes any other feeling in the world! We experience that incredible inner peace knowing that we have a friend in Jesus—and there's nothing that *He* wouldn't do for us!

We can feel free to *be ourselves* and boldly tell God whatever is on our hearts. He longs to be friends with each of us—all we have to do is invite Him into our hearts and lives! Decide today to be *friends with God*!

With a Pure Heart

He who covers his sins will not prosper, but whoever confesses and forsakes them will have mercy.

Proverbs 28:13 (NKJV)

A sure sign that there's unforgiven sin in your heart is when you begin to pray and it just feels awkward and uncomfortable. If you think your prayers are not being heard or not reaching higher than the ceiling, stop and ask yourself *why*. Ask God to bring to your mind any unconfessed sin and then pray for His forgiveness.

God wants you to come to Him with a pure, clean heart, and to do so, you must confess your sins. The Bible says in Psalm 66:18 (NKJV), "If I regard iniquity in my heart, the Lord will not hear." Sin will always separate us from Jesus! So, the first thing we need to do is ask for forgiveness. In 1 John 1:9 (NKJV) we're told, "If we confess our sins, He is faithful and just to forgive us our sins and to cleanse us from all unrighteousness."

There is indescribable relief and joy when you experience God's sweet forgiveness! He will restore unto you a clean heart and place His robe of righteousness upon you. Prayer and communion with your Lord and Savior will come as easily and naturally as talking to your best friend! There'll be no awkwardness or fear, because the distance you felt before will be gone. God hears and responds to your prayers when you come before His throne room with a pure heart!

All About Love

*Many waters cannot quench love, nor can
the floods drown it.*

Song of Solomon 8:7 (NKJV)

———◈———

Love is a word that is used so commonly without any real thought or meaning behind it. People use it to express feelings, although many use the word loosely to *manipulate* the heart! Sadly, some people just don't have a clear understanding of what *love* really is and are searching in all the wrong places.

Everyone needs love—but not the fake, superficial kind of love that the world offers. They need real, qualified, satisfying love which only comes from God, because . . . God *is* love! He is the Originator of love, and without God, there is no love. The Bible tells us in 1 John 4:19 (NKJV), "We love Him, because He first loved us," and in 1 John 4:11 (NKJV), "If God so loved us, we also ought to love one another." It's all about *the love*!

Love is not a word to describe a feeling! Love is not a tool to get what we want. Love is acquired by a connection with God! And He wants us to share His love with each other. God's love is the only love that can truly satisfy the longing in our hearts. Since God is love, we can't possibly love anyone—unless we have a relationship with Him. We can't share what we do not have. We can only experience real love by accepting Jesus Christ into our hearts, and then we can joyfully share with others the most beautiful, reassuring, heartwarming words . . ."Jesus loves you . . . and I do too!"

Failure Is Not an Option

*Say to those with fearful hearts, "Be strong, do not fear;
your God will come, he will come with vengeance; with
divine retribution he will come to save you."*

Isaiah 35:4 (NIV)

When you give your life to Christ and allow Him to have full control, you have nothing to fear because Jesus *never* fails! He will never lead you down a wrong path or tell you to do something that is bad for you. With Jesus . . . failure is not an option!

There are some who miss out on so many blessings simply because they are afraid of failure. Paralyzed by fear, they would rather not even try than to risk failing! Instead of missing out on the life God wants to give you, pray and ask God to remove all fear from your heart and replace it with an extra measure of faith. Pray David's prayer in Psalm 27:1 (NKJV), "The Lord is my light and my salvation; whom shall I fear? The Lord is the strength of my life; of whom shall I be afraid?" Claim this promise in Isaiah 41:10 (NKJV): "Fear not, for I am with you; be not dismayed, for I am your God . . ."

There is no one better to trust than our Lord and Savior. He loves you more than anyone else possibly could! He will *always* have your back. He will never hurt you or disappoint you. If you are crippled with fear, struggling to move forward in your life—remember that faith and trust in God cancels out all fear. And with Jesus, failure is not an option!

Singing Praises to God

*I will sing to the LORD as long as I live; I will
sing praise to my God while I have my being. May my
meditation be sweet to Him; I will be glad in the
LORD. . . . Bless the LORD, O my soul! Praise the LORD!*

Psalm 104:33-35 (NKJV)

———◆———

Singing praises to God is a wonderful way to show your love and thankfulness to your Creator! You don't have to hit all the right notes or even have a melodious voice, because angels are lifting up your songs of praise to Heaven as a glorious, fragrant prayer!

As long as you are singing from your heart, you are honoring God, and *that* warms the heart of our heavenly Father. The awareness of God's presence inspires songs of praise. You need not have a music degree or take voice lessons—just sing from your heart! Too many people miss opportunities to sing praises, even in church. Some mumble along, barely uttering a sound, while others mindlessly sing the words. Oh, how sad!

Instead, don't worry about how you sound or who might be listening. Lift your voice in thanksgiving and praise, giving God the glory He deserves! Singing is a wonderful way to show God just how much you love Him!

We Want Justice

He was led as a lamb to the slaughter,
and as a sheep before its shearers is silent,
so He opened not His mouth.

Isaiah 53:7 (NKJV)

<><>

Injustice is hard to swallow for just about everyone. When someone has been treated unfairly—the first human emotion to creep in is . . . vengeance. We want justice! We want to make them pay for what they have done! Especially if what they did was illegal—yet the judge let them walk away free, without punishment for their crime. That really gets our blood boiling, and we want to see them suffer. We want revenge! Some even plan to retaliate, wanting to cause the offender the most amount of pain. But that is not God's way, and it's not what Jesus Himself set forth for us as an example.

The worst possible injustice of all was when Christ was crucified on Calvary—yet He humbly took the abuse and prayed in Luke 23:34 (KJV), "Father, forgive them; for they know not what they do." The Bible tells us in Leviticus 19:18 (NIV), "Do not seek revenge or bear a grudge against anyone among your people, but love your neighbor as yourself. I am the LORD."

The Bible makes it very clear that Jesus wants us to love those who mistreat us and to pray for them. We're told in Proverbs 24:17 that we're not even to gloat when our enemies fall and stumble. Remember, God loves them just as much as He loves us. He longs to save *all* His children—so, love one another and leave *justice* to God!

Power to Change

*"I will give you a new heart and put a new spirit
within you; I will take the heart of stone out of your
flesh and give you a heart of flesh."*

Ezekiel 36:26 (NKJV)

―――――◆―――――

Sin is a deadly disease that has been passed on from generation to generation since the beginning of time. We're told in Romans 3:23 (KJV), "For all have sinned, and come short of the glory of God." Sin is defined as any thought, word, or action that goes against God's laws or standards. Simply put, sin is rebellion against God!

The good news is, the Bible tells us in 1 John 1:9 (NKJV) that all we need to do is confess our sins, and "He is faithful and just to forgive us our sin and cleanse us from all unrighteousness." Our salvation came at an unimaginable price—for God loved us so much that He gave His only Son—that we might live and have eternal life with Him!

To accept God's amazing gift, we need to allow Him to change us fully and completely. It's not enough that we know *who* God is, we must know Him *personally* and intimately as our Friend and Savior! When we do, God gives us the *power to change* and get rid of all the junk in our lives that is separating us from Him. Remember that God must accomplish something *in* us before He does anything for us or through us.

God's Gift of Time

*It is written: " 'As surely as I live,' says the Lord,
'every knee will bow before me; every tongue will
acknowledge God.' " So then, each of us will give
an account of ourselves to God.*

Romans 14:11-12 (NIV)

Time is a gift that God gives us and so is His gift of *choice* about how we spend it. However, on Judgment Day, we will be held accountable for the choices we made. The decision is ours: we can spend our days living for self—or living for Jesus! God reminded us that our days are numbered through David when he wrote in Psalm 89:47 (ESV), "Remember how short my time is!" Even Job lamented in Job 7:6 (NKJV), "My days are swifter than a weaver's shuttle."

Time is short, and none of us know when we will take our last breath. We must live for Jesus every day, every hour, every minute! As Christians, we know that this earth is temporary and we need to spend each day with Heaven as our goal—using the time God gives us to honor and glorify our Creator!

God has a special plan for each of us, and He will give us all the time required to accomplish the tasks that He has set forth. It's up to us to allow the Holy Spirit to lead, guide, and direct just how we spend *God's gift of time*!

Distant from God

Behold, the Lord's hand is not shortened, that it
cannot save; nor His ear heavy, that it cannot hear.
But your iniquities have separated you from your God;
and your sins have hidden His face from you,
so that He will not hear.

Isaiah 59:1-2 (NKJV)

To know Jesus as our personal Savior should be our most important goal. It is what every Christian needs to strive for. Some people complain that He doesn't *feel real* to them. But for God to be *real* to us, we must spend time with Him through both prayer and the study of His Word. The more time we spend talking with Jesus, the closer we will be. It's also good to surround ourselves with others who *know Jesus*! Godly friends help strengthen our walk with the Lord.

And don't forget about witnessing. Whenever we share God's love with others, we definitely feel close to Him. Whenever our faith dims, or we begin to feel *distant* from God, it's usually because we have decreased our prayer time or stopped praying altogether. To be separated from God is a dangerous place to be! The good news is, there is a remedy, because God is only a prayer away and is waiting patiently for you to run into His arms of love!

Compromising Integrity

*I know, my God, that you test the heart
and are pleased with integrity.*

1 Chronicles 29:17 (NIV)

———— ◆ ————

To be a *Christian* is to be *Christlike*, striving to be like Jesus! Our commitment to Him is reflected not only in our actions but in how we act and what we say. This includes our daily decisions we make—from the small things to the big things! The enemy will entice us to rationalize between right and wrong, but don't be fooled! God has given each one of us the power of choice, and that includes the power to decide between good and evil.

We may be able to rationalize in our minds why it's okay to take a parking spot someone else was clearly waiting for, exaggerate our accomplishments, cut in line at the checkout counter, or steal something no one will notice—but it is not at all the way Jesus would act! Just because our conscience can live with impure thoughts and actions does not make it right or *okay*. Even something we think of as trivial, such as borrowing a CD from a friend and making a copy instead of purchasing it ourselves—is stealing in God's eyes!

Compromising our integrity will always separate us from Jesus! Is it really worth missing out on heaven? Determine in your heart today to live according to God's Word—always striving to be more like Jesus.

Heaven Is Our Goal

"For the Son of Man is going to come in his Father's glory with his angels, and then He will reward each person according to what they have done."

Matthew 16:27 (NIV)

Christians talk a lot about Heaven, but no one can fully comprehend how beautiful and marvelous it will be. It's hard to imagine a place where nothing ever dies, no danger exists, and there are no tears, pain, or sorrow, but each day will be more glorious than the day before! Friends and loved ones will be reunited, we will walk streets of gold, live in mansions, and best of all, we'll be face to face with our Lord and Savior. No wonder it's hard to wrap our minds around it!

As Christians, we can claim God's promise in John 14:2-3 (KJV), "In my Father's house are many mansions: if it were not so, I would have told you. I go to prepare a place for you. And if I go and prepare a place for you, I will come again, and receive you unto myself; that where I am, there ye may be also." What a blessed assurance that *Jesus is coming again*!

Heaven is available to all who surrender their hearts to Jesus. No matter what difficulty or heartache we go through here on earth, we can be comforted with the knowledge that it won't last forever. We have blessed hope! We know that Jesus died so that we might live with Him for all eternity! Our time here on earth is short, and how we choose to spend each day decides our outcome. Let us determine in our hearts to live for Jesus and make heaven our goal!

Victory over Addictions

Yet in all these things we are more than conquerors through Him who loved us.

Romans 8:37 (NKJV)

———◆———

Only Jesus can give freedom from addiction! It doesn't matter what sinful habit it is—smoking, alcohol, drugs, sex, or anything else—*only* God has the power to give you the victory. Even though you cringe at what you're doing and tell yourself you can handle it, the pull of evil will find you yielding to your carnal nature. Before long, you quit trying altogether and fall deeper into the pit of despair.

The problem that many people face is that they try to do it alone. Feeble, human attempts will fail every time—but *Jesus never fails*! Pray and ask God to set you free from the chains that have you bound to the things that are hurting you and others. Claim Psalm 146:7 (NIV), "The LORD sets prisoners free," and John 8:36 (NKJV), "Therefore if the Son makes you free, you shall be free indeed." God's Word is a powerful weapon against the enemy! And the Bible tells us in Mark 10:27 (NKJV), "With men it is impossible, but not with God; for with God all things are possible."

Ask God to give you the strength to set you free from the bad habits that are controlling your life. *God will give you the victory*! Remember to claim Philippians 4:13 (NKJV), "I can do all things through Christ who strengthens me," and the *victory will be yours*!

Be Kind to Yourself

*"Are not five sparrows sold for two copper coins?
And not one of them is forgotten before God. But the
very hairs of your head are all numbered. Do not fear
therefore; you are of more value than many sparrows."*

Luke 12:6-7 (NKJV)

———◆———

When you make mistakes or things turn out all wrong, you may be tempted to beat yourself up, tell yourself that *you're a loser, you should have known better*, and *you're unworthy to be loved*. But when a friend comes to you sharing their troubles, you listen, sympathize, encourage, affirm, and remind them of all the reasons they are loved. So why is that when it comes to your own dark days, you wallow in discouragement and can be your own worst enemy?

You take all the blame for being weak and you can be more cruel and hateful to yourself than an enemy ever would. But don't give Satan any glory! Instead of attending his pity party, treat yourself like you would your best friend. Count your blessings! Praise God for the talents He has given you! Remind yourself of all your wonderful qualities, and then don't forget to give God the credit and thank Him.

Harsh words rarely motivate anyone. Determine today to treat yourself as God would. After all, you are royalty! You are a child belonging to the King of the universe. Be kind to yourself, and you will become the person God created you to be!

Quiet Time with God

In the morning, LORD, you hear my voice;
in the morning I lay my requests before you
and wait expectantly.

Psalm 5:3 (NIV)

Worship is the most important part of your morning as it prepares you to meet the demands of your day! This precious prayer time brings you into a oneness with God and helps in dealing with the stress in your life, facing challenges, solving problems, and preventing the cares of your day from becoming overwhelming! Even the blessings in your life are sweeter because of your time spent with God!

In Bible times, God encouraged His people to meet Him in the morning! Isaiah, Daniel, David, and so many others never missed their morning appointments with God! Plan each day to include special alone time with Jesus. This will take determined effort and willpower because Satan will try every trick in the book to come between you and God, but don't fall for his lies. The devil knows if you neglect to pray—he can separate you from Jesus! He doesn't care how he does it, just so he wins!

But God will give you the strength and courage to resist Satan's temptations! Start your day with prayer, and you'll find yourself praying throughout the day as well—which is the secret of living an abundant life in Christ!

Fearless Trust

So that Christ may dwell in your hearts through faith—that you, being rooted and grounded in love, may have strength . . . and to know the love of Christ that surpasses knowledge, that you may be filled with all the fullness of God.

Ephesians 3:17-19 (ESV)

———— ❖ ————

Why do so many people struggle with trusting God? We trust so many other things quite easily; for example, we *trust* that when we put the key in the ignition, the car will start, and when we get on a plane, we do so because we *trust* that we will arrive safely to our destination. When we sit down on chairs, we *trust* that they won't break, and a hundred other examples could be given of blind *trust*.

So why can't we turn over control and put our full faith and trust in God? Who better to trust than the King of the universe who loves us more than anyone else ever could? The answer may be that we just don't know Him well enough!

The more time we spend with Jesus in prayer and studying His Holy Word—the more we will know Him and love Him. We will be eager to surrender our hearts and lives to Him! Then we will become as trusting as a little child who, when on a high ledge, will jump to his father below, knowing with absolute confidence that he will be safe in his father's arms! Oh, how we all need a *fearless trust* like that!

God's Timetable

The LORD is good to those who wait for Him, to the soul who seeks Him. It is good that one should hope and wait quietly for the salvation of the LORD.

Lamentations 3:25-26 (NKJV)

In this fast-paced world we live in, it seems we are in a constant state of impatience. We are part of the *we-want-it-now* generation! We beep our horns in traffic if the car in front of us doesn't hit the accelerator the moment the light turns green. If the checkout line is too long, we leave the store without the items on the shopping list, and if the doctor takes too long before our name is called, we reschedule!

Our impatience carries over in our prayer life as well, blaming God for our current circumstances. We forget that life moves according to God's timetable, not ours. He knows the end from the beginning and has our best interests at heart. He alone knows just what we need and when we need it! Instead of stressing out about life, learn to trust God and His perfect timing! If we could see into the future, we would learn that following God's plan is the *best* plan, and we really wouldn't want it any other way!

No Tolerance for Abuse

He will rescue them from oppression and violence,
for precious is their blood in his sight.

Psalm 72:14 (NIV)

Verbally, physically, sexually, or emotionally abusing others is a *sin*, and God has no tolerance for it! The Bible says in Zephaniah 1:9 (ESV), "On that day I will punish everyone who leaps over the threshold, and those who fill their master's house with violence and fraud." And in Psalm 11:5 (NCV), "The Lord tests those who do right, but he hates the wicked and those who love to hurt others." God wants us to love and treat one another with respect, and He makes it very clear that He has zero tolerance for abuse in any way, shape, or form!

It's not God's plan that anyone should suffer abuse! Physical abuse is the most obvious, but emotional abuse is every bit as painful and damaging. Ask God to come into your heart and life and transform you. You cannot be a follower of Christ and abuse others—it's *that* simple!

When Jesus is in your heart, there is peace, joy, and love—not anger, harsh words, and abuse. If you are an abuser, *stop and get help*! If you are being abused, get out and get help! Tell someone—don't tolerate it or protect your abuser. It is *not* your fault, and you *don't* deserve it. Jesus loves you more than you could possibly know, and He longs to wrap you in His arms of love! God is a *God of love*—and *He loves you*!

One Big Blur

*"But when he, the Spirit of truth, comes, he will
guide you into all the truth. He will not speak on his
own; he will speak only what he hears, and he
will tell you what is yet to come."*

John 16:13 (NIV)

This busy world we live in can feel like a *merry-go-round* that keeps going faster and faster, spinning out of control! At times it seems like life is just one big blur! That's why it's so important to slow down and become *quiet* so that we can hear God's voice. Unfortunately, sometimes our prayers are *one-sided* because *we* do all the talking and don't take the time to listen for God's answer. If we are quiet, we will hear His *still, small voice* as He speaks to us through the Holy Spirit, as well as by studying His Holy Word.

It's vitally important to pray *before* we have our daily devotions and ask God to guide our worship time. He will give us wisdom and discernment as we read His words so we don't misinterpret what He is saying. Worship time will become much more meaningful, and we'll experience a clearer understanding of the Scriptures.

We'll also enjoy a closer walk with our Lord and Savior, and there's no better place to be than *walking hand in hand with Jesus*! Instead of rushing through our prayers, telling God all our problems, and ending with a quick, "Amen," take time to *listen for His answer*.

Christian Characters

*Therefore, if anyone is in Christ, he is a
new creation; old things have passed away;
behold, all things have become new.*

2 Corinthians 5:17 (NKJV)

Our *reputations* are what people *think we are*, but our *characters* define the very essence of *who we are*! *Character* is revealed by the way we act and how we respond to life situations. Our *reputations* are how people perceive us based upon what they see or hear us do. To perform a good deed now and then is not what defines us as Christians, but rather it's the Christlike way we act every day, not only in the good times, but in stressful situations as well.

If we really want to *be like Jesus*, we need to ask God to cleanse us from sin and then trust Him to guide us each step of the way. It's all about surrendering our wills . . . to God's will. If we are faithful about our surrender, then God will work in us and through us. The Bible says in Philippians 2:13 (NKJV), "For it is God who works in you both to will and to do for His good pleasure."

God has given us the gift of choice and we have the power to control our actions. When Christ's character is reproduced in His people, then He will come to claim us as His own, and what a glorious day that will be! Let us each pray for a deeper desire to have Christ's character within us.

Keep On Keeping On

*But those who wait on the LORD shall renew
their strength; they shall mount up with wings like
eagles, they shall run and not be weary,
they shall walk and not faint.*

Isaiah 40:31 (NKJV)

There are times in your life when you feel like you've hit a rut. Everything that *could* go wrong—*does go wrong*! And just when you think you might be getting ahead, you get slapped down. This can be downright discouraging for anyone. It's human nature to throw your hands up in the air and be tempted to just give up. But instead of being a *quitter—fight harder*, armed with the full armor of God! Keep putting one foot in front of the other and just go forward!

The Bible says in James 1:12 (NIV), "Blessed is the one who perseveres . . .", so choose to be *victorious in Jesus,* not a *victim of the enemy*. When Satan tries to pull you down into the dark pit of discouragement, call out loud, "Jesus, save me!" and immediately you will feel God's presence lifting you up into His arms of safety.

Instead of wallowing in despair, focus on what *God can do through you—not what you can't do*! Staying in the fight builds character and makes you stronger. The trials you experience here on earth will prepare you for eternity. Remember, you're not fighting this battle alone. No matter what, refuse to give up and just—keep on keeping on . . . with Jesus!

Unlimited Power

*"Behold, I give you the authority to trample on serpents
and scorpions, and over all the power of the enemy, and
nothing shall by any means hurt you."*

Luke 10:19 (NKJV)

Christians talk a lot about the *power of God*, but few really, truly believe it! It is evident in their prayer life. They pray *hoping* their prayers will get answered, but not trusting that they will! Some complain that they don't think their prayers reach higher than the ceiling, and they just don't *feel* God's power or presence. We can be assured of this: God's power is not only *real*, but it is unlimited. The mere mention of the name of *Jesus* sends Satan running in fear.

However, God does not release His power just because we want Him to. A loving parent would never tell their child to run in front of a speeding car, because they know the danger. Just as parents protect their children, so our heavenly Father protects us. The Bible says in Psalm 62:11 (NKJV) that "power belongs to God." In our human weakness, we see the world through dark glasses, but praise God He sees the whole picture clearly— the end from the beginning! And how reassuring to know that He has unlimited power to lead, guide, and protect us on our earthly journeys.

We don't know the future, but God does, and He knows what is best for us! That's why it's so important for us to pray, "Thy will be done!"

Nagging Never Works

*Join together in following my example, brothers
and sisters, and just as you have us as a model, keep your
eyes on those who live as we do. For, as I have often told
you before and now tell you again even with tears, many
live as enemies of the cross of Christ.*

Philippians 3:17-18 (NIV)

Nagging doesn't win hearts for Jesus—rather it turns them away! No one wants to be pushed into something they don't want to do. Nor do they need a *guilt trip* to bring them closer to God. Instead, we need to *love* people to Jesus. Live by example! While here on earth, Jesus wasn't *begging* people to serve Him. Instead, He just *loved* them—and crowds followed Him everywhere He went!

By beholding, we become changed. If our friends and loved ones observe our relationship with Jesus—that will do more to win their hearts for Heaven than a sermon or a forced Bible study! We need to remember that we are *not* the Holy Spirit. Only God can change hearts!

We need to trust our loved ones to the only one who can save—and that's Jesus Christ! When we do that, and really *let go*, our burden is lifted! We can accept God's gift of joy and live our lives fully and completely surrendered! Nagging never works—live by example!

Give Me More Faith

He replied, "Because you have so little faith. Truly I tell you, if you have faith as small as a mustard seed, you can say to this mountain, 'Move from here to there,' and it will move. Nothing will be impossible for you."

Matthew 17:20 (NIV)

———◆———

Prayer and faith go hand in hand. So many people pray, *hoping* their prayers will be answered, but not actually believing that they will be, yet faith is an essential ingredient for an effective prayer life. Before we even start to pray, our faith should be working. If our faith is weak, we need to ask God to make it stronger. Faith gives us patience to wait on God's perfect timing and belief that He hears and answers.

One of the best stories of faith in the Bible is the sick woman in the midst of a crowd who touched the hem of Jesus' garment, and instantly, she was healed! Jesus told her in Mark 5:34 (ISV), "Daughter, your faith has made you well." What a beautiful example of how God rewards *faith*!

Jesus also said that if we had faith even as small as a grain of a mustard seed that we could move a mountain! There haven't been any newsflashes of people moving any mountains lately, so it's probably safe to say that everyone should pray, "Lord, please give me more faith!"

Minister for Jesus

*Let each of you look out not only for his own
interests, but also for the interests of others. Let this
mind be in you which was also in Christ Jesus.*

Philippians 2:4-5 (NKJV)

When Jesus said, "Go ye therefore and preach to all nations,"
His message was meant for everyone! He wants us to be
daily witnesses to all we come in contact with, and our actions
should always reflect Christ's character.

There are many ways to witness without having an in-depth
Bible study, such as acts of kindness, a gentle encouraging word,
or a tender smile—which can go a long way in sharing God's
love. However, God knows whether our witnessing is done out
of pride, with a *better-than-thou attitude*, or motivated by a
pure, clean heart, truly desiring that everyone would be saved.

Without a humble, surrendered heart, witnessing can easily
become competitive and prideful, bragging about how many
souls have been won! This is not the kind of *minister* the Bible is
talking about. God is pleased when our lives honor Him—inside
and out, and He is grieved when they do not. Be a minister for
Jesus for all the right reasons and *love as Jesus loved*!

Jesus Is the Joy of Living

You have loved righteousness and hated lawlessness;
therefore God, Your God, has anointed You with the oil
of gladness more than Your companions.

Hebrews 1:9 (NKJV)

Sometimes people can get so busy going through their daily routines, it isn't long before one day just rolls into the next, and before they know it, life becomes drudgery. Their quality of life is so poor that they lose their joy. They wake up each day and just go through the motions of living, then drag themselves home at night, dropping into bed discouraged, depressed, and exhausted, only to get up the next day and do it all over again. Sadly, there are lots of people in this category, but it doesn't have to be this way. There's so much more to life! If only they would surrender their hearts and lives to Jesus. He alone *is* the real *joy of living*!

With Jesus in your life, you can experience real joy and happiness even through the darkest storm. He will pull you out of your daily rut and give you reasons to rejoice and sing! Psalm 5:11 (KJV) says, "But let all those that put their trust in thee rejoice; let them ever shout for joy, because thou defendest them: let them also that love thy name be joyful in thee." Yes, Jesus *is* the joy of living!

Reason to Celebrate

*This was the LORD's doing; it is marvelous
in our eyes. This is the day the LORD has made;
we will rejoice and be glad in it.*

Psalm 118:23-24 (NKJV)

Our world today is hyper-focused on *youth and beauty*. Look around and you'll see it's evident everywhere—in billboards, television, magazines, and advertisements. People starve themselves wanting that perfect body—taking diet pills and spending hours at the gym, while others are in search of the magic anti-aging cream that will make them look twenty years younger. How sad it is that society expects once we turn thirty—we need to start apologizing for being alive!

I'm so thankful our heavenly Father doesn't love us based on how old we are, how attractive we are, or how much we weigh. He created us in His image and loves us unconditionally! We are all beautiful in His sight. God doesn't see our flaws—He sees His child whom He loves without measure!

We need to stop trying to be someone we're not and enjoy the person God created us to be. Focus on who we are inside and not try and meet everyone else's expectations. And, instead of dreading the next birthday, embrace it! Rejoice and praise God for each new day. Just waking up each morning—is reason to celebrate!

We Can't Change the Past

God has rescued us from the power of darkness and has brought us into the kingdom of the Son whom he loves, through whom we have redemption, the forgiveness of sins.

Colossians 1:13-14 (ISV)

Jesus wants us to have hearts filled with peace and joy! The Bible says in John 14:27 (NKJV), "Peace I leave with you, My peace I give to you; not as the world gives do I give to you. Let not your heart be troubled, neither let it be afraid." When our hearts are troubled, it's usually because our faith is weak, and we are relying on *self* and not *God*.

In other words, we are trying to *fix* our own problems. But that never works and is a dangerous road to travel! When we fully put our faith and trust in Jesus, there's no need for fear of what might happen. The beauty of a surrendered life—is that God has it all under control!

Satan tries to keep us in a state of worry by attacking us with condemning thoughts about our past. But never allow the enemy even one moment of pleasure! Instead, look up into the tender, forgiving eyes of our Savior. Although we can't change the past, we can experience the freedom from sin through the precious blood of Jesus! Our past no longer has a claim upon us—*we are free in Jesus*!

December 6

Thy Will Be Done

*And He was withdrawn from them about a stone's
throw, and He knelt down and prayed, saying, "Father,
if it is Your will, take this cup away from Me;
nevertheless not My will, but Yours, be done."*

Luke 22:41-42 (NKJV)

———— ✦ ————

If we really want to know God's will for our lives, we need to spend time in His Word! One of the ways God speaks to us is through Scripture. Sometimes it's hard to know the difference between what God's will is and what our selfish will is, but the more time we spend in prayer and Bible study, the less blurry those lines will be. We will also be more in tune for hearing the voice of the Holy Spirit guiding us to know what to pray for!

Too often we pray and are angry with God for not answering our prayers the way *we want Him to*. However, we should end every prayer with the words, "Thy will be done!" It's the most important part of our prayer and one that requires letting God handle it—however He sees fit! And if God's answer turns out to be different than what we hoped for—trust God to know that *His way* was the *best* way! The Bible says in Proverbs 3:5 (NKJV), "Trust in the LORD with all your heart, and lean not on your own understanding." When we fully comprehend that concept, there's no way we would ever *blame God* for anything!

No Favorites

*"But I tell you, love your enemies and pray
for those who persecute you, that you may be children
of your Father in heaven. He causes his sun to
rise on the evil and the good, and sends rain on the
righteous and the unrighteous."*

Matthew 5:44-45 (NIV)

Jesus died on the cross for each and every one of us. He didn't just give His life to save the smartest, best-looking, cream-of-the-crop sort of person. Jesus loves all of us equally. He doesn't *play favorites*! When we think about how God cares for even the tiniest sparrow, it becomes very clear just how much more He cares for us!

The Bible tells the story of Jesus, the Good Shepherd, who searched and searched for a little, lost lamb. He didn't just value the grown-up sheep that were worth more money—all His sheep were important to Him. So it is with our heavenly Father. Some feel inadequate to be a witness for Jesus, but God blesses even the smallest effort. The key is to *stay close to Jesus*! It is when we wander away that we are in danger. Spend time daily in God's Word and pray about everything—yes, even the small, seemingly insignificant, stuff!

And when you're having one of those days when you just don't feel loved by anyone, remember—you are a child of the King of the universe and it doesn't matter what anyone else thinks—it matters what God thinks! So hold your head high, put a smile on your face, and know that Jesus loves you!

December 8

In Search of Happiness

*Therefore with joy you will draw water
from the wells of salvation.*

Isaiah 12:3 (NKJV)

People around the world are searching for *happiness*, but sadly, never seem to find it. The reason is simple—they are looking in all the wrong places! Many depend on their families or friends to make them happy. Some think if they could just find that *perfect mate—then* happiness would come! Others pursue financial success, working like crazy and then wondering why, even with a boatload of money in the bank, they feel empty at the end of the day. Then there are those who seek happiness in Satan's worldly pleasures, such as alcohol, drugs, and sex—not realizing they are sinking deeper and deeper into the dark hole of despair!

The truth is—happiness is a choice! You can't possibly make someone else happy if you are miserable yourself. Peace, joy, and contentment cannot be obtained through worldly pleasures or through other people. No other person here on earth is responsible for your happiness. It's up to you to choose which path you want to travel, and there is only *one* road to happiness, and that is through Jesus Christ our Lord! He alone has the power to give the everlasting joy that you desperately need. Stop looking to others for fulfillment. Look to Jesus! Choose Jesus! Run to Jesus! And when you do . . . you will find rich, fulfilling, and everlasting joy and happiness such as you have never known!

Slip-Sliding Away

Therefore let him who thinks he stands take heed lest he fall.

1 Corinthians 10:12 (NKJV)

The only way to a happy and joy-filled life is to know Jesus as your personal Savior. The more time you spend with Christ, the more you will love Him and want to be like Him. If you have reached a place in your spiritual life where Jesus no longer feels *real*, then you need to increase your prayer time! Anytime you get out of the habit of personal devotions and worship, you begin to drift away from God. Satan is sure to provide enough distractions in your life to make it easy to *slip away*.

Remember, God does not leave or forsake you—it is *you* who leave and forsake *Him*! It is your own sins that separate you from Jesus. If you start to feel that God has withdrawn His presence, go to Him with fresh, sincere surrender! Allow God to open your eyes and reveal your sin so that you can have pure repentance and experience His forgiveness!

Ask Jesus for Holy Spirit power to defeat enemy attacks. No matter what Satan throws your way, stay close to Jesus—stay faithful!

God's Gift of Joy

Until now you have asked nothing in My name. Ask, and
you will receive, that your joy may be full.

John 16:24 (NKJV)

Only believing, worshiping, active Christians are fully able to experience God's wonderful gift of joy! People who don't know the Lord are continually searching for peace and happiness. They go through the motions of life but do not experience the rich and satisfying joy of serving Christ, our Savior. Oh yes, most will find *moments* of fleeting happiness, but are continually searching for *true inner peace*.

Many think that if they had a better job, a fancy car, money in the bank, and a million other unobtainable goals . . . *then* they would be *happy*! But they couldn't be more wrong! They don't realize that what they are seeking has been there all along—that Jesus has been there with His arms wide open, just waiting for them! Jesus *is* the real joy of living, and it's impossible to live a completely satisfied, happy, joyful life unless we are personally connected to the source of all joy—and that is God!

The Bible tells us in Psalm 16:11 (NKJV), "You will show me the path of life; in Your presence is fullness of joy; at Your right hand are pleasures forevermore." When you are connected with Jesus, no one, not even Satan, can take away God's gift of joy!

Entrance Fee to Heaven

I delight greatly in the LORD; my soul rejoices in my God. For he has clothed me with garments of salvation and arrayed me in a robe of his righteousness, as a bridegroom adorns his head like a priest, and as a bride adorns herself with her jewels.

Isaiah 61:10 (NIV)

There are some people who mistakenly think that they have to be *perfect* before they can come to Jesus! They believe they must stop sinning before Jesus could possibly love them—stop doing drugs, smoking, drinking, cheating, lying, etc. But the truth is . . . all are sinners and one sin is no different than another. If you waited until you were *perfect* to come to Jesus . . . you would ever get there, because *no one is perfect*!

But when you come to Jesus, covered in your filthy rags of sin, He accepts you with open arms! He doesn't wrinkle up His nose with disgust at your stench. No, not at all! Instead, He covers you in His robe of righteousness, wraps you in His arms of love, and holds you close!

Jesus *loves* the sinner but hates the sin. In fact, He loves you so much that He gave His life for you. He has already paid the price for your salvation! Your entrance fee to heaven is paid in full and He is calling out, "Come to Me, all you who labor and are heavy laden, and I will give you rest" (Matthew 11:28, NKJV). Won't you come to Jesus today?

Not God's Fault

Therefore do not cast away your confidence,
which has great reward.

Hebrews 10:35 (NKJV)

When tragedy strikes, most people tend to do one of two things: blame God for their troubles or turn to Jesus for help! Even those who claim to be Christians can find themselves questioning God, wanting answers, demanding to know *why*. Some Christians blame God and turn their backs on Him because they are angry. But the truth is this: we live in a sinful world, and it will remain so until Jesus comes. It isn't God's will that anyone should suffer or die. Quite the opposite! It's His will that we have life and have it more abundantly. But until this evil world is done away with, and Jesus comes and takes us to heaven, we will experience the consequences of sin.

When hearts are heavy, turn to Jesus for comfort. He is the only *Healer of hearts*! He will place His comforting arms of love around us and give us a peace such as we have never known. Our time here on earth is short. It won't be much longer before Jesus comes, and we need to be ready!

We need to recommit our lives to Jesus and live for Him. Stay steady on the course. Stay faithful. Stay connected to our Lord and Savior! Jesus *is* coming soon to take us to live with Him, where there will be no more heartache, tears, sorrow, or death, but each day will be more glorious than the day before!

The Devil's Playground

"I command you today to love the LORD your God, to walk in His ways, and to keep His commandments, His statutes, and His judgments, that you may live and multiply; and the LORD your God will bless you in the land which you go to possess."

Deuteronomy 30:16 (NKJV)

The Bible tells us in Matthew 25:13 (KJV), "Watch therefore, for ye know neither the day nor the hour wherein the Son of man cometh." But God also tells us in Matthew 24 that, by the signs, we will know when His coming is near. Those signs are happening *now*! Unless you have been living under a rock and haven't traveled the world or seen or read the news lately, you can't help but know we are living in the last days here on earth. *Now* is the time to get our hearts right with God!

There's no time to fool around or play on the devil's playground. God is telling us to decide: we are either for Him—or against Him! Jesus tells us in Revelation 3:16 (KJV), "So then because thou art lukewarm, and neither cold nor hot, I will spue thee out of my mouth." We must make a decision of whom we will serve! John 14:6 (KJV) tells us, "Jesus saith unto him, I am the way, the truth, and the life: no man cometh unto the Father, but by me." There is no other way to heaven and eternal life, except through Jesus Christ our Lord! "Choose you this day whom ye will serve" (Joshua 24:15, KJV).

God Is Not Santa Claus

*For he satisfies the longing soul, and the hungry
soul he fills with good things.*

Psalm 107:9 (ESV)

———— ❖ ————

The reason we pray is not to *get things we want*. God is *not* Santa Claus—someone we send our *wish list* to and expect to find everything we asked for under the tree! Our *real reason* to pray is to get to know Jesus as our personal Savior and fall more deeply in love with Him. It's to become one with God so that *His will* becomes our *will*!

Passionate prayer and Jesus are synonymous. Jesus didn't just pray, He prayed passionately! He shared His heart with His heavenly Father . . . and so should we! Prayer is not just words, requests, or praise. Passionate prayer is a love relationship with the most awesome God of the Universe! And when we pray to Him, He will never let us down.

May you be inspired to pray passionately from your heart and to trust Him to answer according to what is best for you. God will open the windows of heaven and pour out so many blessings that you will be totally amazed at the depth of His amazing love!

Help My Unbelief

Jesus said to him, "If you can believe, all things are possible to him who believes." Immediately the father of the child cried out and said with tears, "Lord, I believe; help my unbelief!"

Mark 9:23-24 (NKJV)

Many Christians chastise themselves when bad things happen because they falsely think that God would have answered their prayers if only they had more faith—a child wouldn't have died, cancer would have been healed, a job wouldn't have been lost, and so on. They reason that they just didn't pray hard enough. Once a person starts reasoning like that, they take on the burden of responsibility for the bad things that happen in life.

The next step is guilt! This is a dangerous slippery slope! Satan loves this kind of thinking because it takes the blame off of him. The truth is, bad things are the result of sin, and Satan is the originator of sin!

God does not command perfect faith before working miracles in your life. When you pray, God always hears *and* answers. You may not receive the answer instantly or the way you want it, but He does answer! And you can trust that He always does what is best for us! If you are struggling with guilt or doubt, pray, "Lord, I believe; help my unbelief."

Embrace the Journey

*I will be glad and rejoice in You; I will sing praise
to Your name, O Most High.*

Psalm 9:2 (NKJV)

When life looks the bleakest, there is still much to praise Jesus for! It's easy to rejoice when everything in your life is wonderful, but when you can sing praises to God during your darkest hours—you grow spiritually! Think of Paul and Silas in jail, singing and praising God, even though they had been beaten, starved, and shackled in a damp, dark prison! The apostle Paul tell us in Philippians 4:11 (NKJV), "I have learned in whatever state I am, to be content." That's what we all need to strive for, because whatever we may suffer here on earth won't last forever—it's only temporary!

We can rejoice in all things knowing we belong to the King of the universe, and we have the blessed assurance of eternity with Jesus to look forward to! This sinful world is not going to last, and soon all the heartache and pain will be done away with forever. So embrace this journey with a heart of gladness and anticipation for what each new day holds. Experience the fullness of God's joy that we can only find in His presence! When we increase our prayer time, we can't help but rejoice in the Lord always!

Life Is Not Fair

*Truly God is good to Israel, to such as are pure in heart.
But as for me, my feet had almost stumbled; my steps
had nearly slipped. For I was envious of the boastful,
when I saw the prosperity of the wicked. . . . Until I went
into the sanctuary of God; then I understood their end.*

Psalm 73:1-3, 17 (NKJV)

Don't expect to be treated fairly in life because quite simply—*life isn't fair*! It's inevitable that people will say and do hurtful things that you don't deserve. When someone mistreats you, try to view it as an opportunity to grow spiritually. Don't torture yourself by regurgitating each injustice and everything they did to hurt you.

Instead, ask God to immediately put forgiveness in your heart for the person who did you wrong. Don't be concerned about setting the record straight. Instead of obsessing about other people's opinions about you—keep your focus on God and what *He* thinks of you! Ultimately, it is His view of you that really matters!

Remember, Jesus knows the meaning of *unfair* better than anyone else. It certainly wasn't fair that He was nailed to a cross to die for your sins. But He gave His life willingly, so that He could give you the amazing gift of *eternal life*. Wow! He gave you so much more than what you deserve—so when others treat you unfairly, don't be bitter or angry or even feel sorry for yourself. *Forgive and forget*! Remember that God treats you much better than *fair*! He blesses abundantly more than you could ever ask, think—or deserve!

Recognizing God's Voice

*"Call to Me, and I will answer you, and show you great
and mighty things, which you do not know."*

Jeremiah 33:3 (NKJV)

God has a special plan for each of His children, and oh, how essential it is to listen to His voice. It's so very important to *know* if it is *God* impressing you, or the *enemy*! And when you have prayed passionately to God, and He impresses you to do something . . . *go for it*! Don't hesitate and talk yourself out of it because it sounds unreasonable or *out of your comfort zone.*

When you have surrendered your will to God—you won't be acting like you have all the answers. Instead, you'll be leaning on Jesus and following the path that He has laid out for you! How will you know God's voice? Well, the more time you spend in prayer—the more you will recognize His voice! You can be sure that God will never impress you to do anything that would go against His Holy Word.

It's crucial that you listen for God's voice so that you can be obedient to His will. The Bible says in Jeremiah 7:23 (NKJV), "Obey my voice, and I will be your God, and you shall be My people . . . that it may be well with you." God speaks through Scripture as well as His Holy Spirit, but if you are unsure whether it is God's voice impressing you, then double the time you spend on your knees! Set aside a special time each day to spend time with Jesus, because it's during those quiet times when you'll hear God's voice the loudest!

Go and Sin No More

Therefore do not let sin reign in your mortal body so that you obey its evil desires.

Romans 6:12 (NIV)

There is a huge spiritual battle that is won when we learn to hate the sins in our own lives more than the sins of others! Somehow it seems easier to criticize and judge our neighbor for wrongdoing than it is to see our own mistakes. We tend to justify why what we are doing is *okay*, while being harsh when someone else is doing that same thing!

Sin will always separate us from Jesus! In Matthew 7:1 (KJV) we are told, "Judge not, that ye be not judged." We have a full time job keeping our own lives surrendered—we don't need to look for fault in others. When Jesus addressed the accusers of Mary Magdalene, He quietly started writing their sins on the ground. And of course, each of them started slipping away from the crowd until everyone was gone—because they knew they were sinful and didn't want their sins exposed!

Soon, there was no one left to condemn her! John 8:11 (NKJV) tells us "And Jesus said to her, 'Neither do I condemn you; go and sin no more.'" Jesus showed how much He loves sinners when He tenderly and lovingly told Mary that her sins were forgiven. And here's the important part that so many of us overlook—*go and sin no more!*

No Free Passes

Are not two sparrows sold for a penny? Yet not one of
them will fall to the ground outside your Father's care. And
even the very hairs of your head are all numbered. So don't
be afraid; you are worth more than many sparrows.

Matthew 10:29-31 (NIV)

Why is it that when faced with an emotional crisis—we try and fix our own problems? As Christians, we know God is there to help anytime, day or night, yet instead of turning to Him first, we try to get out of the mess ourselves and end up only making it worse! When we awaken in the night with cold sweats because we're filled with fear, when we've reached the end of our *financial rope*, when our closest friend walks away, or we receive devastating news . . . we need to fall on our knees and go to Jesus *first*!

Instead of feeling sorry for ourselves and attending the *why-me party*, send an SOS to heaven! Being Christians does not give us a free pass to a world without pain! The truth is, Satan works even harder on those who love the Lord!

The devil will work overtime to push every button we have that separates us from Jesus, because when he accomplishes that goal—he wins! There's only one way to live a joy-filled life, and that is to put God first! When we make Jesus the center of everything we do—we can stop worrying and enjoy the abundant life God has planned!

All Year Long

He who follows righteousness and mercy finds
life, righteousness, and honor.

Proverbs 21:21 (NKJV)

Jesus wants us to be generous, kind, and loving to our fellowman. However, some people only take this to heart during the holidays. Many who would normally never reach out to others seem to have more open hearts during this season. Sometimes the most self-centered person can be seen throwing coins in a *bell ringer's cup* as they enter or exit a store. The reason for this behavior remains a mystery, but perhaps they are remembering the childhood lessons learned from their parents about being compassionate toward others, or maybe it's the Holy Spirit working on their hearts. Whatever the reason, it is pleasing to God when we help our fellowman.

God tells us in Matthew 25:40 that when we help someone else, it is like we are *doing it for Him*! God has given us the privilege of being His *hands and feet,* filled with tenderness toward others. God doesn't just mean for us to give physical gifts to the needy. He is also talking about having forgiving hearts and thinking the best of those who have done us wrong! Shower them with His grace and mercy and just *love them*! This is the example that Jesus has set for us. Be compassionate, not only during the holidays . . . but all year long!

Living a Sin-Free Life

*Therefore you shall be perfect, just as your
Father in heaven is perfect.*

Matthew 5:48 (NKJV)

When Jesus came to this earth born as a human baby, He grew up to lead a sin-free life, proving that it *could be done.* It was His close connection with God that made it possible. Each of us can live sinless lives as long as Christ is living within us!

Many early Christians suffered terrible persecution and even gave their lives willingly, with peace and courage. Often they were physically weak individuals, but because of their walk with the Lord, they were able to stand up strong for their beliefs and even endured terrible pain and suffering—all with joyful hearts! Only God's Holy Spirit can give someone the power and strength to do that!

I love the song, "Just a Closer Walk with Thee." The words go like this: "I am weak but Thou art strong, Jesus keep me from all wrong; I'll be satisfied as long, as I walk, dear Lord, close to Thee. Just a closer walk with Thee, grant it, Jesus, is my plea. Daily walking close to Thee, let it be, dear Lord, let it be." May that be our daily prayer—*Let me walk, dear Lord, close to Thee!*

No More Gloom

*For you make me glad by your deeds, L*ORD*; I sing
for joy at what your hands have done.*

Psalm 92:4 (NIV)

Christians should be the happiest people on earth because, when we're filled with the joy of Jesus, we just can't help but smile and shine! We're naturally drawn to others who are excited about life and fun to be around! No one wants to hang out with those who are always complaining or depressed. Being around all that negativity isn't good for anyone, for soon, all that gloom and doom starts to rub off on us. But more importantly, being sad and down in the dumps isn't God's plan. He wants us to have life, and have it more abundantly (see John 10:10).

Spending time with Christians who are happy and excited about life is like a breath of fresh air! Soon we start to feel more positive, and those old negative thoughts fade away. When it seems our hearts are just too heavy to even think about *joy*, all we have to do is pray and ask God for His strength to overcome the *cobwebs of discouragement*. Claim Philippians 4:13 (NKJV): "I can do all things through Christ who strengthens me." God *will* give us the victory!

We can't be shining for Jesus if we are depressed and hanging on to all our pain and heartache. To live the abundant life God wants us to live, we need to give Him all our troubles and choose to live a joyful life that radiates His love!

Giving Up Control

*Therefore, my dear friends, as you have always obeyed—
not only in my presence, but now much more in my
absence—continue to work out your salvation with fear
and trembling, for it is God who works in you to will and
to act in order to fulfill his good purpose.*

Philippians 2:12-13 (NIV)

———◆———

God's way is always *the best way*, and if we knew the end from the beginning, we wouldn't want it to be any different! Why is it that we struggle so much with giving up control? We forget that God loves us more than anyone else ever could and wants only what is best for us!

There's no reason to stumble in the darkness with fear and panic, not knowing which way to turn, when God is right there beside us, ready to help. He's the only one who knows the future, and He alone knows what is best. He longs to spare us heartache and pain and calls for us to come to Him so He can show us the way. We need only to clasp His outstretched hand and surrender *our will*—to *His will*. And when we do, He will safely guide our every step! Our lives will be filled with His amazing love—allowing us to experience the real joy of living!

However, God won't force us to love and obey Him. We must *willingly* give up control and serve Him with obedience and *a joyful heart*. Then, and only then, can God truly use us to shine for Him! Let us pray every day for a *willing spirit*!

Teach Me How to Pray

Likewise the Spirit helps us in our weakness.
For we do not know what to pray for as we ought, but
the Spirit himself intercedes for us with
groanings too deep for words.

Romans 8:26 (ESV)

Often when we pray, we are clueless of really *how* to pray or *what to pray for*. Because we can't see the future, we pray selfishly, asking God to fix our problems the way *we think* He should fix them. But many times, if God gave us what we asked for, there would be a miserable result. That's why it is important to ask God for wisdom and discernment. Our prayer should be, "Lord, teach me how to pray." David, the psalmist, prayed in Psalm 119:144 (NIV), "Give me understanding that I may live." He knew that he needed God's divine direction in his life to help him avoid wrongful actions.

We can claim God's promise in James 1:5, where He promises to grant us wisdom—if we ask for it. Yes, He will give us the understanding and discernment we need so that we know *what* to pray for. And always pray for *God's will to be done!* This is so critically important. If we could see the end from the beginning, we truly would not want it any other way . . . than God's way!

Count Your Blessings

*Bless the LORD, O my soul, and forget not all
His benefits.*

Psalm 103:2 (NKJV)

Even the most upbeat, positive, enthusiastic person experiences a *down day* now and then. It's a normal fact of life that not every day is going to be the greatest! It's human nature to feel sad when something bad happens to you or someone you love. If you hear news of a friend or loved one that is in trouble with the law, or was in a serious auto accident, or any other devastating event, it's only natural to be upset. But there's a big difference between *feeling sad* and sinking into a deep depression and getting angry with God!

The devil loves to keep you emotionally crippled because you can't possibly be shining for Jesus if you are in a state of hopeless despair! As a Christian, you know that evil will exist in this world until Jesus comes, and bad things happen to good people—but you also know that throughout your trials, God is with you each step of the way, for you are not alone.

So instead of blaming God, praise Him! Yes, even in the worst time of your life, you can find things to praise God for. Count your blessings! If you're having trouble seeing them, just look around, and you'll soon see that your problems don't look so bad compared to others. Wipe the tears, put a smile on your face, and ask God to put a song in your heart. It's hard to be depressed when you're praising Jesus.

Shelter in Every Storm

Behold, God is my salvation; I will trust, and not be afraid: for the LORD JEHOVAH is my strength and my song; he also is become my salvation. Therefore with joy shall ye draw water out of the wells of salvation.

Isaiah 12:2-3 (KJV)

God never promised there would always be sunshine, but He does promise that He will be there to guide us through every dark day! He will ride out the storms with us, calm the sea, and give us His sweet peace. With God at the center of our lives, we are able to stay balanced and focused on our heavenly goal. When we are having our darkest day and all seems lost, we should not get discouraged and think for one minute that God has given up on us or we just don't matter—because He does.

Jesus loves us so much that He can't imagine heaven without us! He will protect us in times of trouble and comfort us in times of sorrow and grief. What a blessing it is to serve such an all-powerful, loving Lord and Savior! When we are living within God's will, we can rest assured that His eyes are keeping a loving watch over us, and He is ready to answer when we cry for help. Jesus *is* our shelter from every storm!

Doubt Can Be Healthy

*Test all things; hold fast what is good. Abstain
from every form of evil.*

1 Thessalonians 5:21-22 (NKJV)

———

D oubt is often considered a negative trait, but sometimes *doubt* is a good thing! Without it we wouldn't be able to discern when something doesn't sound *quite right*, so we can avoid going down a wrong path or believing a lie. It also makes us question when things go wrong or we are in situations that don't quite *make sense*. Sometimes doubt can help deepen our faith as we search for answers to questions we can't seem to let go of.

Other times the Holy Spirit uses doubt to help us question false beliefs or to encourage us to search our hearts for pure motives. But make no mistake, Satan also uses doubt to get Christians to doubt God. He wants us to question God's love for us and lose faith in our Creator.

The important thing to remember is to keep our eyes fixed on Jesus! We never have to doubt His love for us! Always listen to the Holy Spirit's prompting so that we will not be led astray. Remember, doubt can be healthy . . . if it motivates us to search for truth!

Corrupted by Sin

I will bless the LORD at all times; His praise shall continually be in my mouth. My soul shall make its boast in the LORD; the humble shall hear of it and be glad. Oh, magnify the LORD with me, and let us exalt His name together.

Psalm 34:1-3 (NKJV)

No matter how much heartache we have in our own lives, there's always someone else who suffers worse than we do. The fact is, we live in an imperfect world that is corrupted by sin, and we will suffer the consequences until Jesus comes. There will be tears, pain, and heartache, but throughout our journey here on earth, we have a wonderful Lord and Savior who will walk the road with us. God doesn't promise a perfect life without pain, but He does promise to be with us every step of the way.

When our burdens are overwhelming and our hearts are heavy, we need not despair—just give our troubles to Jesus. Lay them at His feet—and leave them there! Then take the time to count our blessings, reflecting on all the wonderful things that God has done for us. It's hard to be depressed when we think about our blessings! We need to pray and thank God for every precious gift, and don't forget Calvary and His incredible gift of eternal life! When we get off our knees, we'll feel refreshed and rejoice knowing just how much God loves us. Truly, we have much to praise Jesus for!

Secret of a Happy Life

*Now may the God of hope fill you with all joy
and peace in believing, that you may abound in hope
by the power of the Holy Spirit.*

Romans 15:13 (NKJV)

The secret to real happiness, joy, and contentment is to make God *first* in your life! It's really that simple! When you put *God's will* above your own or anyone else's . . . it changes everything. Remember that God's plan is *always* the best plan! You just can't mess up when you are allowing God to take control because God *never* makes mistakes.

When you are following God's lead and trusting Him completely, you never have to wonder if you are doing *the right thing* or how to fix things yourself! You no longer have problems, because when you give your problems to God, they become *His problems*, and there's nothing too big or too small for Him to handle! Isn't that awesome? Don't wait any longer! The Bible says in Psalm 16:8-9 (KJV), "I have set the LORD always before me: because he is at my right hand, I shall not be moved. Therefore my heart is glad, and my glory rejoiceth: my flesh also shall rest in hope." Recommit your life to Jesus today and discover for yourself—the true secret of living a happy life!

Are You Ready?

"Stay dressed for action and keep your lamps burning, and be like men who are waiting for their master to come home from the wedding feast, so that they may open the door to him at once when he comes and knocks."

Luke 12:35-36 (ESV)

After Jesus ascended into Heaven, we were given this promise in Acts 1:11 (NKJV), "This same Jesus, who was taken up from you into heaven, will so come in like manner as you saw Him go into heaven." *Jesus is coming again*! He is making preparations right now for us to be with Him for all eternity. In John 14:2-3 (NKJV) we're told, "In My Father's house are many mansions. . . . I go to prepare a place for you. And if I go and prepare a place for you, I will come again and receive you to Myself; that where I am, there you may be also." Wow! Just imagine how wonderful heaven will be! It is mind-blowing just trying to comprehend it!

God gives us insight into the timing of His return in Matthew 24:33 (KJV), "So likewise ye, when ye shall see all these things, know that it is near, even at the doors." Read on in verses 36-44 that we know not the day, nor the hour of Christ's return. You see, God's timing is perfect! Although we don't know the exact time—Jesus tells us that by the signs we will know His coming is near! *Now* is the time to get ready! In order to receive God's gift of eternal life—we must have hearts that are surrendered! *Are you ready for Jesus to come*?

Index

Other books by Brenda Walsh available at
www.brendawalsh.com

Battered to Blessed
Brenda Walsh with Kay D. Rizzo / Paperback / 222 p.

Brenda Walsh tells a gripping and powerful story of her personal experience with domestic violence and amazing grace. Battered to Blessed is Brenda's amazing journey from pain to peace and living a whole new life of incredible joy in Jesus! **(Also available in audiobook and a Spanish version.)**

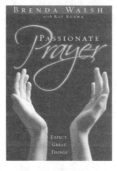

Passionate Prayer
Brenda Walsh / Paperback / 331 p.

Brenda Walsh is one who has learned by experience the power of passionate prayer. This book is filled with miracle stories of God's intervention in her life and the lives of those for whom she has prayed. **(Also available in audiobook.)**

Between Hell and High Water
Brenda Walsh and Kay Kuzma / Paperback / 255 p.

Kay Kuzma and Brenda Walsh have captured the unforgettable tales of survivors of Hurricane Katrina. These riveting stories of life and death, good and evil, hope and despair, will give you courage, faith, and hope as you face your own times of trouble, knowing that whatever happens, God will be there. **(Also available in audiobook.)**

Other books by Brenda Walsh available at
www.brendawalsh.com

Passionate Prayer Promises
Brenda Walsh and Kay Kuzma
Paperback / 230 p.

Do you sometimes have the feeling your prayers are boring and repetitious, or you don't know how to pray? If you want a more exhilarating personal and passionate prayer life, Passionate Prayer Promises is the resource you've been waiting for. (**Also available in sharing and Spanish versions.**)

Prayer Promises for Kids
Brenda Walsh and Kay Kuzma / Paperback / 128 p.

Prayer Promises for Kids is a colorful prayer book of over 100 sample prayers on topics that school-age kids deal with everyday, such as being afraid of bullies, rejection, failure, coping with bad habits, and making friends.

Miss Brenda's Bedtime Stories
Brenda Walsh / Hardcover / 128 p.

Miss Brenda's Bedtime Stories is a collection of five hardcover volumes, each filled with more than twenty-five delightful stories that you will never forget. Each book is filled with exciting character building stories that teach valuable life lessons. Some stories take you halfway around the world, and others will seem as if they could have happened in your own backyard. These true stories, are sure to be loved by children and treasured by parents and grandparents as well. Perfect for reading together before bedtime—or anytime—these stories will warm your heart and draw your family closer to Jesus! (**Also available in audiobook**)

Additional Devotional Resources

For more devotions like these, download Brenda Walsh's free app, *Sharing God's Love*, available on the App Store® for the iPhone or iPad or on Google Play™ for Android devices.

A new devotion will be available to read each day, with the added option of listening to Brenda's audio version.

You can also connect with
Brenda Walsh on: